Psycho Thrillers

ALSO BY WILLIAM INDICK
AND FROM MCFARLAND

*Movies and the Mind: Theories of
the Great Psychoanalysts Applied to Film*
(2004)

Psycho Thrillers

*Cinematic Explorations
of the Mysteries of the Mind*

WILLIAM INDICK

McFarland & Company, Inc., Publishers
Jefferson, North Carolina, and London

LIBRARY OF CONGRESS CATALOGUING-IN-PUBLICATION DATA

Indick, William.
    Psycho thrillers : cinematic explorations of the mysteries of the
mind / William Indick.
        p.   cm.
    Includes bibliographical references and index.

    ISBN 0-7864-2371-4 (softcover : 50# alkaline paper) ∞

    1. Thrillers (Motion pictures, television, etc.) — History and
criticism.   2. Mental illness in motion pictures.   3. Psychiatry
in motion pictures.   4. Motion pictures — Psychological aspects.
I. Title.
PN1995.9.S87154   2006
791.43'6164 — dc22   2005022632

British Library cataloguing data are available

On the cover: Gregory Peck and Ingrid Bergman in *Spellbound* (1945)

Manufactured in the United States of America

McFarland & Company, Inc., Publishers
  Box 611, Jefferson, North Carolina 28640
    www.mcfarlandpub.com

For Michelle

Acknowledgments

The film stills in this book were purchased for book publication at Jerry Ohlinger's Movie Material Store in New York City. The author offers much thanks to Suzanne Johnson and all of his other colleagues in the psychology department at Dowling College. A debt of gratitude is also owed to the entire faculty and administration of Dowling College in Oakdale, New York, for their support of the author's research and writing projects.

Table of Contents

Preface

This book introduces the concept of a "psycho thriller" film genre. A psycho thriller is a movie born of three established genres: the psychological thriller, the horror picture, and the science-fiction film. The defining quality of a psycho thriller is that the film must depict a psychological theme — referred to in this book as "psychological fiction" or "psy-fi" — as a central aspect of the characters or plot. That is, it must be primarily psychological in focus.

Just as science-fiction focuses on the outer limits of scientific possibilities, a psy-fi theme focuses on the fringes of psychological possibilities. Mind control, madness, the parapsychological, the pathological, the paranormal, psychosis, and altered states of reality are the dominant themes of psychological fiction. While psychologists in the real world spend most of their time dealing with mundane research projects or clients with relatively minor neuroses, psychology in the movie world is a roller coaster ride of raving psychotics, mad scientists, super-psychic powers, and mind control nightmares. The psy-fi world presents psychology as a dimension of supernatural and metaphysical wonders.

As one of the premier sciences of the twentieth century, psychology and film came of age together at the same time. The archetypal characters of twentieth century film, characters such as the mad scientist, the psycho killer, and the evil psychiatrist, were often developed in direct reference to the psychological themes that inspired them. While madness existed as a character trait in literature and drama long before psychology as a field came into being, only in the twentieth century has the madman become pathological. For instance, many of Shakespeare's characters — and nearly everyone in *Hamlet*—could be described as "mad," but Norman Bates in

Psycho (1960) was a character driven completely by psychopathology. Bates' behaviors represented real psychological disorders, and his murderous traits were explained through the use of psychoanalysis. In the twentieth century, the crazed killer became a paranoid psychotic, the mad scientist became a pathological narcissist, and the wise old man became a licensed psychologist.

A narrow perspective on the psycho thriller would classify the film type as a subcategory of the science-fiction genre, applying the title only to sci-fi movies that employ psychological themes as the film's primary science. For example, *Dreamscape* (1984) is a prototypical psycho thriller, because the scientific power behind the story is pure psychology (or parapsychology). In this case, Dennis Quaid has a peculiar telepathic ability that allows him to enter into other people's dreams. Non–sci-fi movies, however, often use telepathic or telekinetic abilities as a premise for terror. The horror in *Carrie* (1976) emerges from the lead character's inability to control her own telekinetic abilities. Similarly, the horror in *A Nightmare on Elm Street* (1984) arises from Freddy Krueger's telepathic ability to enter people's dreams. And while the science of psychology in *Psycho* (1960) is not really a driving force behind the story, the psychology provides essential background and explanation of the lead character's behaviors. Psycho killers such as Norman Bates, Jason in the *Friday the 13th* movies, and Michael in the *Halloween* movies all seem to represent psycho thriller characters, even though they do not appear in sci-fi films.

Consequently, the psycho thriller cannot be limited to being merely a subgenre of science fiction. Rather, the psycho thriller could be any film that has either a basic psychological premise as its core theme, or characters that clearly represent specific psychological issues. The prototypical psycho thriller is a movie in which a psy-fi theme — a psychological ability, disorder, or phenomenon — is at the core of the plot. This book devotes chapters to each of the archetypal psy-fi characters: the mad scientist, the psycho killer, the individual with psychic powers, and the psychiatrist. Chapters are also devoted to the classic psy-fi themes of mind control, dreams, memory, and existential issues. The discussion pays special attention to specific films and filmmakers that have contributed to the evolution of the modern psycho thriller.

Though this may be the first book on the subject of psychological science fiction in film, I doubt that it will be the last. As we enter the twenty-first century, interest in all things psychological has never been greater. Filmmakers are feeding this interest with a constant outflow of new movies that explore the outermost limits of the psychological dimension.

Introduction

Every film has a psychological component to it. Broadly construed psychological elements such as neurotic (internal) conflict, identity (character) development, and emotional (dramatic) motivation are necessary ingredients of every story and script. Hence, all movies are psychological. Yet not all movies are "psychological fiction." Not every movie is a "psy-fi" movie. For instance, oftentimes a film is dubbed a "psychological thriller" because the plot centers on the internal conflict within one of the characters—i.e., internal rather than external obstacles. To label a film "psychological" because a character must deal with internal conflict is nonsense of the highest order. Every well-developed film character should deal with internal conflict and struggle with internal obstacles to some degree. Similarly, the psychological thriller is often defined as a movie in which a lot of attention is given to the way the characters influence each other's behavior. Yes, behavior is "psychological," but once again, every good film should pay a lot of attention to the way characters influence each other. Since every work of fiction is inherently psychological, in order to classify a film as psy-fi, the film must depict elements of psychology beyond the ideally ubiquitous features of internal conflict, character development, and motivation.

So what makes a movie a psy-fi movie? In this book, three different elements of the psy-fi film are suggested as defining qualities within the genre:

1. Psy-Fi Characters: A character with a psychological disorder or a person who treats psychological disorders in a lead or significant supporting role.

2. Psy-Fi Powers: Peculiar or in some way significant psychological abilities as a significant aspect of the lead character's role or the movie's plot.

3. Psy-Fi Themes: Overtly psychological themes as a significant aspect of the movie's plot.

In the first chapter, the focus is on the psy-fi character of the psychiatrist. In the past century, the representation of the psychiatrist has developed from stereotypical portraits of evil mesmerists and charlatan quacks in the silent era through the 1930s, to the diametrically opposite but equally stereotypical portraits of the wise, all-knowing, and beneficent psychiatrist of the 1940s, '50s and early '60s, to the menacing but somewhat banal portraits of faceless facilitators and agents of social conformity in the late '60s and 1970s, leading up to the manifold portrayal of modern psychiatrists in contemporary cinema. Chapter Two focuses on psycho killers—psychotics, mad murderers, and serial killers. The focus in Chapter Three is on the mad scientist, one of the most ubiquitous archetypes in story and film, representing a lethal combination of megalomaniacal narcissism and obsessive-compulsive fanaticism.

Psychic powers are addressed in Chapter Four, covering powers such as clairvoyance (the ability to predict future events), telepathy (the ability to "read" minds or communicate psychically), telekinesis (the ability to psychically move objects), pyrokinesis (the ability to psychically start fires), dream projection (the ability to psychically travel into another person's dreams), psychic projection (the ability to psychically travel through space and time), and mind invasion (the ability to psychically enter the virtual world of someone else's mind). Chapter Five will focus on mind control, covering methods such as hypnosis, brainwashing, psychotropic drugs, behavior modification, neurosurgery, and neural implants. Chapter Six will cover the psy-fi depiction of dreams, alternate realities, and altered states of consciousness, while Chapter Seven will focus on the phenomenological and existential dilemmas raised by psy-fi themes such as amnesia, artificial intelligence, virtual reality, multiple identities, false memories, and past lives.

Chapter Eight will briefly cover depictions of psychological disorders that are not frequent psy-fi themes, such as anxiety disorders, autism, depression, dissociative identity disorder, alcoholism, drug addiction, pathological gambling, obsessive-compulsive disorder, post-traumatic stress disorder, schizophrenia, sleep disorders, and others. The final chapter, "Masters of Psy-Fi," focuses on a variety of prolific filmmakers, actors and writers, such as Alfred Hitchcock, John Frankenheimer, Stanley

Kubrick, Brian De Palma, David Cronenberg, Philip K. Dick, and Stephen King, whose works have proven to be extremely influential on the psycho thriller genre.

The conclusion of the book explores the top twenty psy-fi movies of all time, explaining how and why these movies were significant influences on both the psycho thriller genre and the field of film in general. Finally, a comprehensive filmography provides details on all of the films mentioned in this book.

CHAPTER ONE

Doctors of the Mind

PSYCHIATRIST: Tell me more about your dream ... the Cleveland Indians all got jobs at Toys R Us?

JERRY FALK: Yeah. So what can it possibly mean? Look, I can't keep wasting my hour here describing lunatic dreams! I have a date with Amanda. I can't keep running around town on the sly and live like this! Amanda can handle it, but I need help. What do I do? I have to extricate myself from Brooke. It'll break her heart! She wants to marry me!

PSYCHIATRIST: What comes to mind about the Cleveland Indians?

Jerry (Jason Biggs) and his psychiatrist (William Hill)
from Woody Allen's Anything Else *(2003)*

Along with the Western cowboy, the rogue cop, the gangland criminal and the war hero, the psychiatrist is a ubiquitous character in movies, present since the birth of the medium and still viable — if not more so — in contemporary cinema. When the psychiatrist is cast in the lead role of a film, he or she is more often than not given the role of a psychological detective. This type of casting occurs not only because filmmakers tend to make movies about crimes that must be solved, but also because the psychiatrist and the private detective perform parallel jobs. They both reveal the hidden by asking questions, analyzing the subtleties of their subjects' responses, following clues, drawing associations between the seen and the unseen, and otherwise delving into the unknown. The psychiatrist-detective first arose in the 1940s in films such as *Conflict* (1945) and *Spellbound* (1945), and received steady work throughout the latter half of the past century and into the new millennium, in films such as *The Manchurian Candidate* (1962), *The Believers* (1987), and *Don't Say a Word* (2001).

When the psychiatrist is cast in a supporting role, as is typically the case, the character could be good, evil or benign. The psychiatrist could provide help, hindrance, harm, or nothing other than explanation or advice, which could be either right or wrong. The relative flexibility that exists for the psychiatrist character in modern cinema, however, is a somewhat new phenomenon. Throughout the history of film, the psychiatrist has usually been typecast in one way or another, depending completely on the popular attitude towards psychiatry and psychoanalysis at the time the film was made. Early films, for instance, almost always cast the psychiatrist as a devious character who should never be trusted. This "dark age" of the psychiatrist in cinema (1909–1939, approximately) was followed by a "golden age" (1939–1963, approximately) in which psychiatry was depicted as a virtual panacea for all the world's ills, and the psychiatrist was cast as an omniscient, almost godlike hero—a marvelous, mystical mind healer.

The following sections will trace the development and evolution of the psychiatrist archetype in film. It is important to note, before we begin, that the development of the archetype has been a gradational process. Once a character type for the psychiatrist was established, that character—whether charlatan, villain, healer or lunatic—remained available for use by filmmakers at any time, regardless of the particular "age" in which the film might have been made. So, even if a film was made in the "golden age," when extremely positive depictions of the psychiatrist were predominant, retrograde versions of the archetype would still appear, usually in horror films and B movies, in which the psychiatrist was almost always cast as an evil manipulator of innocent subjects. Similarly, even after the golden age of silver screen psychiatry, when the psychiatrist was once again an object of scorn and mistrust, the superhuman, all-knowing mind healer would still appear from time to time, usually in order to give the hero the one important insight needed to save the day. Hence, the great variety of psychiatrist types seen in the cinema today can be seen as a direct result of many years of character development throughout various ages of screen personas. The modern film psychiatrist is only as versatile as the sum of the characters that preceded him. Nevertheless, there is little doubt that the archetype will continue to grow and develop—a perpetuating offspring of both the science of psychology and the art of film.

Headshrinkers

When the psychiatrist character in Victor Fleming's early silent film *When the Clouds Roll By* (1919) first appears on screen, he is introduced by an intertitle, stating: "Here he confirms the popular prejudice of the time against the mushroom growth of dubious psychologists." Indeed, there was an extreme prejudice against psychologists in the first decades of the twentieth century, fueled by a popular mistrust of science and modern medicine, as well as prejudice against both intellectuals and Jews, and in America, prejudice against Europeans. The psychiatrist was perceived as being all of these objects of mistrust wrapped into one person — a Jewish, European, intellectual, scientist-physician who practices dubious techniques such as mesmerism (the colloquial term for hypnotism in the early 1900s).

Terms such as mesmerism and alienists (the colloquial term for psychiatrists) articulated the underlying fear and suspicion felt towards the burgeoning field of psychiatry. The "doctors of the mind" weren't analysts or therapists; they were alienists, implying that they not only worked with alienated portions of human society, but that they actually took part in alienating their unsuspecting subjects from the normal world. To a larger degree, the psychiatrists themselves were aliens— unwelcome intruders in normal, unintellectual, unscientific, Christian, red-blooded, wholesome American society.

The general revulsion and mistrust felt towards psychiatrists in America culminated in the slang term "headshrinker," which originated as Hollywood lingo in the 1930s. Like the witchdoctors and headhunters of primitive societies, the headshrinker distorts and changes the head, though figuratively rather than literally. The term also implies a shrinking or narrowing of the perception of what psychiatrists actually do with their patients. Like the headshrinkers depicted in early films, the term "shrink" is aimed at narrowing the mind, limiting the understanding of a complex topic into a simple stereotype that even the dullest person could comprehend.

Headshrinking became the predominant Hollywood version of what psychoanalysis was all about, and by the end of the 1930s, the set costume for the psychiatrist archetype as well as the blueprints for his character had been firmly established in the cinema. The headshrinker was a short, unattractive, eccentric European with a big nose, wearing a pince-nez and a three-piece suit, sporting a goatee or beard, smoking a cigar or pipe, and spouting a constant stream of unintelligible oedipal psycho-jargon, in a barely comprehensible Viennese accent. As for his character traits, the psychiatrist was always to be suspected of devious trickery, manipulative chicanery, or outright malevolence.

Charlatan Quacks and Malevolent Mesmerists

In the first three decades of film, the psychiatrist was generally cast in one of two ways. He was either a roguish trickster posing as a real doctor, a charlatan quack, or else he was a real doctor who used his evil genius to further his diabolical plots, a malevolent mesmerist. In what is considered to be the first depiction of a psychiatrist on film, the title character in *Dr. Dippy's Sanitarium* (1906) is a charlatan quack. Though he is in charge of an asylum full of lunatics, Dr. Dippy is nearly as crazy as his patients, and has essentially no ability to treat or even control his unfortunate wards. Shortly after this inauspicious debut, the psychiatrist appeared once again as a title character in D.W. Griffith's *The Criminal Hypnotist* (1909), in which the psychiatrist (Arthur V. Johnson) was cast as a malevolent mesmerist, who uses hypnotism to control the minds of unsuspecting dupes in order to hatch an evil plot. Thus the two elemental versions of the psychiatrist archetype were established, character types that would predominate in the depiction of psychiatry for the next 20 years, and would be perpetuated to the present day.

Ten years after D.W. Griffith's unimpressive short, the evil mesmerist character type would come into its own in two extremely popular and successful feature length films. In the German expressionist masterpiece *The Cabinet of Dr. Caligari* (1919), the title character (Werner Krauss) is a perverse psychiatrist who hypnotically commands a powerless somnambulist (Conrad Veidt) into performing his evil, murderous biddings. In Victor Fleming's *When the Cloud Rolls By*, the sinister psychiatrist (Herbert Grimwood) uses similar devices to achieve similar ends. A glaring similarity between both 1919 films is that both evil doctors were actually escaped lunatics from asylums, reaffirming the popular suspicion that psychiatrists are as mad as, or madder than, the patients they allege to treat.

Films of the 1920s and '30s perpetuated the extremely negative versions of the archetype. In Fritz Lang's German series of Dr. Mabuse films, the evil doctor uses his hypnotic powers to further his diabolical plots. And in Tod Browning's *London After Midnight*, aka *The Hypnotist* (1927), Lon Chaney plays a double role as an evil hypnotist who is also a charlatan, using a vampire disguise to trick, terrorize and hypnotize his way into illgotten riches. The masters of horror, Bela Lugosi and Boris Karloff, often found themselves cast as mad doctors who used mind control, hypnotism and other vaguely psychiatric techniques to achieve their sinister, megalomaniacal goals.

In other films, such as Frank Capra's *Mr. Deeds Goes to Town* (1936), the psychiatrist plays a charlatan quack rather than an evil mesmerist.

Werner Krauss as Dr. Caligari (left) and Conrad Veidt as Cesare the somnambulist (right) in Robert Wiene's *The Cabinet of Dr. Caligari* (1919).

Though he is cast as a foolish clown rather than as an evil villain, the stain to the public perception of psychiatry is even more severe, as complete ineptitude is a more believable trait than complete wickedness. When the buffoonish Dr. Von Haller (Wyrley Birch) charged Deeds (Gary Cooper) with insanity because he enjoys playing the tuba, more damage was done to psychiatry as a field than in a hundred films in which mad psychiatrists used hypnotism to conquer the world. Audiences didn't really believe that any psychiatrists were as evil as the ones played by Karloff or Lugosi, but many audiences really did believe that most psychiatrists were as stupid and inept as the one depicted in *Mr. Deeds* and dozens of films just like it.

However, even as the perception of psychiatry in film reached its lowest and darkest point, change was on the horizon. New attitudes towards the field brought about by grand international and domestic events would completely alter the public view of psychiatrists, both on and off the silver screen.

The Talking Cure

Though depictions of the psychiatrist as a quack or a villain would continue into the 1940s and even until this day, the tide had begun to turn by the end of the 1930s, and it turned even more strongly in the war years, partly because of the increased public acceptance of clinical psychology via the need for widespread treatment of "shell shocked" soldiers. Psychiatrists were beginning to be seen as real doctors rather than swindling "shrinks" or villainous mesmerists. Furthermore, understanding of how the therapeutic process actually worked was growing — a growth again due in part to the need to understand traumatized soldiers as the psychologically wounded, rather than as raving lunatics or pathetic madmen. The stigma of mental illness was beginning to clear, and with it, the stigma of being a mental health practitioner.

But while a positive understanding of psychiatry was now in vogue among the masses, Hollywood still needed to present clear and simple versions of the psychiatrist archetype. The film business, after all, is about entertainment, not education. Hence, the therapeutic process was simplified in film as a relatively quick and simple fix. Recovery from trauma, neurosis or even psychosis typically occurred suddenly and dramatically through an emotional catharsis. The psychiatrist would use his incredible intuitive powers to magically uncover his patient's secret hidden issues or traumatic memories. The liberation of these troublesome repressed issues, typically memories from early childhood involving a parent, would result in a catharsis or purging of emotional energy, and thus a complete recovery. Though, on occasion, the psychiatrist would use the retrograde technique of hypnotism, the more common method employed in the post–1930s era was what early psychoanalysts called "the talking cure." By talking with the patient and creating a therapeutic environment based on a trusting and nurturing doctor-patient relationship, the underlying unconscious issues would be revealed and worked through during the discussions in analysis. The patient, facilitated by the psychiatrist, would literally talk his way through his problems and heal himself via derepression and self-understanding.

Hollywood's simplistic take on the talking cure is epitomized in the written prologue to Hitchcock's *Spellbound* (1945):

> Our story deals with psychoanalysis, the method by which modern science treats the emotional problems of the sane. The analyst seeks only to induce the patient to talk about his hidden problems, to open the locked doors of his mind. Once the complexes that have been disturbing the patient are uncovered and interpreted, the illness and confusion disappear ... and the evils of unreason are driven from the human soul.

On the one hand, the cinema aims to legitimize psychiatry by labeling it a science and portraying it with earnest zeal; but on the other hand, the cinema betrays this earnestness by portraying psychiatry as a quick fix, and confusing the matter with blatantly unscientific references to "the evils of unreason" and "the human soul."

Spellbound is a prime example of the classic Hollywood treatment of psychoanalysis. Dr. Petersen (Ingrid Bergman), a beautiful psychoanalyst, inexplicably wears a white lab coat all day for no apparent reason other than a need to look scientific. When the psychologically disturbed John Ballantine (Gregory Peck) enters the scene, various psychiatrists go on and on at every turn about his inscrutable "guilt complex," which is miraculously cured the instant he remembers the details of a childhood trauma. Even the title of the movie implies a sense of witchery, an allusion to the belief that psychological disorders are akin to spiritual possessions, supernatural hexes or evil curses. Though the psychiatrists in *Spellbound* are called "scientists," their role and methods more closely resemble that of exorcists, witch doctors or magicians.

The Wise Old Man

As the psychiatrist archetype emerged from its dark age in pre–1940s cinema, it was once again split into two dominant versions, this time based on gender. Both versions were exclusively positive, as opposed to the exclusively negative versions in the dark age. Both versions also used the talking cure as their primary technique. However, the way in which psychological healing was achieved diverged sharply. Male psychiatrists were typically portrayed as strong, omniscient, benevolent older men. Their presence corresponded quite strongly with Carl G. Jung's description of the wise old man archetype. The wise old man was a strong, all-knowing father figure, much like a god, but on a personal rather than cultural level. Like a father, the wise old man offered the knowledge and support that the hero needed in order to overcome his fears or obstacles and achieve his goals. The male psychiatrist was typically depicted as the wise old man archetype in films of the 1940s, '50s and early '60s.

Transference

In order for the wise old man relationship between doctor and patient to work, the patient had to really trust and look up to his or her psychiatrist. Symbolically, the doctor had to become a surrogate father figure to his patient. He had to become the wise, understanding, supportive and strong father figure which would replace the absent, abusive, negligent or otherwise negative real father figure, which the patient had to overcome. This process of becoming a supportive and positive parental figure to the patient is known as "transference." It is very important that transference take place, because it provides the bedrock of the therapeutic relationship. If the patient does not perceive the psychiatrist as a strong, supportive and wise parental figure, then no trust will exist in the relationship. If the patient does not trust the doctor, the patient will not feel comfortable in disclosing his or her innermost secrets, and therefore no real therapeutic work will proceed. In the case of the wise old man psychiatrist archetype, the therapy commences when the patient begins to trust the older male doctor, and it ends when the patient allows him or herself to be healed by this authoritative father figure. In other words, the therapy begins and ends with a positive and powerful act of transference.

Perhaps the first depiction of the wise old man psychiatrist was in Charles Vidor's *Blind Alley* (1939), later remade in 1948 under the title *The Dark Past*. In both versions of the film, the psychiatrist uses dream analysis to uncover his violent patient's repressed aggressive impulses towards his father. Through the process of transference, the doctor becomes a replacement father figure to his disturbed

Gregory Peck as John Ballantine and Ingrid Bergman as Dr. Constance Petersen in Alfred Hitchcock's *Spellbound* (1945).

patient. This transference allows the patient to understand his own dark, repressed, aggressive impulses towards his biological father, while simultaneously forming a positive, trusting relationship with a new symbolic father figure. This new relationship and self-knowledge leads to the resolution of the patient's aggression issues, as well as his ironic demise. The patient was a psychopathic killer and gangster. His murderous violence stemmed from a repressed desire to kill his father. When this repressed desire is derepressed and resolved through analysis, the killer loses his ability to kill. As such, he cannot shoot back at the cops coming after him in the climactic scene, and he is killed.

The term "transference" involves a lot of issues. In one sense, the patients allow themselves to transfer emotional baggage related to parental or other significant figures in their private lives onto the psychiatrist. Once the baggage is transferred, it can be dealt with in the therapeutic atmosphere of the analysis. On another level, the patient transfers his or her need for a strong and positive parental figure onto the psychiatrist, placing an incredible amount of trust and faith into the therapeutic relationship. And on an even more elemental level, the patient transfers the control of his or her own psyche into the competent hands of the psychiatrist, allowing the good doctor to steer the therapy in the proper direction and eventually arrive at the destination in which the patient's issues will be resolved. In a sense, the patient must fall in love with the psychiatrist, in the same way that a small child will love her father. This is why most of the film depictions of the wise old man psychiatrist archetype involve a young female patient with an older doctor.

In classic films such as *Now, Voyager* (1942), *The Snake Pit* (1948), and *The Three Faces of Eve* (1957), a vulnerable, pretty girl (Bette Davis, Olivia de Havilland, and Joanne Woodward, respectively) must first overcome her fear and mistrust of the older and powerful male doctor (Claude Rains, Leo Genn and Lee J. Cobb, respectively). Once fear and mistrust are overcome, the girl typically falls in love with her doctor, just as a little girl falls romantically in love with her father when she is in the throes of her Electra Complex. The wise old psychiatrist uses this positive transference to establish trust in the therapeutic relationship, while simultaneously working through the transference, making it clear to the patient that she does not really love him, she is only in love with the persona of the powerful and wise father figure. In the final stages of therapy, the psychiatrist leads his patient to a healthy resolution of her issues, which typically leads her into the arms of a different man. The girl's love for the psychiatrist, which is symbolically incestuous, is then transferred onto this appropriate and nonincestuous love interest. Thus, cured by her symbolic father, the psychologically healed girl and her handsome young prince live happily ever after.

The Love Goddess

For most of film history, when a woman was cast in the role of psychiatrist, the dynamic changed completely. In Jungian psychology, the father archetype is the wise old man, and the mother archetype is the goddess. While the wise old man supplies wisdom, strength and power, the goddess provides love. So, while the male psychiatrist in movies heals through the art and science of psychoanalysis, the female psychiatrist almost always heals through love. In the quintessential female psychiatrist movie, Hitchcock's *Spellbound*, and dozens of films just like it, the psychiatrist, Dr. Constance Petersen (Ingrid Bergman), falls in love with a disturbed mental case (Gregory Peck). While she is somewhat of an ineffectual doctor before she falls in love, she is a whirlwind after her fall. Her passion and dedication to save her beloved patient have no bounds. The moral of the female psychiatrist movie is the ever-popular theme, "love conquers all." The female psychiatrist as love goddess archetype fits in well with some common misconceptions about women that were popular in the first half of the twentieth century: First, that women are too emotional to be good scientists or analysts; second, that women doctors and nurses always fall in love with their male patients, (the "Florence Nightingale effect"); and third, that a woman, no matter how successful, is incomplete without a man. Dr. Brulov (Michael Chekhov), the goddess-psychiatrist's training analyst in *Spellbound*, summed it up nicely when he tells her: "Women make the best psychoanalysts until they fall in love ... then they make the best patients."

Interestingly, *Spellbound* featured a picture-perfect depiction of four stereotypical psychiatrist movie characters. Dr. Brulov is a prime example of the wise old man psychiatrist. He is short, very old, eccentric, smokes a pipe, has a goatee, wears old-fashioned horned rim glasses and speaks with a thick Viennese accent. He is also a supportive (although old-fashioned) mentor and father figure to Dr. Petersen. He treats her like a daughter. When she lies to him, introducing Ballantine as her husband, Brulov replies, "Any husband of Constance is a husband of mine," implying that he and Petersen are like family. The psychiatrist-as-father role is expanded to include Ballantine. Later on in the film, when Brulov begins his analysis of Ballantine, he tells him, "I'm going to be your father image. I want you to look on me as your father. Trust me, lean on me."

Petersen is a perfect example of the love goddess psychiatrist, as she immediately falls desperately in love with Ballantine, despite the fact that he is a paranoid amnesiac experiencing psychosis and a severe identity disorder, who may or may not be a murderous psychopath. In the first act of the film, Ballantine himself poses as a famous psychiatrist in charge of a mental asylum. In reality, he is actually a charlatan quack. À la Dr. Caligari, he is an escaped madman on the lam, even more psychologically disturbed than most of the patients in the asylum that he is pretending to run. And finally, the villain in the film is Dr. Murchison (Leo Carroll), a mad psychiatrist in charge of the asylum, who murders another psychiatrist in a jealous rage, and then tries to pin the murder on the mentally confused Ballantine. At the end of the film, Murchison kills himself, a proper end to a retrograde evil psychiatrist type that, no matter how far psychiatry as a field progressed, would just not go away.

Countertransference

Just as the wise old man psychiatrist heals through transference, the love goddess psychiatrist heals through countertransference. In analysis, it is quite normal for the analyst to experience personal feelings for his patient. A certain amount of countertransference is expected. If the patient is putting all of her trust and faith in her therapist, making him a surrogate parental figure, then it is only appropriate that the therapist invest some feelings of care and empathy in his patient, making her a surrogate child. If the therapist does not experience a certain amount of countertransference, then he is not a very good therapist. If he feels absolutely nothing for his patient, then he does not truly care for her, and he is not "putting his heart" into his work. Countertransference, nevertheless, is a double-edged sword. A psychiatrist can care too little, but then again, he could also care too much. The slippery slope of personal emotions in the therapeutic environment can lead to some pretty serious messes, especially in the movies.

A stark dichotomy along gender lines can be seen in the depiction of countertransference in film. When the love goddess psychiatrist falls in love with one of her patients, it typically leads to the patient's complete recovery and redemption. But when a male psychiatrist gives in to his feelings of countertransference and develops a romantic infatuation for his female patient, the results are usually quite unhealthy. However, these negative representations of the psychiatric relationship were rarely seen in the 1940s, '50s and early '60s, a time when Hollywood was in love with psychiatry and psychiatrists could do no wrong. This love story culminated in the years between 1957 and 1963, an era that Gabbard and Gabbard referred to in their book, *Psychiatry and the Cinema* (1999), as "the golden age of psychiatry in the American cinema." These years saw the release of films such as *The Three Faces of Eve, Suddenly, Last Summer* (1959), *Splendor in the Grass* (1961), *David and Lisa* (1962), *Captain Newman, M.D.* (1963), and of course, John Huston's *Freud* (1962). In all of these films (especially the latter), psychiatrists are lionized as selfless healers of almost godlike proportions. The love story came to a bitter end in the years to follow. When the golden age ended, the depiction of psychiatrists in film became so negative, that the image of a male psychiatrist in love with his vulnerable female patient was merely the least of a whole menagerie of evils.

The Return of the Dark Age

In 1963, Bob Dylan sang, "The times they are a-changing." They certainly were. All aspects of cultural life in America were beginning to change at that time. The cultural revolution was glaringly apparent in the cinema. The psychiatrist archetype, embedded in the American collective unconscious as a strong and dependable father figure, began to lose his air of unassailability. Father figures in general were suspect in the movie theaters. Father figures represented the older generation, the patriarchal ruling class, the right wing establishment that was trying to repress the youth movement. The psychiatrist, once an advocate of derepression, was beginning to be seen as a symbol of repression. He was an agent of social conformity, trying to bind the rebellious counterculture in a straitjacket of obedience. To the younger generation of filmmakers in the 1960s and '70s, psychiatrists represented one thing: "the Man."

Signs of change in the depiction of the archetype could be seen in subtle weaknesses of various psychiatrist characters in the 1950s and early '60s. The archetype was beginning to show chinks in his armor. In Henry Hathaway's *Fourteen Hours* (1951), a disturbed young man (Richard Baseheart) stands on a precipitous ledge, sixteen floors above a Manhattan street, threatening to jump. Though the brilliant and capable psychiatrist (Martin Gabel) can explain the young man's problem in an effortless flow of elaborate psychobabble, he cannot help him. The young man will not speak with the psychiatrist because he doesn't trust doctors. Similarly, in Hitchcock's *Psycho* (1960), the brilliant and self-assured psychiatrist (Simon Oakland) can explain in detail all of the murderous psychotic's (Anthony

Perkins) oedipal difficulties, but only after Norman's killing spree is over, and he is safely restrained in police custody.

Another clue to the imminent change to come can be seen in John Frankenheimer's groundbreaking 1962 psy-fi classic, *The Manchurian Candidate*. In this transitional film, based on Richard Condon's novel, two opposing versions of psychiatrist characters are depicted. Dr. Lo (Khigh Dhiegh) is an evil Manchurian mesmerist, similar in every way to the stereotypical mad doctor representations of the psychiatrist that dominated the screen in the 1930s. Dr. Lo uses hypnotism and sinister mind control techniques to brainwash a group of American soldiers, creating a hypnotically controlled assassin out of one them (Laurence Harvey). The only man who can stop this sinister plot is Marco (Frank Sinatra), a soldier who is having recurrent dreams about the brainwashing. Enter a wise and caring psychiatrist (Joe Adams) — the only man who believes Marco's crazy story, and the only one who can help Marco save the country from the communists. This simultaneous depiction of both archetypes in the same film asserts that some psychiatrists are good while others are bad, and that psychiatry as a tool could be used for both good and evil. The golden age's optimistic view of psychiatry had begun to turn decidedly pessimistic by the early 1960s. From that point on, the role of the psychiatrist in the cinema will only become more complex.

Dirty Wise Old Men

As mentioned previously, the depiction of romantic countertransference in film tends to follow a strict gender dichotomy in which the outcome for female psychiatrists is extremely positive, and the outcome for male psychiatrists is extremely negative. Depictions of the wise old man allowing his illicit sexual desire to overcome his professional conscience began to appear more regularly after the waning of the golden age. There were, however, some transitional films that foreshadowed the new trend. Like *The Manchurian Candidate*, Henry King's *Tender Is the Night* (based on the F. Scott Fitzgerald novel), also appeared on screen in 1962 — a precipitous year for screen psychiatrists. In this film, Jason Robards plays a wise and caring psychiatrist with the rather implausible yet oddly portentous name of Dr. Dick Diver. Though he is a talented analyst, he cannot overcome his passionate countertransference for a lovely young patient (Jennifer Jones). Giving in to his love leads to his tragic downfall.

After 1962, the image of the philandering male psychiatrist who routinely seduces his young, vulnerable, female patients would be depicted so many times in film as to become hackneyed and trite. Woody Allen, in particular, would cast this archetypal character in many of his films, beginning with his script for *What's New, Pussycat?* (1965). In Allen's first feature length screenplay, Dr. Fritz Fassbender (Peter Sellers) is a rather silly psychiatrist who call himself a "doctor of the mind," and is completely obsessed with seducing his sexy young patient (Capucine). In Allen's *Everything You Always Wanted to Know About Sex * But Were Afraid to Ask* (1972), Gene Wilder plays a brilliant doctor who falls in love with a female patient. The only problem is, the female patient is a sheep. Obviously, Wilder's downfall is swift and ruinous. In *Zelig* (1983), Allen's psychiatrist is a woman (Mia Farrow). True to form, when the female psychiatrist falls in love with her male patient, he is miraculously cured and they live happily ever after. This denouement contrasts strikingly with the characters in Allen's *Husbands and Wives* (1992), in which a male psychiatrist's (Ron Rifkin) infatuation with his young patient (Juliette Lewis) is depicted as pathetic and disastrous. Only in his most recent depiction of countertransference, *Deconstructing Harry* (1997), has Allen broken the mold, by depicting an unhappy relationship between a man (Stanley Tucci) and his female psychiatrist (Kirstie Alley), though it is clear that their problems do not arise from countertransference, but rather, they are manifestations of Woody Allen's central pessimistic philosophies, in which all relationships are eventually doomed to failure, and psychoanalysis is an essentially worthless, narcissistic and futile pursuit.

Shocking Conformity

For movie psychiatrists in the 1960s and '70s, countertransference was the least of their problems. The pessimistic view of psychiatry that had taken over in cinema as a corollary to the antiauthoritarianism trend in all aspects of American culture began to equate psychiatry with conformity. The "headshrinker" was now an agent of "the Man," and his job was to shrink any and all social misfits into the shape that society wanted them to be in. The counterculture's dim view of psychiatry was not so far off. The bible of the psychological profession — the *Diagnostic and Statistical Manual of Mental Disorders (DSM)* — listed homosexuality as a "sociopathic personality disturbance." Though the *DSM II* removed homosexuality from the sociopathic list in 1968, it was still categorized as a "sexual deviation" until the release of the *DSM III* in 1973, when the orientation was only considered a disorder if it was "ego-dystonic," (harmful to the subject's sense of self). Ego-dystonic homosexuality disorder would eventually be deleted from the manual when the *DSM III* was revised in 1987.

The pathologizing of homosexuality was just one way in which the fields of psychology and psychiatry attempted to normalize human behavior by setting rather rigid and conservative bounds for psychological health. Various aspects of the 1960s counterculture that were considered central to the movement — the sexual revolution, hallucinogenic drug use, "dropping out" of normal society — were considered psychologically aberrant by the practicing psychiatrists of that era. The most dramatic expressions of psychiatry as a mechanism of enforcing conformity is seen in the film depictions of ECT, (electroconvulsive therapy), commonly known as "electroshock treatment."

In the 1960s and '70s, ECT was recast in movie theaters as a torturous, barbaric, medieval practice, in which individualistic mental patients were literally shocked into conformity. Vivid depictions of electroshock treatment were depicted in films such as Samuel Fuller's *Shock Corridor* (1963), *Shock Treatment* (1964), John Cassavetes' *A Woman Under the Influence* (1974), and most notably, in Milos Forman's masterpiece, *One Flew Over the Cuckoo's Nest* (1975). The latter film, based on Ken Kesey's novel, won the Academy Awards for Best Actor (Jack Nicholson), Best Actress (Louise Fletcher), Best Adapted Screenplay (Lawrence Hauben and Bo Goldman), Best Director (Forman), and Best Picture (Saul Zaentz and Michael Douglas). The enormous popular and critical success of *Cuckoo's Nest* escalated the film to iconic status. The extremely negative view of psychiatry portrayed in this film, especially in the brutal and now infamous shock treatment scene, is emblematic of the cinematic representations of the field in those days.

An equally important film released in the same era was Stanley Kubrick's *A Clockwork Orange* (1971), which epitomized the psychiatry-as-an-agent-of-conformity mindset. In the film, young Alex (Malcolm McDowell) is a juvenile delinquent, "whose principal interests are rape, ultra-violence and Beethoven." His full name, Alexander de Large, is an oblique reference to Alexander the Great, inferring that in the ancient days of classical Greece, an adolescent with Alex's talents for leadership, sexual dominance and aggression could have conquered the world, but in the modern days of psychiatry and conformity, Alex's proclivities are considered pathological. Alex is incarcerated and then "cured" of his "ultraviolent" sexual-aggressive tendencies via the "Ludovico technique," which involves a drug that induces intense nausea. Alex is given the drug and then forced to watch violent films, in order for his body and mind to make the primary association that violence is bad and sickening.

The Ludovico technique eerily recalls the behaviorist methods of "shaping" and "conditioning," in which techniques such as aversion therapy are used to control and modify human behaviors. The title of the film, based on Anthony Burgess' novel, alludes to the potential hazards of behavior modification applied at a societal level. The word "orange" is an inference to the Malay root word for man, "ourang" (from which the word orangutan is derived). A "clockwork orange" is a mechanized man — a being that resembles a human but is actually a machine, lacking any freedom of choice or self-determination. The Ludovico technique also recalls the pseudopsychiatric process of brainwashing as well as electroshock treatment, in that the technique is painful and seems to cause some sort of physiological change in the subject's brain. Like *Cuckoo's Nest*, *Clockwork Orange* is an indictment of the field of psychiatry. The filmmakers' contention is that psychiatrists use invasive, insidious, and often brutal techniques in order to force social misfits into an involuntary state of conformity.

When electroshock doesn't work, "the Man" as psychiatrist will opt for the last resort ... full frontal lobotomy. As far as psychiatric techniques for behavior modification are concerned, lobotomy is as invasive as you can get. The doctor's knife actually invades and severs a part of the patient's cerebrum. Lobotomy as an agent of conformity was depicted quite vividly in *A Fine Madness* (1966), in which an iconoclastic poet (Sean Connery) is lobotomized in order to exorcise him of his individuality. In this sense, the process of lobotomy evokes the medieval practice of lepanation, in which barbers bore holes into people's skulls in order to free them of evil spirits. In *Cuckoo's Nest*, McMurphy (Jack Nicholson) is a free spirit, but in the end, his nonconformist spirit is exorcised via a lobotomy. Similarly, at the end of *Clockwork Orange*, the "cured" Alex goes haywire, nearly kills himself, and is returned to the care of his psychiatrists. As he recovers, he remembers, as if in a dream, that the "doctors were playing around with my gulliver, you know, like the inside of my brain." His purple-haired psychiatrist assures him that this was just a dream, but the implication is that he was lobotomized. The twist in this case is that the lobotomy reversed the effects of the sinister Ludovico technique, allowing him to return to his nonconformist, albeit ultraviolent, nature.

Ineffectual Imbeciles

As in the dark age of cinema psychiatry, the archetype was not just depicted as a malevolent force. Sometimes, they were just incompetent boobs, whose feeble attempts to normalize their patients merely emphasized how square and out of touch "the Man" really was. In one of the most memorable nonconformist themed movies of the hippy age, Hal Ashby's *Harold and Maude* (1971), young Harold (Bud Cort) faces three authoritarian agents of social conformity: a priest, a military uncle, and an imbecilic psychiatrist. The psychiatrist (G. Wood) is unable to help Harold with his obvious difficulties in relating to his absent father and officious mother (Vivian Pickles). He only appears sporadically in order to cajole Harold into more "healthy" psychological pursuits, to spout meaningless oedipal dribble in the course of disparaging his new relationship with the much older Maude (Ruth Gordon), and to basically play the part of the buffoonish pseudoscientist as the representative of the middle-aged, authoritarian, right-wing establishment.

The psychiatrist in *Diary of a Mad Housewife* (1970) plays a similar role. Tina Balser (Carrie Snodgrass) is a woman on the verge of liberation, who realizes that she has become unsatisfied with the traditional feminine roles of mother and housewife. Her psychiatrist (who's scenes were not included in the theatrical release, but can now be seen in both the television and video versions of the film) acts as a foil to Tina's burgeoning individualism. His main aim is to convince Tina that her only path to happiness is by conforming to the stifling traditional roles that encage her.

The same theme is played out, with extreme melodrama, in Sidney Lumet's *Equus* (1977)—based on the play by Peter Shaffer. The disturbed youth, Alan Strang (Peter Firth), has a fitting name, as his *strange* obsession with horses leads to an equally strange sexual fetish culminating in a horrific act of psychotic madness in which he gouges the eyes out of six horses. Though his psychiatrist, Dr. Dysart (Richard Burton), cures the boy, he laments his profession and the fruits of his own labor. Though Alan was clearly disturbed, Dysart envied his maniacal passion. Dysart sees psychiatry as a science that robs aberrant individuals of their passion, just as science itself is a belief system that robs humanity of it religious faith ... its spiritual passion. According to Dysart, though Alan was exorcised of his psychological demons and can now rejoin normal society, he will never experience the heights of passion again.

Secular Skeptics

Burton's role as a psychiatric exorcist of passion in *Equus* stands in stark contrast to a role he played the very same year in *The Exorcist II* (1977). In this sequel to the 1973 blockbuster about demonic possession, Burton plays a passionate priest, faithful to his religion and deeply committed to the task of exorcising a demon from an innocent girl (Linda Blair). His foil in this film is a nonbelieving psychiatrist (Louise Fletcher), in her follow-up performance to her Oscar winning role as the psychiatric nurse in *Cuckoo's Nest*. As a scientist, the psychiatrist is naturally skeptical of supernatural or spiritual sources to ostensibly psychological problems. In *Exorcist II,* Fletcher is not only the denying obstacle to the heroic priest, she is also the unwitting cause to the possession, as her extravagant hypnosis machine affords the medium through which the evil demon possesses the girl.

The psychiatrist's role as the dimwitted foil to the faithful hero goes back to the early years of film. As a devout scientist, the psychiatrist is also an atheist, and thereby a skeptic of all things spiritual and supernatural. In horror movies, which frequently feature evil powers of spiritual or supernatural origin, the psychiatrist is easily cast as the secular obstacle of disbelief. For instance, in Tod Browning's *Dracula* (1931), the secular psychiatrist, Dr. Seward (Herbert Bunston), cannot believe that Count Dracula (Bela Lugosi) is actually an evil vampire. Only Professor Van Helsing, a scholar of theology, folklore, and all things mythological, is aware of Dracula's true evil identity. The psychiatrist as the secular skeptic and foil to the faithful hero can be seen in most of the demonic horror movies that were in vogue in the 1960s and '70s, such as: *Rosemary's Baby* (1968), *The Exorcist* (1973), *The Exorcist II, The Omen* (1976) and *Damien: Omen II* (1978). In these founding films of the devil thriller genre, and dozens of films just like them, psychiatrists are nearly always depicted as impotent, powerless, and futile figures when faced with the supernatural powers of true evil.

Faceless Facilitators

A mainstay of the psychoanalyst's office, at least in the early days, was the ubiquitous "psychiatric couch," on which the patient would lie as he recalled his early childhood memories, dreams, and other unconscious issues to his analyst, who would sit attentively behind the couch, notepad and pencil in hand. The psychiatric couch is a relic of the medical origins of the psychiatrist's trade. It replaced the medical examination table. The couch was also meant to offer a place where patients could be extremely comfortable on a physical level, in order to ease hypnosis or to just make the patient feel relaxed and at ease. Finally, the set up was also an aid in the transference process. By lying on a couch with the analyst behind him, the patient could not see his doctor. Theoretically, this allowed the doctor to become a blank slate for transference, making it easy for the patient to project all sorts of issues and associations onto the unseen psychiatrist. Though the psychiatric couch setup is almost never used anymore in real practice, it is still a mainstay in movies, featured in most cinematic depictions of the analyst's office.

Portraying the psychiatrist as a faceless and frequently voiceless figure plays into the perception in cinema that psychiatrists themselves are for the most part ineffectual, unnecessary, and unhelpful. Gabbard and Gabbard (1999) point out that psychiatrists in movies often play a pragmatic role, as faceless facilitators through which film characters can express their innermost feelings, deepest secrets, and unconscious psychological issues. The Gabbards apply the term "ficelle" to this frequently seen role, borrowing the expression from Henry James (1934). The term refers to the invisible strings that the puppeteer uses to control a puppet. In essence, the psychiatrist as a ficelle is merely a replacement for voiceover, the process of dubbing character narration over a scene. Since voiceover is nonorganic to the film — it comes out of nowhere — many filmmakers consider it to be a violation of the illusion of reality that the film is trying to create. However, filmmakers could still provide important backstory, explanation, and exposition about a character while also avoiding voiceover, by showing a seen in which the character, lying on a psychiatric couch, bares his soul to a faceless ficelle.

There are way too many depictions of the psychiatrist as ficelle to provide even a perfunctory rundown, so just a few will be named. In *Klute* (1971), we have little insight into the heroine's (Jane Fonda) conflicted feelings about being a prostitute, but through her sessions with a mainly faceless psychiatrist, we're allowed to hear her feelings about her career, and we can also get a peak at her weak and vulnerable sides. In *The Lonely Guy* (1984), Steve Martin's character's sense of loneliness and alienation are not ameliorated by psychiatry, as he only speaks to his analyst through an intercom. Neither Martin nor the audience ever see the psychiatrist's face. In *Leaving Las Vegas* (1995), the therapist plays an identical role as the one in *Klute,* but to an even higher level of anonymity, as the heroine (Elisabeth Shue) speaks directly to the screen, and we never see her therapist's face. And finally, aside from being the most persistent butt of Woody Allen's one-liner jokes, psychiatrists in Allen's films are quite frequently cast as faceless facilitators, most notably, in *Annie Hall* (1977), *Interiors* (1978), *Hannah and Her Sisters* (1986), *Husbands and Wives* (1992), and *Anything Else* (2003).

The Hugging Cure

As the turbulent 1960s and its long-lasting cultural aftershocks through-out the 1970s finally yielded to the more conservative and right-wing era of the 1980s — the Reagan Era — the perception of psychiatry in the cinema once again changed. There was a decided return to the positive depictions of therapists that reigned in the golden age. But the modern age film psychiatrists had developed in a peculiar way. They relied less on pseudoscientific stoicism and allowed themselves to be warmer, kinder, and more intimate with their patients. In a sense, the later versions of the psychiatrist archetype combine both the talking cure of the wise old man and the loving cure of the goddess. This integrated technique, as epitomized in the most successful psychiatry-themed films of the past twenty-five years, *Ordinary People* (1980) and *Good Will Hunting* (1997), could be dubbed "the hugging cure."

In both films, the course of therapy runs pretty much the same. A troubled young man enters therapy. His psychiatrist, Dr. Berger (Judd Hirsch) in *Ordinary People* and Dr. Maguire (Robin Williams) in *Good Will Hunting*, becomes a father figure to the boy, (Timothy Hutton and Matt Damon, respectively). The fatherly psychiatrist provides both wisdom and love, while a female romantic interest (Elizabeth McGovern and Minnie Driver, respectively) provides a nurturing mother replacement figure. At the end of therapy, the boys are able to overcome traumatic memories through a cathartic release of emotional baggage, and in both cases, the climax of therapy is marked by a dramatic hug between patient and psychiatrist. The hugging cure symbolizes the psychiatrist's ability to heal the psychologically wounded with a combination of both science and love. Though they are as ideal as the psychiatrists of the golden age, these modern age archetypes diverge from the older ones in that they are overtly emotional in their interactions with their patients, displaying anger, impatience, and even hostility, in addition to their ability to show love via physical intimacy — an act which is sternly frowned upon by professional psychiatric organizations.

Psycho-Psychiatrists

Though the depiction of psychiatrists in the modern age of cinema has turned noticeably more positive, the traditional negative depiction of psychiatrists as evil megalomaniacs in horror films, a tradition begun in 1919 with *Dr. Caligari*, remains true to form. If anything, psychiatrists in modern age horror movies are even more malevolent than their dark age predecessors. In the same year that Robert Redford lionized the good Dr. Berger in *Ordinary People*, Brian De Palma created a chilling modern age portrait of a psychotic psychiatrist (Michael Caine) in *Dressed to Kill* (1980). But it wasn't until 1991 that the ultimate psycho-psychiatrist, the sinister Hannibal Lecter (Anthony Hopkins), appeared in Jonathan Demme's *The Silence of the Lambs*. As a doctor who uses his psychiatric skills to torture and destroy his innocent victims, Lecter came to be perceived as the most vile of all cinema serial killers, and would eventually be voted by the American Film Institute as the number one villain in film history. Other notable depictions of psychotic psychiatrists can be seen in the prototypical psycho thrillers, *Raising Cain* (1992), *Conspiracy Theory* (1997), *Disturbing Behavior* (1998), and *Gothika* (2003).

Conclusion

After a century of variation in the portrayal of psychiatrists in film, their depiction is still relegated primarily to the dichotomy of *Dr. Jekylls* or *Dr. Hydes* ... they are either unbelievably good, or incalculably evil. Nevertheless, the primary role of film is to entertain. It is not the job of film to educate, elucidate, illuminate, enlighten, or in any way broaden the perceptions of movie audiences. As such, criticizing filmmakers for portraying stereotypical, incorrect, or oversimplified depictions of psychiatrists (as opposed to accurate or balanced depictions) is like criticizing your dog for not taking out the garbage. It's just not in their job description.

Nevertheless, as we look forward to the next millennium of film, we know for certain that we will see more psychiatrists on the silver screen, and there is much hope for the future. Up till now, there has been little differentiation in films between psychiatrists, clinical psychologists, psychoanalysts, psychotherapists, counselors, social workers, or any other professional that is even marginally related to a mental health field. Similarly, the history of film has shown a glaring lack of balanced depictions of mental health practitioners. As we have seen, they are typically portrayed as saintly, evil, or completely useless. It is entirely possible that we will see more realistic depictions of mental health practitioners in the decades and centuries to come. Whether or not these more realistic psychiatrists will be entertaining on a cinematic level, remains to be seen.

CHAPTER TWO

Psycho Killers

My theory is that everyone is a potential murderer.
Bruno (Robert Walker)
from Alfred Hitchcock's Strangers on a Train *(1951)*

People with psychological disorders have always appeared in movies in numbers highly disproportionate to the actual number of people with psychological disorders in the population at large. In the movies, the killer, villain, or criminal is extremely likely to be a psychopath — a person completely out of touch with reality, and severely mentally disturbed. Certainly, Alfred Hitchcock's *Psycho* (1960) was a landmark film in regards to the depiction of the psycho killer in film, but it was by no means the first. Even within the relatively circumscribed sphere of horror movies and thrillers featuring psycho killers, *Psycho* was not the first of such pictures— though it certainly began a new trend in the horror/thriller genre. The evolution of the psycho killer archetype through the twentieth century parallels film audiences' understanding and acceptance of psychology as a field, and the ability of psychology to provide explanations for people's behaviors and motivations. If there is one aspect of the archetype that has evolved over the decades, it is clearly found within the psycho killer's motivation to kill.

Vicious Monsters and Evil Villains

In the early years of film, the silent era through the 1930s, there were very few "psycho killers" per se. Movie villains who killed their victims were either monsters, such as vampires, mummies, or werewolves, or they were simply sinister, evil men. As for motivation, there was little or none. Monsters killed, generally, as a corollary to their lustful pursuit of a desirable young maiden. Evil villains, such as the Phantom (Lon Chaney) in *The Phantom of the Opera* (1925) or Count Poelzig (Boris Karloff) in *The Black Cat* (1934), typically killed for the same reason. Lust and desire as motivations for murder are quite effective and convincing, though not particularly sophisticated. Lust and desire could be directed at nearly anyone at anytime. Perhaps therein lay the horror of the monster/villain's vicious deeds, but still, more sophisticated motivations would need to emerge.

Sociopathic Gangsters

In the early 1930s, another type of murderous villain arose out of the budding new genre of gangster films. The sociopathic gangster murderers played by James Cagney, Edward G. Robinson, George Raft, and Humphrey Bogart in numerous gangster movies were psychologically disturbed to be sure, but they weren't stark raving mad, like the villains played by Lon Chaney, Boris Karloff, and Bela Lugosi, in the horror pictures of that period. Neither were they monsters. The gangster killers were real men living in a real world who killed for real reasons. The gangster's motivation for killing was success in his chosen field, revenge, and/or survival. The gangster killed in order to be a successful, living, and unfettered criminal. Once again, simple and effective motivations for a rather simple type of character.

In the 1940s, however, the one-dimensional gangster character began to develop in terms of psychological sophistication and motivation. In *Blind Alley* (1939), the gangster killer (Chester Morris) is psychoanalyzed. The audience discovers the psychological root of the character's murderous rage, in this case, a displaced oedipal desire to kill his abusive father. Motivation for this archetype suddenly becomes more psychologically complex, as the character himself is seen more clearly as an individual who is mentally disturbed. A clear watermark is reached a decade later in Raoul Walsh's *White Heat* (1949). James Cagney, the most ubiquitous of the gangster killers from the '30s and '40s, is not depicted as a simple one-dimensional racketeer killing for business, but rather, as a deranged psychopath, completely out of touch with reality, delusional, suffering from paralyzing psychosomatic headaches, and driven mad by an out-of-control oedipal complex, which compels him to kill out of an incestuous desire for his mother's love. In this film, Cagney — the king of the gangsters — progresses the archetype from a mere sociopath who kills for profit or revenge, into a full blown psychopath, who's killing represents deep-seated unconscious urges and psychological disorders. The age of the psycho killer was born.

It should be noted here that psycho killers did appear in films prior to *White Heat* in 1949. Peter Lorre, in particular, was known for playing murderous villains in the '30s and '40s, who were motivated to kill, purely out of psychopathology. His role as the child murderer in Fritz Lang's *M* (1931) stands out as the clearest example, though similar characterizations could be seen in other Peter Lorre films, such as *Mad Love* (1935), *Crime and Punishment* (1935), *Island of the Doomed Men* (1940), *Stranger on the Third Floor* (1940), and *The Face Behind the Mask* (1941). However, a couple of sidebars must also be mentioned in reference to these films. First, though Lorre's mad murderers were, to be certain, psycho killers, the filmmakers did essentially nothing to explain the psychopathology behind the psycho. The killers were just plain crazy. That was all the motivation and explanation deemed necessary at the time. Second, many of these films were either remakes of original German productions, or else heavily influenced by German directors, writers, cast, and crew. As such, the German influence on the part of the killer expressed a different perspective on the character. The German style was less clear-cut than the Hollywood style. There was more room left for ambiguity, the unexplained, the mysterious, and the unknown. These aspects created a "creepy" feel to the Peter Lorre characters, a macabre sense of eeriness that paralleled the expressionist look of the sets and the noir settings. In certain ways, the Lorre films could be said to be way ahead of their time.

Enter the Master

Alfred Hitchcock, the "Master of Suspense," was arguably the most significant filmmaker involved in the development of the psycho killer archetype. Not only did he take the mad murderer away from the gangster genre and back into the horror/thriller genre, he created a more sophisticated and complex psychological profile for his mad villains. Hitchcock began his career in England with a thriller that was more similar to the German thrillers of that period than to the Hollywood films from America. His first feature film of note, *The Lodger* (1927), was clearly influenced by German directors such as Fritz Lang, which is not surprising, as his work prior to the film had been on joint British/German productions. *The Lodger* presents a psycho killer very similar to the Peter Lorre killers that would emerge shortly afterwards. The character of The Lodger is based loosely on Jack the Ripper. He kills women out of some deep-rooted psychological compulsion, which is never even cursorily explained.

Fast forward over two decades later, to 1948, and Hitchcock is still in the early years of his lengthy and prodigious career. By this time, Hitchcock has filmed a few more borderline psychotic characters, most notably, in *Rebecca* (1940), *Suspicion* (1941), and *Spellbound* (1945), when he returns to the familiar psycho killer character, in *Rope* (1948). This time, the killer is more of a sociopath, with a clear and explicitly stated motive for killing, but it's not what you'd expect. The killer has no ulterior motives. He is not killing for lust, desire, revenge, or profit. He is killing simply for the experience of killing. He murders for the thrill of the conquest, and the challenge of committing the perfect crime. Clearly, Hitchcock was onto something in this bleak, short, extremely experimental film. He was working on a new type of killer, a psycho with method behind his madness ... a dark, scary, all-too-human form of modern monster.

The lead characters in *Rope*, John Dall as the psycho killer and Farley Granger as his reluctant partner in crime, were based very loosely on Leopold and Loeb, the infamous "thrill killers" of 1924, a pair of brilliant, Jewish, homosexual, millionaire teenagers who killed a boy merely for the macabre excitement of the act and the intellectual challenge of getting away with it. The case, already outrageous, was made even more of a public spectacle when the great Clarence Darrow defended the boys in court and miraculously saved them from the death sentence. The case of Leopold and Loeb was a mass media event, and it was extremely influential on the public imagination's view of murder, madness, and the mysteries of motivation. Quite a few movie psycho killers were based, either directly or indirectly, on Leopold and Loeb.

While the influence of the case of the "thrill killers" was readily apparent in Hitchcock's *Rope*, it was more subdued in a similar but much more mainstream film, Hitchcock's *Strangers on a Train* (1951). Farley Granger is once again cast as the reluctant partner to a psycho killer, Bruno Anthony (Robert Walker). While Bruno is clearly disturbed, he at least has a practical motivation for murder ... money. Driven by oedipal desires— an overwhelming need for his mother's love and affection, matched by a resentful aggressive urge towards his father — Bruno wants to kill his father in order to inherit his wealth. This well developed psycho killer incorporates a number of motivations:

1. The thrill killer's desire to destroy, along with the associated intellectual challenge of committing "the perfect murder."

2. The criminal sociopath's desire for money.

3. The traditional psycho killer's oedipal impulses toward rivalry and aggression.

The Masterwork

Though murder was an incessant leitmotif in Hitchcock's films throughout the 1950s, as well as in the television series he hosted and produced — *Alfred Hitchcock Presents* (1955) — he would not create another psycho killer until 1960, when he made the film that broke the old mold and created a new one. To a certain degree, the material presented in *Psycho* was not entirely new. Film audiences had experienced psycho killers before. They were familiar with men who were driven to murder by their own psychological demons. But Hitchcock made the sheer terror of this possibility more plausible in *Psycho*, by creating a relatively realistic setting for his macabre story, and casting the killer as a shy, wholesome, innocent looking young man. He broke all the unwritten rules of film narrative by establishing a beautiful young woman (Janet Leigh) as the lead character, and then brutally slaughtering her nearly halfway into the film. The effect, for audiences of the day, was jarring and disconcerting. They couldn't believe what happened. They had lost their bearings. When the heroine was suddenly killed, it was like the audience lost their best friend. They had no one left to identify with, so the audience — unwillingly — was forced to identify with the only lead character left in the film, Norman Bates (Anthony Perkins). In this way, the audience was drawn into the mind of the killer, seeing the story unravel through his distorted eyes.

In the end, Hitchcock explains the psychological motivation for his killer in clear terms. A Freudian psychiatrist provides a psychoanalysis of Norman Bates, describing how his oedipal fantasies drove him to killing his mother and her lover, and then forced him to actually become his mother in order to alleviate his own guilt over killing her. In this denouement, Hitchcock added an original and extremely influential element to the psycho killer character — the split personality. As Norman, the shy, unassuming, dutiful son, was kind and obliging. But when his sexual desire was aroused, his shadow personality — Mother Bates — took over, driving Bates to destroy the source of desire, because the girl was perceived as a rival for her son's love. Another important element in *Psycho* is that it is a production of Robert Bloch's 1959 novel, which was based very loosely on the true story of Ed Gein. The significant point is that, unlike Leopold and Loeb, Gein was a true psychotic with a severe psychiatric disorder and a

Anthony Perkins as Norman Bates and Janet Leigh as Marion Crane in Alfred Hitchcock's *Psycho* (1960).

truly murderous oedipal complex. Even more noteworthy is the fact that Gein, and his fictional counterpart, Norman Bates, were both serial killers.

Altogether, Hitchcock's *Psycho* changed the direction of the psycho killer genre in five specific ways:

1. As the title portends, *Psycho* establishes and deals explicitly with the psycho killer's mental problems and psychological motivations, explaining them openly in psychological terms.

2. The style of the film is realistic, especially in its depiction of violence. The masterful "shower scene," considered incredibly gory and horrific for its day, would go on to influence and inspire four-and-a-half decades of "slasher" movies.

3. The film would establish the serial killer as the psycho killer of choice for nearly all of the future psycho thrillers to come.

4. *Psycho* introduced the character element of split personality (aka multiple personality disorder, aka dissociative identity disorder) into the

psycho killer archetype. This character element would go on to be used in dozens of similar films in the psycho thriller genre.

5. Norman Bates is technically a transvestite, as he dons a dress and wig when his mother's personality takes over his psyche. Transvestitism and transsexualism would go on to become common character elements in the psycho thriller genre.

To a certain extent, the psycho killer's character can be seen to have come full circle, at least in terms of his motivation. In the first few decades of film, murderers were typically evil villains or undead monsters, with little motivation to kill other than lust and desire. In the 1930s, gangland murderers arose ... sociopathic killers whose motivations were money, freedom, and survival. In the 1940s, the true psycho killer emerged, though the psychopath's motivations often seemed rather obscure and oblique, until the masterwork of the genre appeared in 1960. And now, in the postmodern era following *Psycho* and the many, many films it inspired, the typical psycho killer in movies is a serial killer — a modern day monster, an evil villain — who's motivations have been explained and illustrated so many times in so many movies, as to make any psychological explanation for the psychotic serial killer's motives completely redundant and unnecessary. A filmmaker need only point out that a murderer is a serial killer, a "psycho," and his character is immediately developed. Such is the power of an established screen archetype.

Serial Killers

Serial killer movies are so prevalent and come out so frequently that any feasible list would be immediately incomprehensive, as it would be out-of-date the moment it was printed. The only option is to survey some of the most significant serial killer movies in the genre. In the same year that Hitchcock made *Psycho*, Michael Powell made *Peeping Tom* (1960) in England. The film is about a psychopathic serial killer with a deadly voyeuristic fetish. He photographs women and kills them, using a blade that juts out from behind the camera's lens, allowing the killer to snap a shot of his victim's horrified death visage as she dies. We learn by the end of the film that the psycho was tortured as a boy by his father, a psychological researcher obsessed with the study of primal fear, who used his own son as a guinea pig. *Peeping Tom* is in many ways similar to *Psycho*, but while Hitchcock's film was hailed as a masterpiece and drove his career to new heights, Powell's film was denounced as "going too far," and it went a long way towards ruining his very illustrious career. Whether the negative reactions towards *Peeping Tom* were due to different sensibilities in Britain as compared to America, or for other reasons, is a matter of conjecture. Nevertheless, *Peeping Tom* would go on to become a cult favorite among filmmakers and horror buffs. The backstory plot device of an abusive father using his son as a guinea pig in horrific psychological experiments would also become a commonly used character element in the serial killer genre.

Backtracking, briefly, it is necessary to point out that Fritz Lang's *M* (1931) is usually considered the first serial killer film of note. It is truly a wonderful film, very much ahead of its time. The film seems to prefigure the modern serial killer genre, as it focuses primarily on the detectives in search of the killer, rather than the killer himself. Returning to the post–*Psycho* era, Hitchcock's use of realism and a "true" life story in his rendition of Norman Bates inspired a short wave of realistic crime dramas about real serial killers. The best of these movies were *In Cold Blood* (1967) and *The Boston Strangler* (1968). Both films provided much psychological background on the killers, providing interesting and realistic stories about fascinating killers. The tide turned, however, in 1974, with the inexplicable success of the extremely low budget independent film, *The Texas Chain Saw Massacre*. The film made so much money among teen audiences that it inspired a host of other low-budget, teen-oriented, serial killer horror films in the 1970s and '80s, such as *Halloween* (1978), *Friday the 13th* (1980), and *A Nightmare on Elm Street* (1984). These films, and the dozens of sequels and knockoffs they spawned, gave rise to the low budget "slasher" movie genre, in which knife-wielding psychopathic killers slash their way through scores of scantily clad teens in 95 minutes of blood and gore.

The serial killer genre regained much of its prestige with the enormous critical and box office success of Jonathan Demme's *Silence of the Lambs* (1991). The film swept the Oscars in 1992, winning top awards for best actor (Anthony Hopkins), best actress (Jodie Foster), best writing for an adaptation (Ted Tally), best director (Jonathan Demme), and best picture. The casting of a master psychiatrist as an evil, twisted, cannibalistic serial killer created one of the most memorable psychopaths in film history. Demme's success lead to countless new serial killer movies starring A-list actors and directed by the industry's leading directors. Some of the more noteworthy of the new brood of serial killer movies include *Se7en* (1995), for its interesting scenario and plot twists, *American Psycho* (2000), for its postmodern take on the serial killer phenomenon, and *Insomnia* (2002), for its excellent ensemble cast and surreal atmosphere.

Serial Killers in Love

Serial killer movies have become so plentiful that the genre has spawned subgenres of its own. Arthur Penn's *Bonnie and Clyde* (1967) is a story about two gorgeous young lovers (Faye Dunaway and Warren Beatty) who kill and rob their way across the Depression era Midwest. Though they were gangsters, not serial killers, the simultaneously romantic and violent image of the rebellious young outlaws in love inspired similarly themed films. Terrence Malick's debut feature, *Badlands* (1973), was loosely based on the 1958 Charles Starkweather and Caril Ann Fugate case. Caril, a 14-year-old girl, and her teenaged boyfriend, Charlie, killed Caril's sexually abusive stepfather and the rest of her family, before embarking on a killing spree in the badlands of North Dakota. While the character based on Caril, Holly (Sissy Spacek), does not murder alongside her serial killing boyfriend, she does facilitate his evil deeds by forgiving him and looking away. This film is one of the most interesting in the serial-killers-in-love category, as the relationship between Holly and Kit (Martin Sheen) eerily resembles the relationship between a drug addict and his codependent. We get the sense that Kit would not continue his killings if Holly would only discontinue her enabling support and leave him, but unfortunately, she loves him too much to walk away from him, even though he's a vicious murderer.

Despite the violent, sensational subject matter, Malick's film is quiet and understated, with subtle performances by Sissy Spacek and Martin Sheen. It stands in stark contrast to another film inspired by the same case, Oliver Stone's *Natural Born Killers* (1994). Stone's movie is more of a political allegory about violence and the media than a real story. It is an explosion of blood, sex, murder, and depravity, meant to say something about evil, society, love, hate, aggression, the dual nature of man, and stuff like that. Audiences are still trying to figure out what Oliver Stone was trying to say in *Natural Born Killers*. A final entry in this category is *Kalifornia* (1993). This film brought much praise and attention to Brad Pitt at a time when he was just emerging into stardom, for his performance as the sadistic yet somehow loveable serial killer named Early. The film costars Juliette Lewis as Adele, Early's sheepish girlfriend, prefiguring her role the following year as Mallory in *Natural Born Killers*. The characters of Adele in *Kalifornia* and Holly in *Badlands* are extremely similar — both provide love and support for their sociopathic boyfriends, facilitating their killing sprees. *Kalifornia* presents an interesting premise, in which a journalist (David Duchovny) obsessed with serial killers and his girlfriend unwittingly pair up with a serial killer (Pitt) and his girlfriend (Lewis) on an ill-fated road trip to

California. In this sense, *Kalifornia* represents somewhat of a postmodern take on serial killers, as the film focuses on the media's obsession with serial killing, even as the medium itself is a depiction of a sensationalized serial killer.

Transvestite and Transsexual Killers

In a rarely seen early film by Hitchcock, *Murder!* (1930), the murderer reveals himself in the end to be a transvestite. In retrospect, the most interesting element of this movie is that the killer's denouement predates that of Norman Bates in *Psycho* by exactly 30 years. Exactly 20 years later, Brian De Palma made *Dressed to Kill* (1980), a film that is essentially an homage to Hitchcock's *Psycho*. At the climax of De Palma's film, the psycho killer reveals himself to be a transsexual. And then, 11 years later, the serial killer in *The Silence of the Lambs* reveals himself to be a transsexual with the most macabre of transvestite fetishes— the need to dress himself up in the actual skin of his female victims. Why so many depictions of transvestites and transsexuals as serial killers? Apparently, some filmmakers think they're weird and scary. (That's saying a lot, for people who spend most of their time in Hollywood.)

Real-Life Serial Killers

Producers, noting the popular fascination with serial killers, have produced many films based on the exploits of real-life serial killers. Jack the Ripper, the most famous serial killer of all times, has had many movies based on his notorious killing spree. To date, aside from numerous television episodes and documentaries, there have been three feature length films, two television miniseries, and one video game produced under the title, "Jack the Ripper." Many feature length films have also been made that are, to varying degrees, loosely based on the Ripper legend. Some of the more notable Jack the Rippers include: Werner Krauss (the actor who played Dr. Caligari) in *Das Wachsfigurenkabinett,* aka *Waxworks* (1924), Ivor Novello in Hitchcock's *The Lodger* (1927), Jack Palance in *Man in the Attic* (1953), Klaus Kinski in *Jack the Ripper* (1976), David Warner in *Time after Time* (1979), Anthony Perkins in *Edge of Sanity* (1989), and Paul Rhys in *From Hell* (2001).

A selected list of other real-life serial killers who have been immortalized on the silver screen include: Ed Gein in *Psycho*, Albert DeSalvo in

The Boston Strangler, Perry Smith and Dick Hickock in *In Cold Blood*, Charles Starkweather and Caril Ann Fugate in *Badlands*, Charles Manson (and family) in *Helter Skelter* (1976), Henry Lee Lucas in *Henry: Portrait of a Serial Killer* (1986), Ted Bundy in *The Deliberate Stranger* (1986), John Wayne Gacy in *To Catch a Killer* (1992), Carl Panzram in *Killer: A Journal of Murder* (1996), David Berkowitz in *Summer of Sam* (1999), Jeffrey Dahmer in *Dahmer* (2002), and Aileen Wuornos in *Monster* (2003). It is a sad truth that, for some very sick people, the path of violence and destruction has led to celebrity and fame.

Split Personality Serial Killers

The notion that a person's psyche could be split in two was expressed in fiction by Robert Louis Stevenson in his 1886 story, *The Strange Case of Dr. Jekyll and Mr. Hyde,* long before psychologists began to speak of "split personalities," a term which later evolved into "multiple personality disorder," and finally, "dissociative identity disorder." Ancient folk tales about werewolves and vampires, to a lesser degree, assert the notion that the duality of man could, in extreme cases, be split into two different personalities occupying the same person. When movie audiences began to tire of the traditional monster myths and gothic Victorian tales, serial killers were created who—like werewolves—seemed to have a civilized outward persona, masking a hidden, murderous shadow. Nevertheless, movie characters didn't mention anything about multiple personality disorders until Hitchcock put the psychological subtext in front of the frame, in *Psycho.* Since then, it has become rather standard fare for a serial killer to have more than one personality. Like the Big Bad Wolf in Grandma's frock, the ability to hide his true identity from the vulnerable young maiden makes the killer all the more terrifying.

Frankly, the use of multiple personalities in the psycho thriller genre has become hackneyed and trite. In Charlie Kaufman's iconoclastic script for *Adaptation* (2002), a film which ironically revolves around a struggling screenwriter whose psyche splits into two writers—twin brothers, Charlie and Donald Kaufman—an interchange occurs between the two writer personalities. It goes as follows:

> DONALD: The killer, the girl, and the cop all have split personalities. They're all the same person. Isn't that fucked up?
> CHARLIE: The only idea more overused than serial killers is multiple personality! On top of that, you explore the notion that cop and

criminal are really two aspects of the same person. See every cop movie ever made for other examples of this!

DONALD: Mom called it "psychologically taut."

Nonetheless, screenwriters will undoubtedly continue to write thrillers about serial killers with multiple personalities. For other examples of this, see: Brian De Palma's *Dressed to Kill* and *Raising Cain*, Alan Parker's *Angel Heart* (1987), *Color of Night* (1994), *Session 9* (2001), and *Identity* (2003).

Serial Killer Satires

One surefire sign that the dramatic vigor of a genre is waning is the appearance of film satires. In 1996, the thriller *Scream* appeared on the screen, a film which could accurately be labeled "a postmodern slasher movie." The movie is self-referential. All of the characters have seen dozens of slasher movies. They can predict what may happen at each turn. In their dialogue, they reference the very same slasher movies that prefigured the film that they're in. It's almost as if they are looking into the camera and winking. The movie was a hit, spawning two sequels.

It was no surprise in 2000, when *Scream 3* hit the screens, that the film had to compete with *Scary Movie*, aka *Scream If You Know What I Did Last Halloween*, a parody of *Scream* and the entire slasher movie genre. It was also no surprise that *Scary Movie* made more money in its opening weekend than any of the three *Scream* movies made in any of their opening weekends. The writing on the wall seemed clear. When Dracula and the Frankenstein monster began to appear in Abbott and Costello movies in the mid–1940s, making more money than the original monster movies made when they first appeared in the early the 1930s, it indicated to the studios that these monsters had lost their ability to terrify. Now that slasher movie parodies are making more money than real slasher movies, the tides of change — ruled by box office receipts— point toward a new direction. What direction that may be is up to the creative minds of filmmakers, and the fickle tastes of movie audiences.

CHAPTER THREE

Mad Scientists

Home ... I have no home!
Hunted! Despised! Living like an animal! The jungle is my home!
But I will show the world that I can be its master.
I shall perfect my own race of people —
a race of atomic supermen that will conquer the world!
Dr. Vornoff (Bela Lugosi)
from Ed Wood's, Bride of the Monster *(1955)*

What makes mad scientists so mad? Is it their driving ambition? Is it their sacrilegious desire to play God by creating human life? Is it their megalomaniacal aspiration to rule the world? Is it their manic obsession with their scientific research? Or is it their lack of ability to understand the evil in what they do? From a psychological perspective, nearly all mad scientists in psycho thrillers are embodiments of two personality disorders: narcissistic personality disorder and obsessive-compulsive disorder (OCD). The *Diagnostic and Statistical Manual of Mental Disorders (DSM-IV-TR)* (2000), which psychologists use to diagnose psychological disorders, provides a simple list of symptomatic behaviors indicative of clinical narcissism and OCD. Thankfully, the psycho thriller genre has provided a plethora of mad scientist examples, such as Dr. Caligari, Dr. Jekyll, Dr. Frankenstein, and Dr. Moreau, from which to make our diagnoses.

OC Science

In *The Cabinet of Dr. Caligari* (1919), the title character (Werner Krauss) is just an ordinary psychiatrist in charge of a rural lunatic asylum.

But when a new patient (Conrad Veidt) arrives who is a somnambulist, the good doctor is tempted to delve into the research of the fascinating legend of Dr. Caligari, a man who was able to hypnotically control the minds of other men. With precipitous speed, his scientific interest becomes compulsive, as the intertitles document his internal dialogue: "I must know everything — I must penetrate the heart of his secret! — I must become Caligari!" The doctor, no longer a mild-mannered psychiatrist, but the embodiment of the infamous and mad Dr. Caligari, embarks on his diabolical plot to control the mind of the somnambulist, as the intertitle states: "In the grip of an obsession."

Already, Dr. Caligari displays one of the *DSM*'s telltale signs of OCD. He is "excessively devoted to work and productivity to the exclusion of leisure activities and friendships." This is the heart of both the disorder and the mad scientist character ... his mad obsession with his wicked work, and his crazed compulsion to pursue it to the exclusion of anything or anyone else. It is this obsessive-compulsiveness that drives the scientist to great heights of scientific achievement, but at the price of his soul. For the more he dedicates himself completely to his work, the more he cuts himself off from other human beings, and the more mad he becomes.

Another crucial symptom of OCD is that the obsessive-compulsive "shows rigidity and stubbornness." In every mad scientist movie, there is a lover and/or friend who tries to convince the scientist that he is being driven mad by his obsession, and that he should take a break, what we refer to nowadays as a "mental health day." The mad scientist will have none of it. He stubbornly refuses to leave his lab. He must work day and night, foregoing food and rest and the company of others in pursuance of his mad dream. Clearly, this tendency leads to social isolation, which only adds to his madness.

Another *DSM* symptom that isolates the mad scientist from friends and loved ones is his "reluctance to delegate tasks or to work with others unless they submit to exactly his or her way of doing things." In the real world, scientists do not work alone. They work with other scientists, typically in big research teams of colleagues, assistants, and students of all levels. The mad scientist, however, is compelled to work alone, not only because of the mad goals of his experiment, but because of his obsessive "perfectionism" — another OCD symptom — which prohibits him from letting others touch his work, lest their assistance results in an outcome less than what he perceives to be 100 percent perfect. The mad scientist nearly always works alone, or with only one weird lab assistant, typically named "Igor," who is marginalized enough that he is willing to take his master's callous abuse. Ironically, it is the mad scientist's perfectionist and controlling attributes that often lead to the one critical mistake that turns his wondrous creation into a horrifying creature. The best example is seen in *Frankenstein* (1931). Because the doctor has isolated himself from all of his colleagues at the university, he does not have access to the appropriate brain for his creation. His only option is to send his incompetent hunchbacked assistant, Fritz (Dwight Frye), to break into the university lab and steal the brain. Of course, stupid Fritz fouls everything up by dropping the proper brain, and grabbing the abnormal brain of a career criminal. For lack of the right brain, Dr. Frankenstein's manmade man will never become anything more than a monster.

A final OCD tendency from the *DSM* that is apparent in mad scientists is that they are "over conscientious, scrupulous, and inflexible about matters of morality, ethics, or values." At first, we may think just the opposite, as the mad scientist's work is nearly always perceived as blatantly sacrilegious ... an affront to God. However, the sacrilege is all a matter of perception. As a man of science, an heir of Darwin, the mad scientist typically doesn't believe in the existence of an almighty supernatural being. This, however, does not mean that the mad scientist is not religious. To the contrary, he is fiercely religious, and doggedly dedicated to his pious work. The only difference is that for the mad scientist, science is his religion. Science is God. And the way the mad scientist can emulate God, the way that this man can see himself as being made in God's image, is to play God himself, by creating or significantly altering human life.

The best example of the mad scientist as someone who is "scrupulous, and inflexible about matters of morality" can be seen in Paramount Pictures' 1920 version of *Dr. Jekyll and Mr. Hyde*. The story gets moving when Jekyll (John Barrymore), described by an introductory intertitle as "an idealist and a philanthropist," is taken to a sordid cabaret show, where he is deeply conflicted by feelings of lust for a sexy showgirl. The self-loathing and disgust that he feels for himself as a result of his own sexual desire drives him toward an obsessive goal. Driven by an inflexible moral need to distance himself from his base impulses, he wonders: "Wouldn't it be marvelous if the two natures in man could be separated — housed in two different bodies!" His need for moral superiority immediately leads him to the premise that science can be as powerful as God: "Science has wrought other miracles! Why not this?" The result, a full blown descent into obsessive-compulsive mad science: "His imagination afire with this new idea, and his whole being mastered by the exploring passion of the scientist, Jekyll spent days and nights in his laboratory."

Narcissistic Science

According to the *DSM,* a primary trait of narcissistic personality disorder is "a grandiose sense of self importance ... [he] expects to be recognized as superior." But to say that the mad scientist exhibits a superiority complex is a gargantuan understatement. It is more appropriate to say that his character has a god complex. He sees himself as immeasurably superior — superhuman — at least on an intellectual level, to those around him. He even facilitates this narcissistic delusion of grandeur by restricting his company to a single lab assistant, the ubiquitous "Igor" or "Fritz" character, who is typically physically handicapped (a dwarf or a hunchback) as well as intellectually slow or retarded. His attitude results in another *DSM* symptom, he is "interpersonally exploitative," not only of his disabled assistant, but of his poor experimental subjects as well, who did not ask to be brought to life as hideous monsters or physically altered mutants. Here we see three more *DSM* symptoms of narcissism: the mad scientist "lacks empathy," "has a sense of entitlement," and displays "arrogant, haughty behaviors." The latter symptom is most evidently portrayed in *Frankenstein,* when the grandiose doctor shouts out his signature line, "Now I know what it feels like to be God!"

Another symptom from the *DSM* is that the narcissist "is often envious of others or believes that others are envious of him." The mad scientist is likely to complain that his colleagues and superiors at the university laughed at him and his work. He is driven by the need to prove his genius to the entire scientific community, so he can laugh at them, especially when his race of supermutants conquers the world. This feeds into three more *DSM* symptoms, the fact that the mad scientist "requires excessive admiration," that he "is preoccupied with fantasies of unlimited success, power, brilliance, beauty, or ideal love," and that he "believes that he or she is "special" and unique and can only be understood by, or should associate with, other special or high status people." The mad scientist builds a castle of intellectual superiority around himself, and fills the castle with grandiose delusions of godliness, ultimate power, and revenge.

Furthermore, the mad scientist uses his intellectual superiority as a justification for his ungodly experiments. Only he can understand the incredible importance of his work, therefore only he can be the judge of whether his experiments are moral or not. The mad scientist justifies his immoral work and his unethical means, such as the illicit use of human corpses and the barbaric practice of human experimentation, through his claim of intellectual superiority, and his belief that the ends of human creativity justify the means of unethical research. Like Prometheus, the mad scientist has the forethought to see that his creation must have the fire of the gods to exist, even if the fire is attained through immoral means. And like Epimetheus, Prometheus' shortsighted brother, the mad scientist realizes his folly only as an afterthought, subsequent to the mayhem and destruction that ensues after his demented creature runs amok in an orgy of violence. And finally, like Faust, the mad scientist's uncompromising and unethical dedication to science is a virtual deal with the devil, an evil enterprise based on creativity but ultimately ending in destruction.

Social Science

It is significant to note that the traditional mad scientists, such as Dr. Jekyll and Dr. Frankenstein, were members of the aristocracy or wealthy ruling class. This aspect of the mad scientist archetype relates to a basic mistrust that ordinary people in past centuries have had of not only the scions of science, but also to a mistrust of the oligarchy. The Marxist doctrine holds that the ruling classes create a political and economic system in which the members of the proletariat are merely powerless automatons under the control of their wealthy masters. This doctrine corresponds eerily with the basic plot of an aristocratic scientist creating a poor and powerless creature condemned to a miserable life of bondage and servitude to a haughty and arrogant master. The mad scientist is nothing short of a master-tyrant. The monster, his hapless creation, is merely a serf in his dominion. The eventual rise of the monster against his master is symbolic of the working class' struggle against the ruling class.

Another critical characteristic of the mad scientist is his tendency toward isolation. The mad scientist is an isolated genius, a man who alienates himself from others by making his work the most important thing in his life, to the preclusion of love and normal human relations. In pursuing his diabolical research, the mad scientist feels compelled to hide himself away in a remote castle, dark dungeon, or secluded crypt ... away from the prying eyes of meddling laymen and observers. Certainly, isolation is necessary for the mad scientist, as his work is inherently immoral and illegal, but it also alludes to a deeper need in his character, his need for control. Mad science is all about control. The mad scientist is a control freak, desperately trying to control his world and the people around him as if they were test tubes in his laboratory. Like the gods in the heavens, it is not enough for the mad scientist to be intellectually superior; he must prove his superiority by creating a being or race of beings that he can have complete control over. The irony of the mad scientist plot is that he typically loses control over his creature immediately after he creates him, and the rest of his story revolves around the struggle to regain control over the monster-creature run amok.

A complementary note of irony in the mad scientist's story revolves around his isolation from the woman he loves. In the first act, the mad scientist typically alienates himself from his female love interest by locking himself away in his laboratory and focusing solely on his unholy work. By the end of the second act, the mad scientist's monster has escaped his control, and has typically abducted the virginal love interest and carried her off to his lair. In the third act, the mad scientist realizes the error of his ways, and understands that his love for the girl is much more important than his scientific obsessions. His challenge now is to become un-isolated. He must choose love over science. This choice is displayed symbolically when the mad scientist destroys his own creation in order to save the life of the woman he loves.

A final irony is seen in the relationship between the mad scientist and his monster. A basic existential question is raised in the mad scientist genre, in which mortals act like gods by creating Man. The plot raises the question: If a man can create a man, then is that man a god? This underlying question is the subtext behind the relationship between the mad scientist and his monster, which is symbolic of the relationship between God and man, and to a lesser extent, the conflicted relationship between father and son. In the first act, the mad scientist negates the existence of God in favor of his own creative powers of science. The monster's wild and deadly rampage in the second act represents the ordinary man's basic fear of science and the unnerving realization that the modern age is gradually replacing God with science. In the third act, the mad scientist must repent for both his narcissism and his heresy. He must admit that, like Prometheus, he was a rash and irresponsible creator. Like Faust, he must repent for allowing himself to become allied with the devil. And, like a dutiful father, the creator must encounter his creature and put him to rights. The mad scientist absolves himself of his sacrilege by destroying his creature and admitting that it was wrong of him to venture into the gods' domain. By the end of his tale, the mad scientist must humbly admit that there are some things that men were simply not meant to know, and that, in the repentant words of Dr. Frankenstein: "there are boundaries that ought not to be crossed!"

But in order to understand the mad scientist, we must look beyond the psychological diagnoses, and explore the historical evolution of the archetype. Traces of the mad scientist can be seen in ancient characters, such as the tribal witch doctor, the pagan high priest, and the ancient

Greek myths of Prometheus and Pandora. The modern archetype of the mad scientist, however, is most closely tied to the image of the medieval alchemist, a controversial character that treads the line between virtue and sacrilege, and whose cryptic formulas and odd experiments gave rise to the first rays of the dawn of science.

Goethe's Alchemist

In the Middle Ages, the black arts, though banned by the church, were practiced in secrecy by alchemists. Forced to hide in dark dungeons and cryptic workshops, these men dedicated their lives to the search of the elusive Philosopher's Stone, the divine chemical which would transmute base metals into gold and even confer immortality to man. In their day, the alchemists were the embodiment of Prometheus, dedicated and creative geniuses in search of the elixir of life, the universal medicine, and the irresistible solvent. Despite great risk to their own lives, they delved into God's domain in order to discover and retrieve the divine secrets of the universe. Although their work was often dubious and typically illusory, the alchemists were the predecessors of modern science. The image of the obsessed alchemist working furiously over his bubbling potions, pouring over his cryptic texts and huddling over sulfuric flames in his dark, hidden workshop, provided the template for the modern day image of the mad scientist.

The conflicting reactions of both reverence and fear that medieval people felt towards the alchemist made him one of the most enduring subjects of legend and literature. On the one hand, the alchemist broke from tradition, law, and society by engaging in the black arts and tempting the fury of God. But on the other hand, the alchemist pursued his passions because of his uniquely human attributes of curiosity and his desperate need to understand the workings of the Lord. The alchemist's admirable characteristics — his genius, his determination, his inquisitiveness, and his genuine desire to help mankind — made him a character worthy of compassion and even respect, even if his reckless powers and blasphemous narcissism made him a character to be feared and mistrusted. These dramatic conflicts are what made Dr. Faust into one of the most popular legendary characters of the Middle Ages.

The medieval tales of Faust were based on the real life story of a magician and alchemist named Faust, who lived in Germany in the early part of the sixteenth century. His name first appeared in literature in *Historia von Dr. Johann Fausten* (1587), in which Faust makes a deal with

Mephistopheles (the devil incarnate), who increases Faust's knowledge and powers, but at the price of his soul. The most famous version of the Faust legend was eventually written by Goethe in the early nineteenth century. Goethe's epic poem diverges from the earlier versions of the legend by making Faust a more sympathetic character. Goethe's Faust makes his pact with the devil because of a true desire to use the illicit knowledge to help humanity. Consequently, at the end of his story, Faust is acquitted of his crimes rather than cursed with eternal damnation. This more sympathetic attitude towards the ancient alchemist is indicative of the age in which Goethe lived, an age of burgeoning science and reason, an age in which knowledge and understanding were beginning to be seen as virtues nearly as divine as the Christian virtues of humility and faith. Goethe's archetypal hero, a man of hubris, genius, passion, and intellectual curiosity, would become the fundamental prototype for a modern mythological hero, a man who's work and vision would fly in the face of nearly two thousand years of Christian dogma ... a man of science.

The Age of Science

The nineteenth century ushered in a new age of human imagination. The Age of Reason, a term coined by Thomas Paine in 1795 as the title of his influential book, was an apt name for a new world view that was spawned by the new philosophies and sciences of the Enlightenment. Logical and scientific theories were replacing the old theological ones. Charles Darwin (1809–1882) provided a new explanation for the creation of humankind with the publication of *On the Origin of the Species* (1859), the "book that shook the world." Evolution and Darwinism had indeed changed the world by the time Darwin published his definitive thoughts on the subject in 1871, in *The Descent of Man*. By the latter half of the century, Nietzsche had already declared that "God is dead!" Medicine, chemistry, physics, and other sciences were established fields, and new technologies such as electricity and the telephone were changing the way people lived. But while modern science and the Industrial Revolution were vaulting the world into a new age, the beliefs, superstitions, and fears of the average man were still rooted in ancient myths and legends.

By the end of the nineteenth century, a definite rift was apparent between the intellectuals and scientists espousing the new technologies and the average people on the street, referred to unceremoniously as "the masses." This rift existed on both political and socioeconomic levels. The doctors and scientists were, as a rule, highly educated; most were descended from wealthy if not aristocratic families. While the new technologies were invented with the promise of a better, braver new world, the average working man only experienced harder and more perilous labor in the coal mines and factories owned by the wealthy ruling class. As cold hard science began to replace traditional devotion to religion, a basic sense of mistrust started to arise amidst the working classes. The masses mistrusted the new brand of surgeons, who were somehow able to dispassionately cut up and dissect human bodies as if they were so many links of sausage. This mistrust was fueled by lurid rumors of demented vivisectionists who would cut up live human subjects in order to see the functioning workings of their insides, and medical "body snatchers" who would steal corpses from gallows and graveyards (and even occasionally resort to murder) in order to provide fresh cadavers for dissection at medical universities.

In the nineteenth century, scientists such as Louis Pasteur studied invisible microscopic germs, and the Curies studied unknown elements that carried forth obscure but deadly forms of death. Like the medieval alchemists, these scientists were delving into dark, mysterious areas— venturing into God's domain. Many people believed that these experiments were immoral, evil, and potentially dangerous. What if the microbiologist inadvertently unleashes a ghastly disease that could infect millions? What if the chemist mistakenly releases dangerous elements that can poison the countryside? What if the physicist discovers an awesome godlike power that can destroy the entire planet? These fears were instinctual responses to the unknown, yet in retrospect, we must admit that to a very large degree, the fears were entirely justified. Now, in an age of deadly nuclear weapons, toxic environmental pollutants, and horrible manmade biological agents, we're forced to wonder if the uneducated masses were right in wanting to force the Pandora's box of scientific inquiry shut.

The fear of medical science in the nineteenth century stemmed from a general fear of the unknown, and it was this fear that gave birth to the mad scientist archetype in its fully developed form. Victorian novelists such as H.G. Wells, Mary Wollstonecraft Shelley, Robert Louis Stevenson, Nathaniel Hawthorne, and Jules Verne all created mad scientist characters that incorporated the old fears of the unknown into the new fears of scientific discovery. As the nineteenth century gave way to the twentieth, the ordinary man's fears were given new meaning when World War I introduced the use of new technologies to create terrifying pain and destruction in massacres that could never have been conceived before. Machine guns, submarines, airplane bombers, chemical toxins, and biological weapons were all employed to destroy the flesh of young soldiers, as the politicians sat in their mansions and the scientists worked in their laboratories, creating new and more horrific weapons of mass destruction. Meanwhile, soldiers returned home by the million in pine boxes, or with disfigured faces, missing limbs or mangled bodies ... only to find medical science unable to help them.

Silent Science

One of the earliest films, Georges Méliès's *Le Voyage dans la lune (A Trip to the Moon)* (1902), featured a now infamous ending, in which the moon — seen as a large human face — frowns as an invasive rocket ship protrudes from his eye. The message is ingeniously antiscientific ... man is beginning to meddle in areas in which he does not belong. The silent feature films of the 1920s echoed the pacifistic sentiments of post-World War I Europe and America. As a corollary to the antiwar trend, there was also an antitechnology feel to many silent films, which tended to offer a bleak view of the superscientific world of tomorrow. In addition to a general mistrust of medical science and the physical sciences, there was also a wary attitude towards the new social science of psychology, and its avid proponents, psychiatrists.

Robert Wiene's expressionistic classic, *Das Kabinett des Doktor Caligari (The Cabinet of Dr. Caligari)* (1919), considered to be the first feature length horror film, is a story about a mesmerist (Werner Krauss) who hypnotically commands a somnambulist (Conrad Veidt) to carry out his evil biddings. The film evoked contemporary anxieties about psychiatrists such as Sigmund Freud, who used dubious techniques like hypnotism, typically referred to as "mesmerism" back in those days, in reference to Dr. Anton Mesmer, the eighteenth century physician and occultist, whose methods of thought control were mistakenly associated with the technique of hypnotism. The average filmgoer was easily convinced that a man with the ability to control other people's minds could easily control their bodies and their behaviors as well. The film reverberated with audiences' fear of the new and unknown, in this case, psychoanalytic theories of the unconscious and esoteric psychiatric techniques such as hypnotism and dream analysis.

It is also not a coincidence that the film itself was intended as a sociopolitical allegory of the Great War — the somnambulist symbolizing the working-class soldier, and the doctor representing the evil ruling-class master, who commands a powerless dupe to kill other innocent people. There were also a number of Silent Era films that depicted medieval tales of alchemy and sorcery. Paul Wegener directed two celebrated versions of the Golem legend, *Der Golem* (1915) and *Der Golem, wie er in die Welt kam* (1920). The tale of the Golem is part of Eastern European Jewish folklore, in which a sixteenth century rabbi uses mystical spells and potions from the Kabala to bring life to a clay creature, in order to protect his village from anti-Semitic pogroms. The theme of creating a man from clay through magic and alchemy is a precursor to the mad scientist plot of human creation via modern medicine and electricity. The Gothic imagery in the Golem films, as well as the character of the misguided creator, Rabbi Loew, would become significant influences on later film depictions of the mad scientist, such as Dr. Frankenstein.

The legend of the infamous alchemist, Dr. Faust, was also filmed numerous times in the early years of film, most notably by F.W. Murnau in 1926. But undoubtedly, the most memorable mad science movie of the 1920s was Fritz Lang's futuristic classic, *Metropolis* (1927). Like Wiene's, Murnau's, and Wegener's films, Lang's epic was also made in the German expressionistic style, but Lang's film was set in the terrifying future rather than the gloomy past. As such, *Metropolis* depicts the work of a true mad scientist — Rotwang (Rudolf Klein-Rogge) — who creates an android double of a rebellious woman in order to incite the working classes to riot. More significant than the mad scientist characterization, however, is the overt sociopolitical message of the film. Society in *Metropolis* is divided into two clear classes. The "thinkers" are the wealthy and educated ruling class, who live above ground in an opulent Eden, while the poor and exploited "workers" live underground in a dismal pit of smoke and dirt. The most moving scenes in the film depict the workers trudging listlessly into the smoky bowels of Moloch, the machine-god devised by the thinkers to rule the workers' gloomy underworld. Though *Metropolis* was a metaphorical vision of the future, its message was clearly designed for the audience of its day. The film depicted the working class's fear and resentment of the ruling class, as well as their mistrust of the new science and technologies that seemed to only benefit the rich, while the poor remained exploited and overworked in the industrial age hell of factories and sweatshops.

An interesting detail in *Metropolis* is that Rotwang wears a black glove over a crippled hand. It is very common for the mad scientist to be deformed or crippled to a certain degree. The ultimate example of this theme is the title character in Stanley Kubrick's *Dr. Strangelove or: How I Learned to Stop Worrying and Love the Bomb* (1964), in which Strangelove (Peter Sellers) is paralyzed from the neck down. As with traditional depictions of any villain, physical handicaps or deformities are external symbols of internal deformities. The crippled villain has a crippled soul. In the mad scientists' case, physical deformities add another layer of irony to their character, as their work typically entails the narcissistic dream of creating a perfect being, who is completely free of deformity or weakness. The mad scientist's physical inferiority, his inferiority complex, becomes such a driving force in his psyche that he becomes obsessed with the vision of creating a superior being ... the projection of his own unconscious fantasies of physical perfection.

While the 1920s saw the gradual development of the mad scientist archetype, it did not truly come of age until the 1930s, when the silver screen suddenly exploded with a host of classic film depictions. The definitive film versions of the most significant mad scientist characters were all released around the same time: *Frankenstein* and *Dr. Jekyll and Mr. Hyde* in 1931, and *The Island of Lost Souls* (aka *The Island of Dr. Moreau*) in 1933. No one can say for certain why the mad scientist plot became so popular among film audiences at that particular moment in history, though it must be noted that the archetype's popularity reached its zenith when the American economy was at its all-time low, in the murky depths of the Great Depression. In the early 1930s, the futuristic promises of a brave new world, a world in which science and technology would ease the toils and troubles of the common man, were seen as the empty promises of a corrupt and irresponsible ruling class. Social unrest spurred by the Depression revived a sense of mistrust among the working classes against government and authority, reawakening the old prejudices against science, industry, and the intelligentsia. In the mind of the average moviegoer, the mad scientist was merely a sly reflection of the mad forces at work in government and industry, men who fooled around with what they did not understand and caused the bottom to fall out of the economy, resulting in distress for the rich and disaster for the poor.

The Modern Prometheus

When Mary Wollstonecraft Shelley penned her infamous novel in 1818, the title, "*Frankenstein: The Modern Prometheus*," alluded to the original inspiration for the mad scientist archetype. The mad scientist is a creative genius, who is obsessed with the notion of creation. Like Prometheus, the mad scientist has incredible creative powers, and sees himself as a god. Often times, as in the case of Dr. Frankenstein, the mad scientist actually aspires to create a new race of beings, a "manmade race of gods and monsters." His compulsive obsession with human creation and his narcissis-

tic insistence that he alone has the right to take on such an awesome task
are the integral features of his character — the qualities that make him a
"mad" scientist.

In the first act of the 1931 Universal production of *Frankenstein*, we
encounter the baron Dr. Henry Frankenstein (Colin Clive). Dr. Frankenstein embodies all of the previously mentioned characteristics of the mad
scientist: he is rich, aristocratic, despotic, isolated, secretive, iconoclastic, passionate, a creative genius, a control freak, narcissistic, self-
centered, ruthless, obsessive-compulsive, and oh yes ... quite mad! In the
creation scenes, director James Whale created an indelible image of the
mad scientist at work, in part by embodying the persona of another real
life mad scientist, Nikola Tesla (1856–1943). Tesla was an uncontested
genius in the field of electricity, the father of alternating current and
super-sci-fi brainchildren such as radar, remote control, death rays, and
robots. Frankenstein's laboratory is decorated with Tesla coils that snap,
crackle, and pop with electrical arcs and flashing sparks. Other features
of the Frankenstein lab that have become standard mad scientist equip-
ment are sparkling cyclotrons, Van de Graaff generators (metal globes that
produce streaks of static electricity) and a plethora of interconnected test
tubes and beakers containing colored liquids, which may or may not
be boiling over a Bunsen burner or perpetually frothing of their own
accord.

The Gothic setting, the dungeon laboratory of a remote castle in a
dark, dreary, distinctly medieval European landscape, recalls the dungeon
workshops of the alchemists of old. Other alchemical origins of the
Frankenstein myth were infused into the story by Mary Shelley. It is
believed that Konrad Dippel (1673–1734), an infamous German alchemist,
served as a model for her character of Dr. Frankenstein. Like Shelley's
character, Dippel was a vivisectionist who was deeply interested in the
reanimation of dead tissue. He studied medicine at the University of Geis-
sen, in the same region as Darmstadt, where the actual Castle Frankenstein stood. It was even rumored that Dippel performed many of his
heretical experiments at Castle Frankenstein, as his University registra-
tion was signed with the epithet, "Franckensteina." And finally, like Dr.
Frankenstein, Dippel was an extraordinarily controversial figure in aca-
demia, for both his heretical experimentation and his nihilistic philosophies.

A leitmotif of heresy runs throughout the Universal film. Frankenstein's means of breathing life into his creature — via electrical current
from bolts of lighting — is clearly evocative of the Prometheus myth, in
which the hero steals fire from the gods. It is also worthwhile to note that

Zeus himself was known for throwing lighting bolts down from the heavens, while Frankenstein accomplishes his ungodly deed by catching lightning bolts from a storm. Finally, Frankenstein's maniacal ranting at his moment of triumph—"It's alive! It's alive!"—capped off with a line that just barely made it past the censors—"Now I know what it feels like to be God!"—leaves little doubt that this character is cursed with a god complex.

In Universal's sequel film, *Bride of Frankenstein* (1935), the archetypal symbolism is drawn out even further. A new character, the demented Dr. Pretorius (Ernest Thesiger), is introduced to play a Mephistopheles type to Frankenstein's Faust. Pretorius lures the research wary Frankenstein back into the laboratory, and toasts their evil partnership with a now infamous line: "To a new world of gods and monsters!" Pretorius is an even more exaggerated example of the mad scientist archetype. His wild, bushy, gray hair reminds the viewer of another eccentric scientist, Albert Einstein, while the name "Pretorius" is reminiscent of both the words "Prometheus" and "notorious." Furthermore, Pretorius' plan is not just to create one monster. By making a mate for Frankenstein's original monster, Pretorius aims to make an entire race of manmade men. Pretorius himself may have been a nod to another infamous historical character, Paracelsus, a sixteenth century alchemist who claimed to have created a homunculus ... a miniature human being. In a rather amusing scene in *Bride of Frankenstein*, Pretorius shows the young doctor his own homunculi, little costumed men and women in glass jars, which ironically appear to be much more advanced than the simple stitch-and-shock job for which Pretorius is trying to enlist Dr. Frankenstein.

The third act of both films provides an excellent example of the ubiquitous mad scientist plot, in which the monster attacks and abducts the scientist's love interest. The doctor must then confront his own creation in order to save the life of his love. Interestingly, in the original ending of both films, Dr. Frankenstein dies—just retribution for his crimes against nature. But in both cases, the studio forced James Whale to tack on happy endings, in which the doctor and his love interest escape with their lives, while the monster (Boris Karloff) is destroyed. The tacked on happy endings imply not only a general desire in film audiences for movies to end on a positive note, but a general willingness of film audiences to have sympathy for the mad scientist character. By the 1930s, mass audiences were much better adjusted to the new technologies afforded to them by modern science. Film itself, a technology regarded as magic when it was first introduced in the late nineteenth century, had now become the primary medium of storytelling to mass audiences. Though wary of mad scientists, in the end, the repentant Dr. Frankenstein is forgiven his trespasses by his audience.

Dr. Jekyll and Dr. Moreau

At least four early film versions of Robert Louis Stevenson's cautionary novel, *The Strange Case of Dr. Jekyll and Mr. Hyde* (1886), in various lengths, were made prior to 1920, which was a banner year for the mad doctor. Four additional film versions of the tale were released in 1920, including a German production directed by F.W. Murnau and starring Conrad Veidt, and Paramount's production starring John Barrymore, in his signature role. The American film, under the shortened title, *Dr. Jekyll and Mr. Hyde,* featured a breathtaking performance by Barrymore as the mad doctor, and introduced to screen audiences the archetypal mad scientist folly of self-experimentation. This ubiquitous plot device is merely another aspect of the scientist's madness, in that he is so obsessed with his work and compulsive about pursuing it, that he cannot even stop himself from subjecting his own body and mind to the obvious risks and dangers.

As with Dr. Frankenstein, the definitive film version of the Dr. Jekyll character appeared on screens in 1931—a seminal season for mad scientists and monsters. Paramount's second and best feature length production of Stevenson's tale starred Fredric March in an Oscar winning performance. Two years later, Paramount released *The Island of Lost Souls* (1933), a feature based on H.G. Wells' novel, *The Island of Dr. Moreau* (1896), starring Charles Laughton in the title role. Jekyll and Moreau share all of the archetypal characteristics of the mad scientist: they isolate themselves from society, they hail from the upper classes, they are obsessed with their work, they display a desperate need for complete control, and they crave the domination of others. In particular, both doctors are obsessed with mastering the division between the civilized and primitive sides of human nature. Jekyll explores this division by concocting a potion to separate the two sides, resulting in a split in his own identity. Moreau's potion, on the other hand, transforms wild animals into humans, but to his frustration, the mutant subjects eventually regress to their more primitive forms. Most significantly, both doctors also engage in unethical research on humans. Jekyll uses himself as a subject, while Moreau, in due course, uses a captive as an unwilling human subject. Dr. Caligari, in *The Cabinet of Dr. Caligari*, is another mad scientist who engages in unethical research on an unwilling subject.

Fredric March as the mad scientist, Dr. Jekyll, in Rouben Mamoulian's *Dr. Jekyll and Mr. Hyde* (1931).

Unethical Experimentation, Unwilling Subjects

The fear that scientists would use unethical methods of experimentation on human subjects was a justified concern in the 1930s. In 1933, the U.S. Public Health Service began a long-term study in Tuskegee, Alabama. Three hundred and ninety-nine African American men with latent syphilis were recruited into the program, but they were not informed that the study was investigating the long-term effects of *untreated* syphilitic infection. The men were simply told that they had "bad blood," and received no treatment for their condition until the unethical program was exposed in 1972. As a consequence of refusing treatment to these men, 128 subjects died of syphilis, over 40 of the subjects' wives contracted the disease, and 20 of the subjects' children were born with congenital syphilis. The fact that the Tuskegee syphilis study was conducted by respectable scientists employed by the U.S. government in a federally funded program that was clearly unethical as well as blatantly racist, emphasizes the point that the fear of mad science was not, and is still not, an irrational fear.

The characters of Jekyll and Moreau were written in the nineteenth century, a time of intense reaction to Darwin's recently published treatises on evolution. The resulting theories about the genetic basis of humanity bloomed in both scientific and political circles, giving birth to the eugenics movement of the early twentieth century. America was the first country to write eugenics-based philosophies into law. Pennsylvanian eugenicists in 1905 convinced their state legislator to introduce a law giving doctors the right to forcibly sterilize patients who were considered to be "feeble minded." Laws supporting involuntary and compulsory sterilization were soon adopted by states across the country, as sterilization was used to end the reproductive lives of any person deemed "unfit" by the state. "Unfit" individuals included the "feeble minded" (mentally retarded), criminals, epileptics, and people suffering from other "genetically-based" disorders. Compulsory involuntary sterilization rates remained relatively low, however, until the Supreme Court upheld the right of the state of Virginia to force mental patients to undergo sterilization in 1927. From that point on, sterilization rates increased exponentially across the country throughout the 1930s—incidentally, at the same time that mad scientist movies were at their peak of popularity. Compulsory sterilization fell into decline in the 1940s, when another Supreme Court decision ruled against punitive sterilization of prison inmates, but more significantly, because of the new association between eugenics and the Nazis.

Ironically, the Nazi-German eugenicists claimed that the inspiration for their eugenics policy came from the American sterilization programs. The Nazis, however, used compulsory sterilization much more broadly. While the United States only sterilized a total of 64,000 victims in its 40-year history of state-enforced eugenics, the Nazis sterilized nearly half a million people in just the first four years of its program, before the regime's resources were directed toward the war effort and the more drastic methods of racial cleansing employed in the concentration camps. The evils of American and German compulsory sterilization would pale in comparison to the sheer horror of the genetic and biological experimentation that would be inflicted upon the Jews by the Nazis. The most infamous of the Nazi scientists/torturers was the insidious Dr. Mengele of Auschwitz, also known as "the angel of death." Mengele performed horrific experiments on his captive subjects, ostensibly in search of the genetic path to racial purity, but his overt sadism and the sheer joy he took in his ghoulish work leads one to believe that science was merely a secondary concern to the evil angel. Though Jekyll and Moreau were products of fiction, they were the literary and cinematic precursors to mad scientists such as Mengele, who not only matched the madness of his fictional forerunners, but surpassed them in utter sadism, depravity, and inhumanity.

The Age of Madness

The world as we knew it changed at 8:15 A.M. on August 6, 1945, when an atomic bomb was dropped on the city of Hiroshima, Japan. It was the dawn of the nuclear age, or as science-fiction writers had taken to calling it, the "Age of Madness." The nuclear proliferation of the Cold War arms race was true madness, as mad scientists and politicians brought the world to the brink of nuclear Armageddon, and kept it there — teetering precariously on the edge — for over 40 years. As a result, a new brand of mad scientist was born ... the nuclear physicist. Perhaps the most iconic of the new breed of madmen was Herman Kahn, the American physicist who conceived the Cold War armaments doctrine of "mutually assured destruction," typically referred to with the acronym, "M.A.D." The notion of resting the world's security on a delicate balance of super-deadly thermonuclear weapons was indeed mad, as it almost certainly would have ended with the assured destruction of all mankind. Kahn's doctrine was satirized in Kubrick's Cold War classic, *Dr. Strangelove or: How I Learned to Stop Worrying and Love the Bomb* (1964), with the M.A.D. doctrine represented as a Soviet "doomsday device," and Kahn himself represented as the inspiration for the title character, played brilliantly by Peter Sellers.

Nuclear physicists of the twentieth century brought the Promethean roots of the mad scientist archetype full circle. Just as Prometheus stole fire from the gods by lighting a torch on the sun, nuclear physicists harnessed thermonuclear energy, the force that fuels the sun, and in doing so endowed man with the awesome destructive power of the gods. J. Robert Oppenheimer, one of the real life prototypes of the nuclear age mad scientist, described the feeling of being a modern day Prometheus in a 1950s television interview, by quoting from the Upanishads: "I am become Death, shatterer of worlds." Oppenheimer himself was shattered by guilt for his leading role in inventing the atomic bomb, remarking: "we did the work of the devil," and later opposing the development of the hydrogen bomb. Now with the power to destroy the entire world many times over, the nuclear mad scientist became an even more conflicted character type. Oftentimes racked with guilt, and more often than not vaguely German, the mad scientist became one part Oppenheimer, two parts Albert Einstein, and one part Werner von Braun — the brilliant Nazi rocket scientist who was co-opted by the Americans after the war. Despite his loyal work for the Nazis, including rocket development programs that utilized thousands of concentration camp victims as slave labor, Von Braun became a key figure on the American side of the Cold War, helping America to build long-range ballistic missiles, and later building the rockets for NASA that launched the first man to the moon.

Sci-fi movies of the 1950s, such as *The Blob* (1958), *Godzilla, King of the Monsters* (1956) and *Them!* (1954) frequently dwelled on the dangers of mislaid radiation from nuclear weapons testing. Whereas Frankenstein built his monster intentionally with the nineteenth century fire technology — electrical power — nuclear age mad scientists mistakenly created monsters by mishandling the twentieth century fire technology — nuclear power. Incidentally, the huge mutant insects in 1950s B-movies such as *Them!* and *The Deadly Mantis* (1957) played upon a primordial human fear and revulsion of bugs. In the Bible, pagan cults worshipped "Baal Zevuv," Hebrew for "lord of the flies." The name has been passed down in history as "Beelzebub," a representation of the devil. Though the monsters in big bug movies were not literal demons or pagan gods, they certainly did the work of the devil, instilling as much fear and awe as Satan himself. Another common feature in '50s B-movies were extraterrestrial space beings with supersized big brains. The fears evoked by these big-brained aliens paralleled contemporary fears of egghead scientists and their big-brained colleagues in the sociopolitical intelligentsia, who had brought the entire globe to the brink of destruction.

Postmodern Madness

By the latter half of the twentieth century, the mad scientist archetype had become so well worn and familiar that the character itself was recognizable as kitsch and/or camp. No longer a universal source of fear and dread, the mad scientist was ripe for parody. He could be trivialized or even laughed at. The first sign that the modern mad scientist had switched over to postmodern spectacle was in Universal Pictures' *Abbot and Costello Meet Frankenstein* (1948), which was a huge financial success. The film's humorous take on mad scientists and their monsters opened the door for a slew of camp comedy thrillers in the 1950s and '60s, such as *I Was a Teenage Werewolf* (1957), the highly successful "Monster Mash" (1962) pop song, and the extremely popular television show, *The Munsters* (1964–1966). Increasingly, mad scientists appeared as kitsch caricatures of themselves, cast as the outrageous antagonists in TV shows like *Batman* (1966–1968), *Gilligan's Island* (1964–1967), and *The Monkees* (1966–1968). The postmodern mad scientist was also ubiquitously cast as the antagonist in serial films such as the James Bond movies and Pink Panther films. The archetype reached the height of camp in 1975's *The Rocky Horror Picture Show*, when the mad scientist was cast as Dr. Frank-N-Furter (Tim Curry)— dressed in high heels, fishnet stockings, and a black lace bustier, and singing: "I'm just a sweet transvestite from transsexual, Transylvania."

In the twenty-first century, the mad scientist has become so trite that serious depictions of the character are rarely seen. Dr. Evil (Mike Myers) in the *Austin Powers* movies (1997, 1999, 2002), Green Goblin (Willem Dafoe) in the *Spider-Man* movies (2002, 2004), and the megalomaniacal mouse in the popular cartoon series, *Pinky and the Brain* (1995–1998), are all postmodern takes on the aging archetype, in which the character elicits chuckles and guffaws rather than gasps of fear. A recent trend has been to substitute the traditional mad scientist part with an avaricious executive who employs a staff of scientists to realize his narcissistic, diabolical plots. For instance, Superman's nemesis, Lex Luthor, was initially written as a traditional mad scientist character in the original 1930s comic books. In the twenty-first century cartoon series, Luthor is depicted as a greedy corporate executive of a vast multimedia empire.

Now that the Age of Madness has somewhat come to an end, and the Age of Technology is rapidly evolving into the Information Age, modern science is opening up new dimensions of possibilities through the advents of instant internet access, cybernetic nanotechnology, and human genome manipulation. What once was considered heresy has now become mundane scientific innovation. What was feared in the nineteenth and early twentieth centuries— organ and limb transplants, superintelligent robots, human-resembling androids, and robot-resembling cyborgs— is no longer science fiction, but science reality. Nevertheless, the ancient fears have not gone away. The president of the United States still finds it necessary to ban scientific research on human cloning. Similar bans on stem cell research and genetic modification recall old fears and policy mistakes concerning eugenics and compulsory sterilization. So, while certain versions of the archetype have lost some of their power to terrify, science itself is always progressing. Therefore, the scientist as a Promethean deliverer of ungodly power and dangerous technology will always retain the ability to frighten the masses. The uneasy identification that audiences make with the mad scientist at the unconscious level is that, perhaps, we are not the children of a divine benevolent god. Perhaps, instead, we are just the hapless creations of an irresponsible creator, a creator whose qualifications to create life are as dubious as Dr. Frankenstein's or Dr. Moreau's — a creator who may be as mad as the maddest scientist ever to appear on film.

CHAPTER FOUR

Psychic Powers

Why should any phenomena be assumed impossible? The universe begins to look more and more like a great thought, than a great machine.

Sir James Jean
as quoted in the film, Psychic Killer *(1975)*

Psy-fi authors and filmmakers owe a debt of gratitude to the CIA and other intelligence agencies for their secret research in the area of paranormal psychic abilities. Under top secret projects such as MKULTRA, MKSEARCH, Project Bluebird and Project Artichoke, intelligence agencies explored the outermost capacities of the human mind. In the interest of national defense against the "red scourge" of communism, cold warriors sought any edge they could in their covert battles against the soviets. After all, it was well reported that soviet researchers were exploring the operational possibilities of clairvoyance, telepathy, astral (psychic) projection, and other potential psychic abilities. Countless highly trained spies could be spared death or capture by the enemy if a highly attuned psychic super-spy could attain the same information from the safety of a CIA psych lab. Clairvoyant psychic spies could foretell what the enemy was planning on doing, or what they were furtively pulling off in the shadows of secrecy, thousands of miles from American soil. Telepathic psychic spies could read the minds of enemy agents, soviet officers, or even invade the minds of Russian diplomats. Some psychic spies were even being trained to psychically project themselves across time and space, to locate enemy missile sites in the far reaches of the Siberian tundra.

Though it will never be fully known how much, if any, of the government funded research into psychic powers bore fruit, the fact that they engaged in this kind of research is fuel enough for the active imaginations of psy-fi writers and directors. The fact that most of the data and details about the research was never fully released makes the experiments that much more engaging. Who knows what mysteries these mad scientists revealed? What strange, sinister powers of the mind did they unleash on the world? What evils did they bring to bear? We have only the medium of psycho thrillers to deal directly with these deep, dark questions.

Recurrent Themes

There are certain themes in movie genres that constantly reoccur. Like the notions that vampires fear crucibles, or that werewolves can only be killed by a silver bullet — once an idea is created by screenwriters, it becomes part of the lore of that specific genre, and it is recapitulated in subsequent films. Thus, films are much like folklore, in that they create stories and legends that perpetuate themselves through the telling and retelling of the same stories. So when Brian De Palma, in *The Fury* (1978), depicted nose bleeds as a symptom of someone experiencing an intense psychic power, the notion was repeated by other filmmakers in later films, such as in David Cronenberg's *Scanners* (1981) or David Koepp's *Stir of Echoes* (1999). Filmmakers even embellished on the theme, by depicting blood emitting from other orifices— eyes and ears— indicating the presence of hyper-psychic activity within the cranium.

Other recurrent themes are more general dramatic leitmotifs. In most psychic power movies, for example, the special power could be perceived as both a gift or a curse. In Cronenberg's *The Dead Zone* (1983), Johnny Smith (Christopher Walken) is tortured by the macabre ability to see into other people's future, especially when that future involves a horrific death. However, his curse is also a blessing for mankind, because he can use his power to the save the world from a nuclear apocalypse, by killing the mass murdering madman who will become the future president of the United States (Martin Sheen). A corollary to the blessing/curse dichotomy is the issue that the power could be used for either good or evil. In *Dreamscape* (1984), two characters have the ability to psychically project themselves into other people's dreams. One character uses the power to do good, the other to do evil. The hero (Dennis Quaid) uses dream projection to save the president of the United States (Eddie Albert), who is going to be assassinated in his dreams by the villain (David Patrick Kelly). (The presence of the president of the United States, by the way, is not a recurrent theme in psy-fi movies ... it is a recurrent theme in *all* movies.) The idea, that when someone dies in their dream, they also die in real life, has become a recurrent theme in psy-fi movies, used most notably in *The Matrix* (1999). When someone dies in the computer generated dream world known as "the matrix," their physical body also dies. Why is this so? Why are vampires thwarted by garlic? Recurrent themes do not have to be logical, they just have to be established.

Another common recurrent theme is that psychics are typically perceived by others as crazy, abnormal freaks. The most compelling application of the psychic-as-freak theme can be seen in Brian De Palma's *Carrie* (1976), in which the title character (Sissy Spacek) is abused and harassed by her sadistic schoolmates for nearly the entire picture, until her humiliation, anger, and rage explodes in an orgy of bloody telekinetic violence. The climax in *Carrie* denotes another recurrent theme. By the end of the picture, the hero will not be seen as a defective freak or mutant, but rather, as an advanced being with highly evolved powers, casting the psychic as, in essence, the next step on the evolutionary ladder.

Psychic Detectives

In what may be the quintessential psycho thriller, *The Dead Zone*, a man (Christopher Walken) suffers severe head trauma in a car accident. He wakes up after many years in a coma to discover that he has the ability to predict the future of any person he touches. The ability to tell the future has been known by many names: clairvoyance, prophecy, second sight, e.s.p. (extrasensory perception), fortune telling, divination, soothsaying, prognostication, precognition, etc. The gift is one of the oldest mystical/spiritual beliefs, predating the bible and modern religious thought. There are psychological researchers who espouse the existence of ESP, and there are those who denounce it. Outside of the psych lab, there have been many instances of the police using "psychic detectives" to help them find bodies and locate criminals. Again, the relative success and accuracy of these psychic detectives has been lauded by some and condemned as hokum by others. Regardless of whether the actual power exists or not, clairvoyance has been the subject of countless television shows, documentaries, and movies.

In *The Dead Zone*, Johnny uses his powers to help police locate a psycho killer. Similarly, in *The Gift* (2000), the heroin (Cate Blanchett) is a clairvoyant called upon to locate a missing girl. In Spielberg's psy-fi classic, *Minority Report* (2002), based on Philip K. Dick's 1956 short story, an entire system of law and order is set up under which policemen arrest

Christopher Walken as Johnny Smith in David Cronenberg's *The Dead Zone* (1983).

people before they even commit their crime, as the super psychic "precogs" can predict exactly when and where an individual will break the law. Though not all ESP themed movies are about psychic detectives, the use of the power to solve crimes is the most popular psy-fi leitmotif, given the tendency for filmmakers to make films about criminals and the people who catch them.

Clairaudience and Clairsentience

The term clairvoyance is derived from the French terms "clair" (clear) and "voyance" (mind reading). Unlike the mind reader, the clairvoyant can see psychic information clearly, without having to go through the mind of another. However, psychic information can also be received through other senses. Clairaudience is when the psychic can hear the voices of spirits or entities from beyond, without seeing them. Whoopi Goldberg's character in the blockbuster hit, *Ghost* (1990), was a clairaudient. She could hear the deceased hero's (Patrick Swayze) voice, but she could not see him. Another variation on the theme is clairsentience, the ability to feel the feelings or physical sensations of the beings from beyond, without actually hearing or seeing them. Forest Whitaker's character in the blockbuster hit, *Species* (1995), was a clairsentient. Describing himself as an "empath"—as opposed to a telepath—he was able to feel what the predatorial alien villain (Natasha Henstridge) had felt at each stage of the hunt. Clairsentients are supposedly able to psychically sense smells and tastes as well.

Psychic Communication

Telepathy, the ability to communicate psychically, involves two separate processes: mind reading—the ability to perceive other people's thoughts, and thought transmission—the ability to transmit thought's into other people's brains. Sometimes these separate abilities are cast as being mutually exclusive, other times, telepaths retain both types of powers. For example, Dr. Spock (Leonard Nimoy) in the *Star Trek* (1966) series of television shows and films is capable of performing the infamous "Vulcan mind meld," during which he can read his subject's mind, as well as communicate his own thoughts to his subject psychically. The title character (Alec Baldwin) in *The Shadow* (1994) has "the power to cloud men's minds," enabling him to read minds as well as deliver telepathic commands. Similarly, Jedi knights in the *Star Wars* series of films have the ability to intercept thoughts and transmit their thoughts into other people's heads, as "the Force has power over the weak minded." However, while the sinister alien beings in *Dark City* (1998) can communicate freely with each other, because "they share one group mind," they cannot read or transmit thoughts into the minds of humans.

It should be noted that psychotics, especially paranoid schizophrenics, often believe that they are the victims of thought transmission and "thought broadcasting"—the fear that others can hear your thoughts. Since schizophrenics typically experience auditory hallucinations, hearing voices inside their head that they cannot control, it seems natural that they might fear that their own internal dialogues might be beyond their own control, causing their thoughts to be transmitted to others without their consent. Combine this troubling notion with other psychotic symptoms of schizophrenia—delusions, paranoia, magical thinking—and you can understand why schizophrenics often claim that the CIA or FBI is monitoring their thoughts.

Psycho-spiritualism

When we consider the prevalence of schizophrenia, a disorder that affects nearly 2.2 million American adults (about 1 percent of the population at large), we begin to comprehend the scope of the phenomenon, not so much as a disorder, but as a universal human tendency. Psychologists who espouse this perspective point out that everyone is prone, in varying extents, to "positive psychotic symptoms," which include paranoia, delusions, grandiose thinking, magical beliefs, etc. The fact that all humans are prone to the most overt symptoms of psychosis, auditory and visual hallucinations, in certain situations—such as being dehydrated, under tremendous stress, in a heightened state of arousal, under the influence of drugs or alcohol, while meditating, or in a dream state—supports the theory that the tendency towards schizophrenic behavior is innate to all people. Individuals who are labeled clinically psychotic or schizophrenic may be better understood as ordinary people at the high end scale of schizophrenic tendencies. The American Psychological Association itself has allowed for varying degrees of schizophrenia, in designating the *DSM* classifications of "schizoid personality disorder," "schizotypal personality disorder," "schizoaffective disorder," "scizophreniform disorder," and other diagnoses indicating varying degrees in the length and intensity of psychosis.

In essence, we are all schizophrenic ... more or less. To a certain degree, we all hallucinate, even if it's just in our dreams. We all experience, to varying extents, paranoia, delusions, grandiose thoughts, magical beliefs, etc. Certainly, the universal human tendency toward the religious belief in all-powerful supernatural beings that control every aspect of our lives and destinies can be construed as essentially schizophrenic trends towards magical thinking, delusions, and even paranoia. Hence, ancient mystical/spiritual beliefs in gods, devils, prophecies, demonic possessions, and spiritual unions, can be linked theoretically to modern beliefs in extraterrestrials, ESP, past lives, collective memories, and telepathy. Enter psy-fi movies, to express this psycho-spiritual link theatrically in the form of film.

People with the paranormal ability to commune with spiritual or divine beings have been referred to as prophets, mediums, oracles, and—of course—psychics. In psycho thrillers, the line between psychic powers and spiritual powers are often blurred. In Kubrick's *The Shining* (1980), based on Stephen King's 1977 novel, there are two characters who commune with spiritual presences. Danny (Danny Lloyd) is a young boy with an imaginary friend named "Tony," an invisible supernatural entity who gives him counsel from beyond. His psychic gift is referred to as "shining." Danny's father (Jack Nicholson) also encounters spiritual beings—ghostly spirits haunting a resort hotel—who eventually take over his personality and drive him to kill his family. The premise of a young child being able to commune with the spirit world is another recurrent psy-fi theme. For some reason, people are prone to believe that children's minds are more open to extraordinary influences, because children are innocent, suggestible, impressionable, and unrepressed. In *The Sixth Sense* (1999), a young boy (Haley Joel Osment) is able to "see dead people." In a somewhat similar film, also released in 1999, the young boy (Zachary David Cope) in *Stir of Echoes* can also communicate with dead spirits. His father (Kevin Bacon) begins to experience the same ability when a door to his subconscious mind is opened, after he is hypnotized at a party.

Stir of Echoes recalls elements from both *The Shining* and *The Sixth Sense*. As in *The Shining*, ghost-telepathy is a genetic trait, handed down from father to son. Also, in both films, there is an older black man who can instantly recognize the psychic ability in the young boy. In *The Shining*, the man (Scatman Crothers) calls the ability "shining." In *Stir of Echoes*, the man (Eddie Smith, Jr.) calls it "x-ray eyes." In both *Stir of Echoes* and *The Sixth Sense*, ghosts speak to human mediums only to express specific needs, typically having to do with their untimely deaths. And in all three films, the father character—including Bruce Willis in *The Sixth Sense*, who plays a father figure to the boy—becomes obsessed or possessed by the ghostly spirits, unable to reconcile their supernatural experiences with their adult, rational understanding of the natural world.

Telekinesis

The paranormal power to move objects using only the force of one's mind was depicted most notably by Brian De Palma in *Carrie* (1976), a film based on Stephen King's 1974 novel. *Carrie* could be considered the quintessential telekinesis themed movie. Not only was the film a tremendous mainstream success, it spurred the great surge of psychic power movies in the late 1970s and early '80s. Unlike *The Exorcist* (1973), in which a young girl's telekinetic power stems from a demonic possession, *Carrie* is not a supernatural thriller. Carrie White (Sissy Spacek) is an average, ordinary girl who realizes that she has a paranormal power, which many people believe to be a real, existing psychological ability. The focus on psychological phenomenon as opposed to supernatural or extraterrestrial phenomenon makes *Carrie* a "pure" work of psychological fiction. De

Palma followed up *Carrie* with *The Fury* (1978), a film more significant for its theme than for its quality. In *The Fury*, children and teens with superior psychic powers are gathered and trained by the CIA to become psychic weapons. In this film, the political conspiracy and mind control themes of *The Manchurian Candidate* and the psychic power theme of *Carrie* are merged into one film, a psy-fi political thriller, which would become the template for many of the psycho thrillers to come.

Following *Carrie* and *The Fury*, telekinesis would become a somewhat common psy-fi theme in movies. Typically, the power evoked terror, such as in *The Medusa Touch* (1978), *Scanners* (1981), and *Friday the 13th Part VII: The New Blood* (1988). Sometimes, the power was used in dramatic, inspirational stories, such as in *Powder* (1995) and *Phenomenon* (1996). And occasionally, the power was used to dispatch comedic set pieces, such as in *Modern Problems* (1981), *Zapped!* (1982), and *Matilda* (1996)—which is based on a Roald Dahl book. *Carrie* and *Matilda* are interesting contrasting takes on the telekinesis theme. Both stories are about girls who have trouble fitting in, with uncaring parents and hateful schoolmates, who discover their telekinetic abilities and use them for revenge. But while Stephen King's story is horrifying, vicious, and disturbing, Roald Dahl's is whimsical, funny, and delightful. It would be hard to imagine two more completely opposing versions of the same basic premise.

Pyrokinesis

The ability to set fires with the power of one's mind is a rather odd notion which has found a home in the psycho thriller genre. Pyrokinesis is related in theory to the supposed phenomenon of "spontaneous human combustion"—when a human body blisters, smokes or bursts into flames spontaneously, without any external spark. The ability to create fires psychically first appeared on film in Cronenberg's *Scanners* (1981), in which pyrokinesis is merely one of the many psychic powers retained by the multi-psychically talented "scanners." The quintessential pyrokinesis movie is *Firestarter* (1984), based on psy-fi master Stephen King's 1980 novel. In *Firestarter*, Drew Barrymore stars as the young girl with the gift/curse of pyrokinesis. Her parents were both guinea pigs in unethical psychic experiments run by a secret government intelligence agency. They develop super-psychic powers which they pass down to their daughter. Naturally, mayhem ensues as she is pursued by shadow government agencies who want to use her as a psychic weapon. *Wilder Napalm* (1993) presents a comedic take on the power, as a trio of pyrokinetics (Dennis Quaid, Debra Winger and Arliss Howard) compose a combustible love triangle. Recent pyrokinesis movies include the Japanese film *Kurosufaia* aka *Cross Fire* (2000) and the *Firestarter* sequel, *Firestarter 2: Rekindled* (2002).

Dream Projection

Also known as dream telepathy, dream projection, the ability to project yourself into someone else's dream, is another psy-fi standard. The quintessential dream projection movie was made in the halcyon days of psy-fi movies, the early 1980s. *Dreamscape* (1984) stars Dennis Quaid as the good dream projector who must thwart the evil dream projector (David Patrick Kelly) from killing the president (Eddie Albert). Released the same year, writer-director Wes Craven's *A Nightmare on Elm Street* (1984) is about a deceased serial killer, Freddy Krueger (Robert Englund), who invades the dreams of teenagers. The surprise hit spawned a total of seven sequels, if you include the campy postmodern films: *New Nightmare* aka *A Nightmare On Elm Street 7: The Real Story* (1994), in which Freddy, angered at being killed off in the last sequel, attempts to murder Wes Craven, and *Freddy vs. Jason* (2003), in which Freddy faces off against Jason from the *Friday the 13th* movies.

The Matrix trilogy (1999, 2003, 2003) must also be mentioned here, as the premise of the films is the collective dream projection of nearly the entire human race into the computer generated digital dream world that is the matrix. In another addition to the genre, *In Dreams* (1999), a clairvoyant mother, appropriately named Clair (Annette Bening), is haunted in her dreams by an evil serial killer (Robert Downey, Jr.) who has abducted her daughter. The stellar cast, engaging screenplay, and masterful direction by Neil Jordan make *In Dreams* one of the best movies within the limited subgenre of dream projection themed psycho thrillers.

Psychic Projection

Also known as remote viewing and astral projection, psychic projection is the ability to psychically leave one's own body and travel through time and space. The first depiction of this phenomenon was way back in 1956, in the psy-fi/sci-fi classic, *Forbidden Planet*. The film is an outer space take on Shakespeare's *The Tempest*, in which a group of astronauts land on a lonely planet inhabited by a mad scientist, Dr. Morbius (Walter Pidgeon) and his sexy young daughter, Altaira (Anne Francis). Morbius and Altaira share a psychologically incestuous relationship on the lonely planet, and Morbius feels threatened by the intrusion of all the handsome, burly young astronauts. His jealous rage is psychically projected into a mysterious "Id" monster (an obvious nod to Freud), which kills off the astronauts one-by-one so that Morbius could keep his daughter all to himself.

The theme would not be picked up again until a strange Russian film, *Solyaris* aka *Solaris,* appeared in 1972. The movie became a cult classic, and was recently remade in Hollywood by the industry giant, Steven Soderbergh. *Solaris* (2002) stars George Clooney as a psychologist who travels to a lonely, distant space station to investigate strange deaths among the astronauts. The theme, reminiscent of *Forbidden Planet*, is played out in a much more complex and sophisticated manner. It seems that alien intelligence is able to get into people's minds and allow them to project their memories of lost loves, regrets, and guilt complexes into physical manifestations of actual beings. In this film, the psychic projections are not the killers, per se, they are merely the representations of inner demons that drive the characters to madness and suicide. Barry Levinson made a very similar film in 1998. Based on a novel by Michael Crichton, *Sphere* seems to be equally inspired by *Forbidden Planet*, Kubrick's *2001: A Space Odyssey* (1968), and the original *Solaris.* In the film, a group of scientists (Dustin Hoffman, Sharon Stone, Liev Schreiber, and Samuel Jackson) descend into the dark depths of the ocean to explore an ancient wreck of a downed spaceship. The mysterious golden sphere within the ship casts a telepathic spell over the scientists, causing them to project their deepest unconscious fears and anxieties outwardly, manifesting their latent psychological issues into real, terrifyingly destructive phenomena.

In the latter half of the 1970s, three low budget horror movies would depict killers who use psychic projection as their modus operandi: *Psychic Killer* (1975), *Patrick* (1978), and Cronenberg's *The Brood* (1979). The latter film would become the most significant, not just because it was an early film by David Cronenberg, but because of Cronenberg's highly inventive and disturbing script, and his excellent directing. In *The Brood*, Cronenberg's first film with "real" movie stars, an evil and extremely disturbed woman (Samantha Eggar) is separated from her husband and daughter and placed in a very strange, experimental mental institution. Her mad psychiatrist (Oliver Reed) applies an ultra-weird experimental technique — "psychoplasmics" — which he hails as "the ultimate therapeutic device." The technique enables patients to manifest their internal psychological demons into external physical manifestations. When Eggar's character suspects that her husband is plotting to separate her from her daughter permanently, and that he is having an affair, her jealous rage is projected into physical demons that take the form of murderous deformed children. The scene in which Eggar "gives birth" to her evil brood of misshapen mutant hatchlings is truly one of the most disturbing images ever shot onto film.

Recently, *The Butterfly Effect* (2004) explored an intriguing premise, in which a young man (Ashton Kutcher) has the psychic power to project himself back into his memories and actually return, temporarily, to prior events in his life. In an interesting twist to the psychic projection theme, the protagonist travels in time rather than space, and can only appear as himself, at a younger age. Nevertheless, by making slight but crucial adjustments to decisions he made during a few moments in his childhood, he completely alters not only his own entire life history, but the lives of everyone he knows. In keeping with the psychic power movie tradition, the hero's strange power is a genetic trait, inherited from his father. Another recent addition to the genre, *Suspect Zero* (2004), explores the phenomenon of remote viewing. Like many of his psycho thriller compadres, the super-psychic (Ben Kingsley) in *Suspect Zero* is a veteran of secret government research in psychic powers. He can psychically project himself to specific locations, where he can witness the misdeeds of practicing serial killers.

In *Brainstorm* (1983), special effects wizard Douglas Trumbull presents the virtual world inside of people's brains, as the usual suspects — brilliant parapsychology researchers funded by a shadowy government military agency — develop a way to literally tap into someone's head and create a videotape of someone's mental world. The plot turns even darker when the powers that be direct the system toward paramilitary purposes, i.e., psychological torture, induced psychosis, and even mass murder ... when they discover that viewing a brain tape of a man's death has a lethal effect. Psychic power movies, unfortunately, tend to be rather formulaic, following either the psychic-powers-as-military-weapons scenario or the psychic-powers-used-to-track-down-a-serial-killer scenario. *The Cell* (2000) follows the latter formula. Jennifer Lopez play a talented therapist who uses sci-fi hi-tech gadgetry to further an experimental new technique that allows her to literally enter her subject's mind. In the film, "the neurological connectic transfer system not only maps the mind, it sends the signal to another party." She enters the twisted, terrifying labyrinth of a serial killer's mind in order to discover where he has hidden his last victim, so that she can be rescued before it's too late. The procedure, however, is extremely dangerous. "It's like the old wives' tale, where you die in your dream, you die in real life." As with all dream projection movies — i.e., *Dreamscape, The*

Matrix, A Nightmare on Elm Street— the end of life is a metaphysical constant that transcends both the conscious and unconscious dream states. Dream death results in real death.

Just when psy-fi movies in this subgenre began to get a bit tired from overusing the two basic formulas mentioned above, a brilliant and inventive screenwriter arrived to remind us of how creative and fascinating these themes could be. In Charlie Kaufman's breakthrough screenplay, *Being John Malkovich* (1999), a disgruntled puppeteer (John Cusack) discovers a portal into the mind of actor John Malkovich. Thrilled at the experience of being John Malkovich, Cusack's character returns through the portal again and again until he masters the mind of Malkovich, and controls him like a puppet. Kaufman's most recent produced script is *Eternal Sunshine of the Spotless Mind* (2004), another fresh take on mind and identity. In the film, a brilliant psychologist (Tom Wilkinson) has invented a way to enter the human brain and erase all memories of a specific person. The psychologist uses the method to help people overcome failed relationships, by erasing all memories of the relationship and the former significant other. However, when Joel (Jim Carrey) and Clementine (Kate Winslet) erase each other from their respective memory banks, they discover that true love is not necessarily in the mind, it's in the heart. Kaufman's script (based on an original screen story by Kaufman, director Michel Gondry and Pierre Bismuth) won the 2005 Academy Award for best screenplay.

The Digital World

Back in the early 1980s, the notion of a human mind entering the digital world of the computer was a bit far out, even for the broadly conceived plots of *Scanners* (1981) and *Tron* (1982). In David Cronenberg's *Scanners,* the protagonist has the ability to telepathically control the mind of a supercomputer, and in Disney's *Tron,* a brilliant computer programmer (Jeff Bridges) is digitalized and projected into a supercomputer's cpu. Now, in the age of the Internet, with human society and the digital world interfacing on a daily basis, these concepts may seem less outrageous. If humans can develop telepathic powers beyond their normal senses, why can't these telepathic powers be used to commune with the minds of supercomputers? This theme was played out recently in *X2* (2003), when Professor Xavier (Patrick Stewart) uses his super-telepathy to enter the digital world of Cerebro, the supercomputer that is somehow connected to the life force of every human and every mutant on Earth. There is little doubt that the interaction between human psychics and artificial intelligence will be seen again in psycho thrillers to come.

Alien Super-Psychics

For some reason, it has become readily accepted that alien beings have psychic powers. For instance, Vulcans like Dr. Spock (Leonard Nimoy) in the *Star Trek* TV shows and movies, and Jedi knights like Obi-Won Kenobe (Alec Guiness) in the *Star Wars* movies, all possess psychic powers such as telepathy, telekinesis, clairvoyance, and psychic projection. In *Dark City* (1998), the aliens also have super-psychic powers: "They had mastered the ultimate technology — the ability to alter physical reality by will alone." To increase their threat: "They have machines buried deep beneath the surface that allow them to focus their telepathic energies." Through a telepathic mind meld of their "group mind," referred to as "tuning," they can telekinetically change the physical shape of the dark city where their human captives live. Why are aliens so often gifted with psychic powers? Possibly, this trait represents a common belief that the development of psychic powers represents the next step in human evolution. So, since aliens are always assumed to be more evolved than humans, they naturally have advanced psychic powers.

Psychic Supermen

A corollary to the psychic alien theme is the notion that some exceptional human beings will independently make the evolutionary leap towards psychic advancement. Since evolution works through the natural selection of randomly occurring genetic mutations, the exceptional individuals "gifted" with paranormal abilities will typically be considered abnormal mutants or freaks. Such is the case in psy-fi depictions of multitalented super-psychics. In *The Fury*, the psychic teens (Andrew Stevens and Amy Irving) have powers that include telepathy, telekinesis, and clairvoyance. While they are harassed and ill-treated by their "normal" peers, their exceptional abilities give them powers beyond belief. The exact same theme is played out in *Scanners*. In fact, both movies submit the notion that super-psychic mutants have the ability to blow up other people's heads with the power of their minds. The exploding head scenes in *The Fury* and *Scanners* represent the archetypal images of the psychic power movie genre. The films also epitomize the ubiquitous psychics-as-weapons theme and psychics-as-freaks theme in psy-fi movies.

In the cult classic film, *Village of the Damned* (1960), and its sequel, *Children of the Damned* (1963), the terrifying children with super-psychic powers, assumed to be alien spawn, actually turn out to be "Man ... advanced a million years." Recently, super-psychic mutants have been cast as superheroes. In *The Shadow*, the title character (Alec Baldwin) uses his powers of telekinesis and telepathic mind control to fight criminals and evil super-villains. In the extremely popular *X-Men* (2000) and its sequel, *X2* (2003), and upcoming threequel, *X-Men 3* (2006), heroic genetic mutants with powers such as telepathy, telekinesis, clairvoyance, pyrokinesis, and other more incredible powers, use their psychic abilities to thwart the diabolical plots of other villainous mutants who plan on conquering the world. Super-psychics in psy-fi movies have emerged from the shadows of secret government labs as gallant superheroes. Though they may be mutants, and may even be considered freaks, it is their spectacular uniqueness that makes them great.

The 10 Percent Myth and the Power of Belief

What can be said about the widespread beliefs that some humans have psychic powers, that all humans potentially have psychic powers, and that the human race as a whole will develop psychic powers as a function of evolution? Whether these beliefs are reality or fantasy is a matter of conjecture. Some people like to point to the old myth that "humans only use 10 percent of their brains." This belief, of course, is preposterous. Humans use 100 percent of their brains. Though, at any given moment, we might only be using 10 percent or so for a specific task, to wonder what the other 90 percent of the brain is up to is like wondering what the rest of the muscles in your body are doing while you are only exercising a few of them. Despite the claims of some believers, who like to assign the unused 90 percent of the brain to potential psychic abilities, PET scans, CAT scans, MRI imagery, and any knowledgeable neurologist can demonstrate quite clearly that there is no unused portion of the brain. Nevertheless, psychological fiction is not involved in actual truth. The authentic existence of psychic powers in the real world is more or less irrelevant. It is the pervasive tendency for people to believe in psychic abilities that drives the imagination and keeps the genre alive. The power of belief is the real power behind psychic abilities. Even if 90 percent of our brains are not reserved for psychic activity, the belief in mind over matter will always prevail.

CHAPTER FIVE

Mind Control

> If both the past and the external world exist only in the mind, and
> the mind itself is controllable — what then?
>
> *George Orwell* 1984 *(1948)*

The fear of mind control is real. Our thoughts and behaviors
are influenced by a million external factors. The government, the media,
our employers, our families, our peers ... our whole lives are, to a
certain degree, manipulated and controlled by others. Marginalized sections of the population, mental patients and prison inmates, have
routinely been subjected to invasive methods of mind control such as
compulsory lobotomies and electric shock treatments, as well as being
forced to ingest (or being forcibly injected with) psychotropic medication, and forced to undergo insidious behavior modification procedures.
But for the rest of us, mind control is more subtly invasive. Media adver-
tisements, political propaganda, corporate misinformation campaigns,
pop culture images, and a constant bombardment of slogans and jingles
from TV, radio, newspapers, magazines, the Internet, and other mass
media, all cloud our minds, screen our perceptions, and impair our judg-
ments.

The most basic existential question — *"Who am I?"* — arises from the
problem of mind control. Are my thoughts and behaviors my own, or are
they merely reflections of external forces. Do I have free will and control
over my own life, or is free will a myth? For most of the twentieth century, psychological responses to the problem of free will came from within
the parameters of the two dominant psychological paradigms.

Freudian Mind Control

The psychoanalytic paradigm, represented most prevalently by Sigmund Freud and the schools of psychoanalysis he inspired, offered a somewhat deterministic view on free will. Human behavior is a compromise between the basic animal drives, sex and aggression, and external social forces such as parental control and societal restraints. Since the animal drives are biological, and the social forces are external, people actually have very little free will. At the unconscious level, our emotions and motivations are controlled primarily by neurotic conflicts and primary associations instilled in us early on in childhood. There is little hope in actually controlling the unconscious forces that rule our lives. The best we can do is to try to understand them.

Skinnerian Mind Control

The alternate approach was supplied by the behaviorist paradigm, represented most prevalently by the American psychologist, B.F. Skinner, and the schools of behavioral psychology that he inspired. Behaviorists were even more deterministic. As Skinner once said: "My image in some places is of a monster of some kind who wants to pull a string and manipulate people. Nothing could be further from the truth. People are manipulated; I just want them to be manipulated more effectively."

The strict Skinnerian approach maintained that all human behaviors are shaped over time by external forces through the process of operant conditioning. As we develop, every behavior results in an external response, which is positive, negative or neutral. Hence, every behavior is either positively or negatively reinforced, resulting in either the repetition or eventual extinction of these behaviors. Human behavior, therefore, is merely the total sum of the responses we receive from external forces. There is absolutely no free will. Our identities are shaped, manipulated, and controlled in entirety by outside forces in our environment. Once again, there is little hope in taking complete control of our lives. The best we can do is to try to understand how we become the products of our own environment, and then try to manipulate our environments in order to attempt to shape our own behaviors.

Humanism and Free Will

The third force in psychology, Humanism, did not come along until the latter half of the twentieth century. Represented by psychologists such as Carl Rogers, Abraham Maslow, and Rollo May, the humanists insisted that people actually do have control over their own minds and lives. In fact, they believed that most neuroses and anxieties stemmed from a feeling of being out of control, a feeling of being a powerless and unwilling participant in one's own life. However, we may become empowered by becoming self-conscious—conscious not only of our own existence—but of our ability to control and master our own identities. Humanistic terms such as self-consciousness, self-actualization, and individuation, all refer to the same basic idea. By uncovering and implementing our own sense of free will, we can define our own identities, determine our own existences, and control our own minds.

Each of the three psychological paradigms offered its own contribution to the psycho thriller genre. The psychoanalytic technique of hypnotism presupposes the notion that there is a part of the mind, the unconscious, which we are not aware of. By inducing a hypnotic trance, hypnotists can reveal thoughts, memories, and emotions that are hidden deep within the unconscious. And, through the technique of hypnotic suggestion, the hypnotist can evoke behaviors in his subject that he would typically not do. Hence, a stage hypnotist can get his subjects to bark like dogs, act like chickens, hop like frogs, etc. The most basic question regarding hypnotism has always been: Can a hypnotic subject be compelled into performing deeds that are abhorrent to him? Can we be hypnotized into doing something against our own will? Most (but not all) psychologists and hypnotists believe that this cannot be done. Nevertheless, a plethora of psycho thrillers use as a basic premise the notion that hypnotism can be used as a form of mind control, and that hypnotic subjects will perform even the most ghastly of crimes, while under their hypnotist's spell.

The behaviorist technique of conditioning presupposes the notion that the bodies and minds of human beings can be controlled completely by manipulating their environments. If B.F. Skinner can use conditioning to get pigeons to play ping-pong, then psy-fi psychologists created in his image can surely get human subjects to do just about anything. In psycho thrillers, mind control via behavior modification and conditioning is typically aided with other external forces, such as psychotropic drugs, neurosurgery, neural implants, neurosensory remote control, or other hi-tech gadgets. Whether the means of mind control are achieved psychoanalytically, through hypnosis, behaviorally, through conditioning, or physiologically (through psychopharmacology or neurosurgery), the ends of mind control are usually foiled humanistically. In the third act of the mind control themed movie, the unwilling subjects will typically become aware of their own predicament, and by implementing their own free will, they will take control of their own minds and behaviors. Naturally, their first act of self-determination will always be the destruction of the evil agent of mind control. Thus, the implicit message of these psycho thrillers is that, while psychoanalytic and behaviorist psychologists claim that our minds are utterly controlled, we know deep down inside that all human beings do have free will, and that once free will is released, no external force is powerful enough to control the mind of an independent, freethinking human being.

Hypnocontrol

George Du Maurier's (1834–1896) last and most famous novel, *Trilby* (1894), was also his first best seller. In his book, Du Maurier created a character who would become an archetype of the psycho thriller genre. The malevolent "Svengali" used extraordinary hypnotic powers to control the life and mind of Trilby, a beautiful, helpless young maiden. By capitalizing on the popular nineteenth century prejudices against science, doctors, and anything vaguely psychological, Du Maurier evoked a seemingly natural fear of mind control, made to appear entirely plausible, via the advent of hypnosis. Hypnocontrol would become the dominant psy-fi theme in the century of films to follow.

Though the story of the innocent young Trilby and her evil puppet-master, Maestro Svengali, would be filmed many times in the silent era, the definitive version would not appear on screen until 1931 (the watershed year for psycho thriller archetypes) when John Barrymore took on the role of the sinister *Svengali*, in one of his most memorable performances. A dozen years earlier, the Svengali type was presented in a variation on the theme, in Robert Wiene's classic, *Das Kabinett des Doktor Caligari* aka *The Cabinet of Dr. Caligari* (1919). In the film, the wicked Dr. Caligari (Werner Krauss) uses hypnocontrol to command his somnambulist, Cesare (Conrad Veidt), to do his evil biddings, stating: "Now I shall learn if it's true that a somnambulist can be compelled to perform acts which, in a waking state, would be abhorrent to him.... Whether, in fact, he can be driven against his will to commit a murder."

The deviation from the *Svengali* script exists in the genesis of the hypnotist/somnambulist relationship. We learn from the doctor's diary that Cesare came to him as a patient while he was the director of a lunatic asylum. Cesare's somnambulism was a preexisting condition. The idea that a person could somehow naturally fall into a hypnotic trance is a remnant of a popular misconception of the nineteenth century, which perceived hypnosis as a psychic power, similar to telepathy.

In the 1800s, it was believed that some people had the innate psychic ability to put others into a state of hypnotic trance. It was also believed that some people had the unfortunate tendency to fall into hypnotic trances with little provocation. It can be understood why these misconceptions existed. Some people, such as stage hypnotists and professional hypnotists, do show exceptional talents and abilities in their trade. It has also been noted that a few exceptional individuals, such as the infamous Rasputin (1864–1916), were reputed to have mystical powers bordering on hypnocontrol. It is now accepted that anyone can learn the basic techniques of hypnotism — they require no spiritual, mystical, or psychic powers. Similarly, there are certain physiological and psychological conditions, such as narcolepsy, epilepsy, and catatonic schizophrenia, which may give the impression to an uneducated observer that the sufferer has slipped into a hypnotic trance. Nevertheless, while some people are more "suggestible" than others, making them easier to hypnotize, it is not possible for someone to merely slip into a hypnotic trance, unless they are under the influence of a hypnotist, psychotropic drugs, or a powerful method of self-hypnosis.

Despite these realities, in the fantasy world of movies, it is readily accepted that some people (especially psychiatrists, vampires, aliens, and powerful older men) have the ability to instantly hypnotize people with merely a prolonged gaze into their eyes and a commanding suggestion. It is also readily accepted that some people (especially pretty young women) can be instantly hypnotized, ostensibly because of their weak minds. The hypnotist/somnambulist relationships in *Caligari* and *Svengali* seem to evoke the misconception that the hypnotic trance is a product of a complementary association — the matching of a natural born puppet-master with a natural born puppet. This association is seen quite clearly in *Svengali,* as John Barrymore's makeup and costume in the film are quite deliberately lifted from Rasputin, the Siberian mystic who purportedly mesmerized the weak-minded tsarina, Alexandra Romanov, controlling her mind and, in turn, indirectly influencing the direction of the Russian empire.

Though Rasputin was a real historical figure, his legend is mainly derived from gossip, rumors, and conjecture. As such, Rasputin is as much a product of fiction as Svengali. By combining the story of Svengali with the image of Rasputin, Hollywood made a significant connection between the evil mesmerist's ability to control the mind of the individual, and his ability to control the will of an entire nation. In psycho thrillers, this sinister connection can come to fruition in three different ways:

1. The hypnotist, like Rasputin, can control the mind of the person controlling the nation.

2. The hypnotist, like Caligari, can use a hypnotized assassin to bring about his rise to power.

3. The hypnotist (or hypnotic regime) could use hypnocontrol techniques on a mass level to control the minds of every individual in the nation.

The Rasputin Type

A year after his highly praised performance in *Svengali,* John Barrymore appeared with his brother Lionel and sister Ethel in *Rasputin and the Empress* (1932), though in this film, brother Lionel played the part of the Siberian mystic. The character of Rasputin was reprised several more times for the screen, most notably, in *Rasputin: The Mad Monk* (1966), in which Christopher Lee played the title role. The Rasputin type of governmental mind controller can be seen in many other films, especially in the sci-fi and fantasy genres. In *The Lord of the Rings* trilogy (2001, 2002, 2003), Christopher Lee reprised his Rasputin type characterization as the evil wizard, Saruman, who retains hypnotic control over Theoden (Bernard Hill), the King of Rohan. Christopher Lee, of course, was well prepared to play a character who possesses mystical hypnotic powers. He played Count Dracula and various other vampires in his many horror movie roles, and vampires—for some reason — typically have hypnotic powers. Lee also played the sinister Jedi knight, Count Dooku (aka Darth Tyranus), in George Lucas' *Star Wars: Episode II—Attack of the Clones* (2002). Like vampires, mad scientists and aliens, Jedi knights also possess hypnotic powers, because, as Obi-Wan Kenobe (Alec Guiness) explained in the original *Star Wars* (1977), "The Force has power over the weak minded."

The Manchurian Candidate

The Caligari type of hypnotist, who gains power through the murderous misdeeds of his mind controlled assassin, was epitomized in John Frankenheimer's cold war classic, *The Manchurian Candidate* (1962). Though the Manchurian hypnotists in the film utilized a variety of mind control techniques, such as "brainwashing," mind altering drugs, and behavioral conditioning, their hypnotic control over their subjects was the

Laurence Harvey as Raymond Shaw (right) and Frank Sinatra as Ben Marco (left) in John Frankenheimer's *The Manchurian Candidate* (1962).

centerpiece of their plan. A key feature of the film's plot involved the use of a posthypnotic suggestion, "Why don't you play a nice game of solitaire?" Upon hearing this phrase, Raymond Shaw (Laurence Harvey) would play solitaire. When he turned over the Queen of Diamonds, a posthypnotic "trigger" was activated in his brain, causing him to fall immediately into a trance, in which he would follow any order given to him, including orders to kill.

In Richard Condon's original novel, there was an extremely disturbing oedipal relationship between Raymond and his mother. The Manchurian hypnotists actually chose Raymond, in part, because he was weak-minded and completely susceptible to mind control, the effect of being browbeaten and dominated by his castrating mother for his entire life. The taboo sexual nature of the mother/son relationship was downplayed in the film version of Condon's novel, but the antagonistic love-hate quality in the interactions between Richard and his mother (Angela Lansbury) remained on screen. *The Manchurian Candidate* would go on to become one of the most influential of all psy-fi films, though it still remains in a class of its own ... a dramatic political thriller, many times imitated but rarely equaled. Ironically, it may be that the only other psy-fi political thriller to match Frankenheimer's film in complexity and sophistication is Jonathan Demme's 2004 remake, starring Denzel Washington and Liev Schreiber.

The Mind-Controlled State

Though generally used to control the minds of individuals, hypnotic techniques could also be used to control the minds of millions. The regimes of Hitler and Stalin were both renowned for their use of propaganda and invasive media in order to control the hearts and minds of their people. Hitler in particular is often referred to as being a "mesmerizing" speaker, with the power to draw his audiences into a nearly hypnotic trance. In the movies, the theme of mass mind control is generally set in the not-too-distant future, an era in which mankind inevitably exists in a totalitarian state of enforced conformity and government sanctioned mind control. Prime examples of this theme can be seen in the film versions of George Orwell's *Nineteen Eighty-Four* (1984) and Aldous Huxley's *Brave New World* (1998), as well as George Lucas' *THX 1138* (1971) and *The Matrix* (1999).

Psychotropic Drugs

According to the movies, the most expedient and effective means of controlling the minds of millions involves the use of mind-numbing or emotion-controlling medication. There is a scene in *One Flew Over the Cuckoo's Nest* in which Nurse Ratched threatens McMurphy, indicating that if he's not willing to take his medication orally, she can arrange for it to be administered anally. The forced medication of mental patients in hospitals provides a point of reference for science fiction writers. If society today is allowed to force a marginalized segment of the population to take psychotropic medication in order to conform their behaviors to the contemporary societal norms, then society tomorrow may be allowed to force the entire population to take psychotropic medication in order to make everyone conform to whatever behaviors are considered optimal in a future age. Conspiracy theorists warn us that forced medication may occur covertly, as well. For example, there are those who believe that the federalized fluoridization of public drinking water is actually part of a government mind control conspiracy.

The real fear in the twenty-first century is not that the government will force everyone to take psychotropic medication, but that the more subtle and indirect influences of psychological organizations and pharmaceutical corporations will convince everyone that they should voluntarily medicate themselves. According to some, the pathologization of America is occurring right now. Television and radio commercials, running 24 hours a day, seven days a week, ask us to diagnose ourselves for psychological disorders. They ask us simple questions, like: "Feeling sad? Anxious? Tired? Restless? You may be suffering from depression or anxiety. To learn how Zoloft may help..." Zoloft, Prozac, Paxil, Wellbutrin ... you may need these drugs. Why? To make you feel better. To help you fit in. To make you feel like everybody else.

In today's society, psychotropic drugs offer the promise of better living through chemistry. They promise a pharmacologically induced utopia in which all complaints, whether physiological or psychological, can be solved by a pill. A world in which drugs represent both the cause and solution to everyone's problems. Of course, for most people, medication prescribed by competent psychiatrists offers relief from serious and genuine mental illnesses. But others, such as Dr. Peter Kramer — the psychiatrist who wrote the landmark bestseller, *Listening to Prozac* (2001) — warn us that powerful drugs such as Prozac can offer emotional balance, but at the cost of individuality. Sometimes there are reasons why we may feel depressed, anxious, tired, or restless. These may be symptoms, signs that there is something wrong in our lives that we should try to fix. By using drugs to eliminate the symptoms without curing the disease, we consign ourselves to a lifetime of dependency on external substances in order to treat internal problems. The greater fear, on a societal level, is that the terror of not fitting in, the desperate need to conform, will drive nearly everyone to the drugstore, to buy the pills that will make them look, feel, and think exactly how society at large determines they should look, feel, and think.

It is these fears that are played out to maximum effect in psycho thrillers such as *THX 1138* and *Equilibrium* (2002). George Lucas' first step toward deification in the world of film was the making of a short, *THX 1138: 4EB*, as a film student in the University of Southern California film school. The student film won him first prize in the 1967–68 National Student Film Festival, leading to a scholarship from Warner Brothers to observe the making of *Finian's Rainbow* (1968), with Francis Ford Coppola as director. Coppola became a mentor and patron of Lucas.' They eventually became friends and partners, forming American Zoetrope in 1969. Their film company's first project was a feature length production of *THX 1138*. The film was released in 1971 to dismal box office, but was recently digitally restored and rereleased on DVD. It presents a futuristic dystopian society, in which sex and all emotions are outlawed. Strict conformity is rigidly maintained via the forced ingestion of powerful psychotropic drugs. Lucas' bleak view of the future stands in stark contrast to most of his later work — mainstream and upbeat films such as *American Graffiti* (1973) and the *Star Wars* and *Indiana Jones* movies.

A similar premise is played out in *Equilibrium*, which seems to have been inspired in equal amounts by Orwell's *1984*, Aldous Huxley's *Brave New World*, François Truffaut's film of Ray Bradbury's novel, *Fahrenheit 451* (1966), and Lucas' *THX 1138*. In the film, the futuristic society is called "Libria," and its citizens are "Librians." Everyone in Libria leads a dismal life of state enforced conformity, as all emotions have been banished, a task made possible by required daily ingestions of "Prozium," a drug that inhibits all emotions. Along with feelings, any product eliciting emotion, such as books, pets, art, music, sex, fancy wallpaper ... is strictly forbidden. Feeling anything is a capital offense. Though the premise and plot are already hackneyed, some of the language is original and interesting. The terms "Librians" and "Libria" are oblique references to Librium and Lithium, "mood stabilizers" prescribed to people diagnosed with bipolar disorder (formerly referred to as manic-depression) in order to rein in emotional highs and lows. The drugs that Librians are required to take, "Prozium," is apparently an amalgamation of Prozac and Librium/ Lithium. *Equilibrium* presents a psy-fi dystopia of a "Prozac Nation" to the nastiest degree, a world in which social peace and tranquility are finally achieved, but at the price of emotional freedom and individuality.

Films such as *THX 1138* and *Equilibrium* borrow much from Aldous Huxley, who may have been the first author to predict the use of psychopharmacology as an agent of conformity at the population-wide level. In his 1932 novel, *Brave New World*, every citizen is required to take daily doses of "soma," a psychotropic drug that keeps everyone both physiologically and psychologically content. The idea is simple. Content minds and bodies do not resist the government. They do not protest, rebel or revolt against the powers that be. Content minds and bodies conform to the system. Huxley's ideas would go on to become the basis of the popular conspiracy theory that the CIA introduced LSD into mainstream society in the 1960s in order to depoliticize the youth movement, and that the government tacitly allows low income neighborhoods to be plagued with drugs, in order to pacify the most oppressed segments of the masses. Conformity, in Huxley's world, is also achieved through behavioral conditioning, by means of repetitive messages delivered during sleep, propaganda, invasive media, and other methods. However, we must admit that the most powerful means of conformity are the psychological tendencies of human beings themselves. Countless social psychology experiments have repeatedly shown, to a frightening degree, that ordinary people display the tendencies to conform to the social roles assigned to them, and to mindlessly obey authority figures without question.

Unwitting Subjects of Mind Control

In Dr. Philip Zimbardo's infamous Stanford prison experiment, carried out in 1971, college students took on the roles of prison inmates and prison guards in a mock prison created in the basement of Stanford University's psychology department. Within a few days of the experiment, the mock guards began to physically and psychologically abuse their mock inmates, even though they all knew it was just an experiment. The study had to be prematurely aborted due to the suffering of the subjects. Why did the guard students become brutal, nasty sadists? Why did the inmate students become compliant, sheepish conformists? According to Zimbardo, they were all just conforming to their assigned social roles.

A similar social psychology experiment, Dr. Stanley Milgram's equally infamous Obedience to Authority study, carried out in 1974, displayed that most ordinary people were willing to administer electric shocks of up to 450 volts to protesting victims, who shrieked out in pain and even collapsed in their chairs from apparent heart attacks, simply because an authority figure dressed in a white lab coat commanded them to continue their role in the experiment. The victims, of course, were Milgram's confederates — actors — who did not receive any real shocks, but the subjects administering the shocks did not know the truth until after the study. Why were ordinary people so willing to torture other apparently innocent people? According to Milgram, "It may be that we are puppets — puppets controlled by the strings of society" (1974). So, while mind controllers in psycho thrillers often employ powerful drugs and sophisticated methods of behavior modification to achieve their ends of social conformity, these tools are only minor aids to the true agents of mass mind control, the all-too-human traits of conformity to social roles, and obedience to authority.

Behavior Modification

The psy-fi depiction of the behaviorist model of mind control was epitomized in Stanley Kubrick's film of Anthony Burgess' novel, *A Clockwork Orange*. Once again, we are in a futuristic society, though invasive methods of mind control as a means of enforcing conformity among the masses are only first being introduced. Burgess predicted, reasonably, that before mind control techniques are employed on the population at large, they will be tested on marginalized sectors of society — mental hospital patients and prison inmates — people that society would consider to be in dire need of socialization, thus legitimizing the use of invasive procedures. In the beginning of the story, Alex (Malcolm McDowell) is a juvenile delinquent, who displays his need for behavior modification in his vicious acts of theft, assault and rape, referred to by Alex as "ultraviolence" and "the old in-out, in-out."

Alex is imprisoned and chosen as the guinea pig for an experimental mind control procedure, "the Ludovico treatment," which is pure Skinnerian behavior modification. The procedure itself is referred to with the euphemism, "aversion therapy," a common term for a process of behavior modification using "aversive" consequences (i.e., physical punishment) as a means of negative reinforcement, designed to eliminate undesirable behaviors. Though Alex is injected thrice daily with a psychotropic drug, the key to the treatment is the creation of negative associations between visions of violence on a movie screen and aversive responses in Alex's body and brain. The scenes in which Alex is forced to watch films of brutal beatings, Nazi death camps, and of a girl being gang-raped, with his head in a vice, his scalp draped with neural electrodes, his eyelids propped open by metal prongs, and his eyeballs moistened by a continuous flow of saline solution, are the most dramatic depictions ever filmed of a behavior modification procedure gone awry.

Burgess' original manuscript for his 1962 book had twenty-one chapters. In the twentieth chapter, Alex's artificial change of character is reversed by a neurosurgical procedure, prompting his sardonic remark, "I was cured all right!" In the twenty-first chapter, Alex is released from the hospital. He returns briefly to his life of crime, but soon abandons violence and larceny on his own accord, employing free will to control his own mind and behaviors. Burgess' publisher at Norton insisted that the twenty-first chapter be dropped, ending the novel with the bleak and pessimistic notion that Alex, after all of his mind control misadventures, will simply return to his life of ultraviolence. Kubrick's film also ends Alex's story at the twentieth chapter, with Alex saying — "I was cured all right!" — as visions of sex and violence flash through his head, to the soundtrack of Beethoven's "Ode to Joy."

Neural Implants

A rather new method of mind control has been made feasible via the advents of neurosurgery, microchips, and nanotechnology. It is now possible (at least according to psy-fi writers) to implant a tiny neural implant in someone's brain, affording reliable and remotely accessible behavior management to mind controllers of all ages. Glenn Close, who played the Svengali character in Jonathan Demme's remake of *The Manchurian Candidate*, used similar methods of mind control in her role as the "Martha Stewart style" Svengali in Frank Oz's 2004 remake of *The Stepford Wives*. The similarities between these two movies are manifold: they are both remakes of classic psycho thrillers, released in 2004, featuring Glenn Close as the mind controller, who uses hi-tech neural implants to control her victims. It seems clear that as we proceed into the twenty-first century, neural implants will become the mind control method of choice.

Though it is a rather unimpressive movie, *Disturbing Behavior* (1998) is worth mentioning here, because it displays the ease in which postmodern filmmakers can infuse mind control themes into their movies. After a century of psy-fi films, filmmakers can employ the archetypes without even the slightest need to establish character or storyline. We immediately understand that the school psychiatrist is an evil mad scientist, seeking absolute control over the teen students in his school. We are completely unsurprised when he declares, shortly before his demise, "Science is God!" Similarly, we really don't need to know how his mind control procedure actually works. We've been briefed on the idea before, in dozens of other psycho thrillers. The neural implant is inserted. Brainwashing à la *Clockwork Orange* type apparatus proceeds. Parents, of course, are in league with the psychiatrist's mad science, both working together towards the common goal of instilling unquestioning conformity into their unwitting teens. When the heroic boy-girl duo of teen rebels (James Marsden and Katie Holmes) uncover the fact that their school psychiatrist was once a researcher in the field of psychopharmacology, the girl's interpretation is immediate and conclusive ... "Mind control!" How does a 16-year-old high school junior know that all psychopharmacologists are obsessed with mind control? Obviously, she's been to the movies.

CIA Mind Control

Thanks to secret government funded research in barbaric experimental methods of mind control, psy-fi filmmakers will never go hungry for paranoid conspiracy plots. According to John Marks, author of *The Search for the Manchurian Candidate: The CIA and Mind Control* (1979), and Colin Ross, author of *Bluebird: Deliberate Creation of Multiple Personality by Psychiatrists* (2000)—who both based their research on many thousands of pages of formerly top secret CIA documents, recently declassified under the Freedom of Information Act—the CIA was actively engaged in mind control research throughout the 1950s, '60s and '70s. CIA funded research experiments ran the gamut from hypnosis aided by powerful psychotropic drugs—"narco-hypnosis"—to invasive brainwashing methods employing electroconvulsive therapy—"electro shock"—and other more insidious techniques. All of this unethical experimentation was justified by government officials, military officers, and psychiatrists under the cold war mentality that the ends of national security justified the means of barbaric psychological torture on innocent, and oftentimes unwilling human subjects.

Mind control experiments began during World War II, when the army and the OSS (the Office of Strategic Services, later to be restructured as the CIA) practiced narco-hypnotic interrogation techniques on captured enemy soldiers and spies, in order to elicit vital wartime reconnaissance. The technique found some success, leading narco-hypnotic interrogators to wonder if the same method could be used to hypnotically program an enemy soldier to assassinate a Nazi official, i.e., Hitler. Wartime research went into the possibility, though there was no proof of any operational World War II era "Manchurian Candidates." But when the war against the Nazis ended, the cold war against the soviets began, and mind control research carried on, full speed ahead, now aided by ex–Nazi psychiatric researchers, co-opted by the U.S. government for use in the cold war, under CIA secret project PAPERCLIP—the attaching of former Nazi researchers onto covert U.S. projects.

The search for the Manchurian Candidate picked up steam when the CIA began experimenting with a powerful new psychotropic drug called D-lysergic acid diethylamide (LSD). The agency stressed the outright goal of "controlling an individual to the point where he will do our bidding against his will and even against such fundamental laws of nature as self preservation" (Marks, p. 25). In other words, government sanctioned mad science. CIA top secret project BLUEBIRD focused on the use of drugs such as LSD to induce a hypnotic trance of extreme suggestibility, during which programming could occur. The range of possibilities for narco-hypnotic programming was unlimited. Aside from creating "Manchurian Candidate" assassins out of enemy agents, we could also program our own agents hypnotically, so that if they were captured, they would not even consciously know what secret plans they were intended to deliver. We could create the ultimate superspy. When project BLUEBIRD was transformed into project ARTICHOCKE in the mid–1950s, the researchers were given the green light to pursue "terminal" experiments in their search for reliable mind control weapons. The word "terminal" meant that the life of the subject may be terminated.

The only well-documented case of mind control research resulting in death is the sad case of Dr. Frank Olson. The only reason that the details of this case are known rather than being destroyed along with most of the other research files, is that Dr. Olson was not really a subject, he was a researcher. Apart from blatantly destructive human experimentation with LSD (such as a CIA sanctioned study conducted by Dr. Harris Isbell, Director of the Addiction Research Center in Lexington, Kentucky, in which seven inmates were kept on increasingly high dosages of LSD for 77 straight days) the head of the agency's mind control research department, Dr. Sidney Gottleib, found it necessary to study the affects of LSD dosing on unwitting subjects, which he frequently practiced on underling researchers at the agency. In November 1953, Dr. Gottleib spiked the drinks of a group of army chemical researchers with LSD. Dr. Frank Olson had a very "bad trip," exacerbated by the fact that he had no idea that he was under the influence of the most powerful hallucinogenic drug known to man. He thought he was going insane. Several days later, extremely depressed and utterly confused, as he was never told about the secret drug, the mild mannered researcher leapt to his death out of a tenth-floor window in New York's Statler hotel.

Olson's wife, Alice, was not told about the LSD, yet she firmly denied for 22 years following the incident that her husband committed unprecipitated suicide. When the story was leaked by a former agent in 1976 and appeared in *The Washington Post*, Alice Olson sued the government.

President Gerald Ford offered her a personal apology, and Congress passed a bill to pay her $750,000 in compensation. This was the only case of the government apologizing and compensating for its decades of unethical research in mind control, and the only reason this case was revealed was because it was a mistake, leaving a paper trail outside of the CIA's control, and not really part of any specific research project. In 1973, Gottleib and CIA director Dick Helms had all of the records of the CIA's drug testing research destroyed. Over two decades of evidence of government sanctioned research conducted at well-known university hospitals such as Johns Hopkins and Cornell, as well as federal prisons and state mental asylums, is gone forever. The hundreds or even thousands of research subject casualties whose lives were destroyed by the CIA and their psychiatric researchers will never be known or recognized.

Depatterning

Though the tragic case of Dr. Olson is the most famous example of CIA mind control research, the more shadowy example — the sinister case of Dr. Ewen Cameron — remains the most infamous. Olson's death did nothing to impede Gottleib's work, who continued his directorship of CIA mind control research as it persisted into the 1960s and '70s, as the project was renamed MKULTRA and later renamed project MKSEARCH. Dr. Ewen Cameron, founder of the psychiatry department at McGill University and former president of both the American Psychiatric Association and World Psychiatric Organization, realized that the creation of an operational "Manchurian Candidate" would require more than narco-hypnosis. The subject's personality and identity would have to be completely wiped away — "brainwashed" — and then a new identity replaced in its stead. He experimented exclusively in Canada and solely on mental hospital patients, who were unaware that they were being used as guinea pigs in CIA funded experiments. Cameron referred to the first part of the process as "depatterning," which involved horrendous sessions of electroshock, up to 40 times more intense than normal shock therapy, administered up to three times a day for intervals of several days at a time, followed by massive doses of strong narcotics. The torturous process, which would often last for months, left the subject in a "vegetable-like" state, with virtually no memories left. He called the second part of the process "psychic driving," in which a new identity was programmed into the subject. Psychic driving involved placing the subject in an isolated room, in a state of total sensory depravation, and playing tape loops of specific messages that would play incessantly for over 16 hours a day, often combined with electric shocks and/or LSD, for several weeks or even months at a time. Psychic driving offered "direct, controlled changes in personality," according to Cameron. Because he and researchers like him were sanctioned and funded by the government, their horrific experiments were allowed to be carried out with complete immunity to the law.

Iatrogenic Multiple Personality Disorder

Other research projects in mind control, which may or may not be ongoing, focus on the use of radio- or microwaves transmitted directly into the brain, neurological implants, and "iatrogenic multiple personality disorder"—the deliberate creation of multiple personalities. The latter phenomenon is well documented, not as CIA research, but in the true life story of publishing heiress Patty Hearst, who was kidnapped by the Symbionese Liberation Army, brainwashed — via a brutal process of rape, sensory deprivation, and psychological torture — and programmed to become an operational terrorist and bank robber. There is some evidence that one of her kidnappers, Donald DeFreeze, was himself a subject of CIA mind control experimentation, as a prisoner at Vacaville State Prison. Not believing that she was a victim of mind control, a federal court sent Hearst to prison for her participation in SLA robberies. She served two years before her sentence was commuted by President Jimmy Carter in 1979. Besides the very well-documented Hearst case, there have been numerous anecdotal tales of iatrogenic multiple personalities, in addition to the widespread conspiracy theories that Kennedy assassins Lee Harvey Oswald and Sirhan Sirhan, as well as John Lennon assassin Mark David Chapman, were all "Manchurian Candidates." The truth of any of these theories of CIA mind control is not known, and may never be known.

Psy-Fi CIA

Since the declassification of some CIA files in the late 1970s, indicating their involvement in covert mind control research, the involvement of secretive government agencies such as the CIA, FBI, and NSA in mind control movies has become a recurrent theme. In *Jacob's Ladder* (1990), the title character (Tim Robbins) is a member of a Vietnam War platoon that is used as a terminal experiment in the research of a psychotropic drug referred to as "the ladder," which is supposed to release the primal aggression in its subjects. "The ladder" is intended to turn the unmotivated Vietnam era soldiers into the ultimate killing machines. The film's premise alludes to actual LSD research performed on unwitting soldiers in the Vietnam era, conducted by both CIA and army intelligence researchers. In the film, the dosed soldiers go mad, butchering each other in a frenzied massacre of drug-fueled slaughter.

In *Conspiracy Theory* (1997), Mel Gibson plays a character obsessed with conspiracy theories about the CIA and other shadow organizations. His paranoia is linked to the fact that he himself is a former CIA "Manchurian Candidate," whose memories have been erased in a manner suggestive of Dr. Cameron's real technique of depatterning. The evil psychiatrist (Patrick Stewart) in *Conspiracy Theory* is eerily reminiscent of the real Ewen Cameron, even down to the faint Scottish accent, which the Scottish born Cameron bore all his life. *In the Dark* (2003) is a made for Canadian TV movie about the lingering aftereffects of mind control research, much of which was conducted by Dr. Cameron in Canada. Michael Murphy plays a man who was psychologically tortured 30 years ago while a patient in a Canadian mental hospital. The film makes direct references to "depatterning" and a doctor much resembling Ewen Cameron. Murphy, like many of Cameron's real life subject-victims, never recovered from his horrific experiences, and was never able to adjust to normal life. Like real life casualties of CIA mind control experiments, the experience not only ruined the subject's life, but the lives of his family as well. Unlike the real casualties, the Canadian film deals with a cabal of CIA men trying to cover up the potentially scandalous information. The real casualties have no firm memories of the period of time in which they were "treated."

The recent remake of *The Manchurian Candidate* (2004) casts "Manchurian Global," a vast corporation that is part of the infamous "military industrial complex," as the shadow organization behind the secret mind control conspiracy. In modern parlance, there is essentially no difference between the CIA and the multibillion dollar global corporations, such as Lockheed Martin, Boeing, and Halliburton, that function as part of the military industrial complex. Both organizations are so big that they are above the law. They both thrive on war and the threat of war, as hundreds of billions of dollars of their revenue comes from the government defense budget. Both organizations have deep ties within the highest orders of the government as well as the highest seats of global corporate power. And both organizations have access to the psychiatric and technological brilliance of mad scientists.

Alien Mind Control

When alien invaders come to Earth, they are usually empowered by pervasive, typically telepathic forces of mind control. The groundbreaking *Invasion of the Body Snatchers* (1956) was the first film to depict aliens coming to Earth and controlling us from within, by replacing humans with alien duplicates. In *Village of the Damned* (1960), children born of human women are actually the spawn of aliens who share one common group mind. They can read each other's minds, they can read human minds, and they have incredible powers of mind control over everyone. The same evil alien spawn appear in the sequel, *Children of the Damned* (1963). Five years later, alien telepathy took over the minds and bodies of the resurrected zombies in George Romero's *Night of the Living Dead* (1968). And less than a decade after that, Steven Spielberg's *Close Encounters of the Third Kind* (1977) depicts friendly aliens who nevertheless ruin the lives of a select group of innocent earthlings, by filling their minds with obsessions about a specific geographic location, which they are all compelled to go to in order to make their close encounter with the alien kind.

A psychosexual twist on alien mind control can be seen in *Lifeforce* (1985), in which an alien vampiress is depicted as a beautiful naked girl. When men encounter this alien, they are the victims of beautiful-naked-girl control. They are rendered helpless by their lust as the sexy girl approaches them and gives them the kiss of death, which sucks the "lifeforce" out of their bodies. One wonders if her telepathic mind control abilities would have been nearly as powerful if she were old, ugly, or fully dressed. A similar theme is played out in *Species* (1995) and *Species II* (1998), in which a parasitic alien monster takes the form of a sexy blonde (Natasha Henstridge), who uses both her telepathic mind control and her sexual allure to find suitable mates that will impregnate her, so she can breed a race of monstrous alien half-breeds.

Unusual Mind Control

There a few psy-fi depictions of mind control that defy categorization. In David Cronenberg's *Shivers* (1975), a slimy parasite gains complete control over its human hosts, turning them into psychosexual zombies with hyperactive libidos, who must have sex immediately with anyone in their midst. The effect is somewhat of a cross between *Night of the Living Dead* and *Species*. In *The Matrix* (1999), the future is a postapocalyptic world in which artificial intelligence rules. The minds of humans are completely controlled, existing in a computer generated dream world called "the matrix," as human bodies are used as batteries to power the machines. And in *X2* (2003), the evil Stryker (Brian Cox)—a military scientist who wants to exterminate all mutants—uses brain fluid from his own super-mutant son to control the minds of other mutants. The mind control agent is introduced directly into the brainstem through a hole in the back of the neck, which looks like a bad cigarette burn. This film raises the all-important question ... could the CIA be working on developing super-mutant brain fluid for the purposes of mind control?

Hypnotic Situational Comedies

It requires mentioning that hypnotism is an extremely common plot device in situational comedies, on both the big and small screens. The following are just a few examples of the widely used motif. In *I Was a Teenage Werewolf* (1957), an insecure teen (Michael Landon) goes to a psychiatrist to overcome his shyness. The psychiatrist (Whit Bissel) uses hypnotism to regress the teen into a primal evolutionary state, a teen werewolf who promptly runs amok in a murderous rampage at his school. In *Office Space* (1999), Peter (Ron Livingston) visits a hypnotherapist to help his relationship with his girlfriend. After falling into a trance—a state of deep relaxation—the morbidly obese hypnotherapist (Michael McShane) has a heart attack and dies, before he can bring Peter back to consciousness. Peter now embarks on a life in which he has no anxieties. He doesn't care about losing his dead-end job or his harping girlfriend, he only does what he wants to do, living in the moment and enjoying each day as it comes. Hilarious complications obviously ensue. In *Shallow Hal* (2001), Hal (Jack Black) only wants to date women who are physically perfect. Self-help guru Tony Robbins hypnotizes Hal, forcing him to see only the inner beauty in the women that he meets, leading him into a relationship with an extremely fat girl (Gwyneth Paltrow). Hilarity ensues, you get the point.

With his proclivity towards infusing psychoanalytic themes into his films, it is no surprise that Woody Allen has used hypnotism to comedic effect in several of his movies. Scenes of hypnotism take place in the following Woody Allen films: *Take the Money and Run* (1969), *Zelig* (1983), *Broadway Danny Rose* (1984), *Alice* (1990), and *The Curse of the Jade Scorpion* (2001). Clearly, hypnotism in-and-of-itself has become a camp and hackneyed act. It has lost all of its ability to terrify audiences, and is now used essentially to amuse. As with any technology or new science, at first we are scared of it, then we get used to it, then it becomes banal. Neural implants seem scary to us now, but in fifty years, they may seem as harmless and amusing a threat as the use of hypnosis on unwitting subjects. While the exact themes, procedures, and technologies to come remain a mystery, one thing remains certain ... for every threat to free will that may arise in the future, there will be a psycho thriller made to capitalize on those fears.

CHAPTER SIX

The Dream World

BEN MARCO: My dreams seem more real to me than what I actually remember happened over there (*Kuwait*). It's like somewhere along the line, I got brainwashed or something, and I'm just like, all scrambled up.
RICHARD DELP: We have all been brainwashed, Marco... .
BEN MARCO: What about my dreams?
RICHARD DELP: What if all this is your dream, and you are still back in Kuwait?

Marco (Denzel Washington) and Delp (Bruno Ganz)
in Jonathan Demme's The Manchurian Candidate *(2004)*

Film is a dream. Film is a fantasy ... a product of human imagination projected in the form of illusory images onto a screen. If films are dreams, then dreams within a film are dreams within a dream. It's like walking into a dark room, seeing a light in a window, and looking out the window, only to find another dark room, with another lighted window. Dreams and films both offer a glimpse into a different world. They allow us to peek into the mysterious realm of what Carl Jung called the "collective unconscious," the realm of myth, archetypes, legend, and imagination. The place where all stories are born.

Dreams in film represent an added level of complexity. Films, which are filled with symbolism, psychological associations, and iconic imagery, must be analyzed in order to be fully understood. Dreams in films contain the same symbolism and imagery, and must be analyzed in the same way, but not in reference to the "real world." Dreams in films must be analyzed in reference to the film world from which they are born. As such, film dreams can represent a myriad of meanings. They could represent hidden secrets in a world of shadows. They could represent childhood desires in a world of adult repression. They could even represent the truth in a world of fantasy. But whatever dreams mean in film, it is rarely simple. Film dreams are often as sophisticated, complex, and esoteric as the dreams we have in our own lives.

Dreams as Truth

Typically, dreams are employed in film as windows into the true nature of things. For example, in both versions of *The Manchurian Candidate* (1962, 2004), Franco's only insight into his insidious brainwashing backstory is through terrifying dreams, which appear like flashbacks of repressed events, though the scenes are suitably surreal, to signify to the viewer that they are dream representations of reality. The use of surreal atmospheres and expressionistic sets are the modus operandi for filmmakers when depicting the dream world. Visual elements often used within dream sequences include: fog, smoke, soft focus, eerie music, odd camera angles, distorted sound, slow motion, dim lighting, and irregular costuming. One of the most famous movie dream sequences appeared in Hitchcock's *Spellbound* (1945), in which the sets for the famous dream sequences were designed by the most renowned of the surrealist painters, Salvador Dalí. The sets in *The Cabinet of Dr. Caligari* (1919) were all expressionistic works of art, designed to evoke a dreamlike quality, as nearly the entire film is actually the disturbed dream of a raving madman.

Since dreams often represent the only truth in a conspiratorial world of lies and deceit, analyzing the dream to reveal its true meaning becomes the central task of the film. The protagonist is sometimes helped by an expert in dream analysis, a psychiatrist, as in *Spellbound*. Other times, the hero must do it mainly on his own, such as in *The Manchurian Candidate*. Often times, the dream does not reveal a secret conspiracy, but rather, a repressed memory vital to the character's development, as in *Blind Alley* (1939), and the remake of the film, *The Dark Past* (1948). In both films, dream analysis is used to reveal the repressed memories of parental abuse that drive a madman to murder. One of the most interesting twists on this theme can be seen in Alex Proyas' *I, Robot* (2004). In the film, a psychologist (Bridget Moynahan) that specializes in the "personality simulation" of robots, who is referred to derisively by the hero (Will Smith) as a "robot shrink," must analyze the dream of a super-advanced robot in order to reveal a secret artificial intelligence plot to take over the world.

The Dream World: Ray Bolger as The Scarecrow and Judy Garland as Dorothy
Gale in *The Wizard of Oz* (1939).

Dreams as Personal Fantasy

Another common theme is the use of dreams to express a character's
deepest wishes and fantasies. Most of *The Wizard of Oz* (1939) takes place in
a dream world, which is an expression of Dorothy's (Judy Garland) wish to
go "over the rainbow," to a place more beautiful and exciting than her drab
existence in Kansas. On a deeper level, the dream world of Oz can also be
interpreted as a fantasy in which a little orphan girl fulfills her deepest
wishes— her desire to be reunited with her mother, symbolized by the figure
of Glinda the Good Witch (Billie Burke), and her father, symbolized by the
figure of the Wizard of Oz (Frank Morgan). In *Abre los Ojos* (1997), and its
Hollywood remake, *Vanilla Sky* (2001), we see a more complex take on this
theme. The stories take place entirely in the dream world of the protagonists
(Eduardo Noriega, Tom Cruise). Some of the dreams are true memories.
Some dreams are fantasies in which the protagonist wins the heart of his true
love (Penélope Cruz in both films). And some dreams are horrifying nightmares, in which his world of fantasy comes crashing down upon itself.

Daydreams

Typically, sleeping dreams in film are filmed surrealistically, while daydream reveries are brief and filmed realistically. Oftentimes, the short daydream scenes trick the audience. We think something is really happening, but then realize that it was just a daydream. A standard example is a scene in which the hero is treated poorly by an obnoxious person, his boss, for example. The hero then hits his boss or somehow harms him, only to cut to a shot of the hero doing nothing. Hitting the boss was just a daydream, but it gave the audience a brief thrill, because they thought it really happened, and it also offered insight into the hero's state of mind. Sometimes, the daydream represents a fantasy of what may happen, such as in Martin Scorcese's *The King of Comedy* (1983), in which Rupert Pupkin (Robert De Niro) engages in frequent reveries of his imminent fame and celebrity. Other times, the daydream represents a fear of what may happen, such as in *Parenthood* (1989), when a neurotic father (Steve Martin) daydreams that his troubled son, in the future, will go on a mad shooting spree atop a university clock-tower. While depictions of sleeping dreams create a world of surrealism in a film, frequent daydreams offer a sense of personal surrealism for a specific character, offering the audience a unique insight into a character's psyche and fantasies.

Anxiety Dreams

In *I, Robot*, a genius inventor, Dr. Lanning (James Cromwell), creates a super-advanced robot. Not only does he instill in his robot the ability to dream, he also records in its memory banks an actual dream of crucial importance. According to the creator's theory, the experience of the recurrent dream will raise anxiety in his creation, causing it to focus on the meaning of the dream so it may eventually reveal its secret and discover a hidden and significant truth about itself. According to traditional psychoanalytic dream analysis, our own recurrent dreams perform the exact same function. Regardless of who or what created our minds, we all dream. Anxiety dreams, especially recurrent anxiety dreams, are messages sent from our unconscious minds to our conscious selves. They express fears and worries about our own situations and potentially dreadful things to come. By focusing on these dreams, analyzing them, and understanding them, we come to learn crucial knowledge about ourselves.

Examples of famous anxiety dream sequences include the dream from *Stranger on the Third Floor* (1940), in which the protagonist (John McGuire) sees himself railroaded into jail after a kangaroo court case, and then executed for a crime he did not commit. Another example can be seen in Tim Burton's *Pee Wee's Big Adventure* (1985), in which Pee Wee (Paul Reubens) has horrific recurring dreams of his beloved bicycle being destroyed by terrible monsters. And in Hitchcock's *Vertigo* (1958), the acrophobic Scottie (James Stewart) is haunted by terrifying dreams of falling to his death.

Dreams as Alternate Realities

The Wachowski brothers' *The Matrix* (1999) presented a computer generated digital dream world, in which humans in a postapocalyptic Earth exist as unconscious slaves to their artificial intelligence masters. Completely unaware of their captive state, humans live in a dream world created by computers, while their bodies—asleep in pods—are used as batteries to run the machines. The innovative and incredibly successful blockbuster provided a very interesting and modern twist on the theme of mind control, including the possibility of a collective dream world in which different psyches can simultaneously exist and interact.

In a very different film, *What Dreams May Come* (1998), an imaginative and fantastic dream world is presented as an endless landscape of three-dimensional oil paintings. The film deals directly with Hamlet's dilemma in Shakespeare's play, when he muses to himself while contemplating suicide:

> To die, to sleep—
> To sleep—perchance to dream: ay there's the rub,
> For in that sleep of death what dreams may come
> When we have shuffled off this mortal coil,
> Must give us pause.

Though the characters in the film are actually in the afterworld rather than a dream world, the implication is that our perception of the afterlife is created by our own imaginations. We paint the sets of our own heaven and hell, just like we paint the sets of our own dreams.

Dream Projection

One of the most fascinating elements of *The Matrix* is the concept of dream projection—the notion that people can enter into other people's dreams and even interact with the dreamers. This concept presupposes the belief that dreams constitute a parallel dimension, an idea owing much in theory to Jung's notion of the collective unconscious. In Jung's theory, symbolic unconscious images created by people who are separated by time and space are shared through the archetypes expressed within the intermediary processes of myth, art, film, and storytelling. In the psy-fi concept of the dream world, the intermediary process is removed, and people can actually enter into a communal dream, a collective dimension of shared associations and symbolic images. *The Matrix* depicts a dream world in which all human beings can interact, sharing unreal time and space.

Dreams as Alternate Existences

A corollary to the notion of a shared dream world is the notion of multiple existences via the dream dimension. The idea is, in our dreams, we can experience entirely different lives from our original, primary existence. This concept has been addressed by films in two ways. In *Jacob's Ladder* (1990), Jacob (Tim Robbins) is a soldier in Vietnam, a victim of army mind control experiments. The experiment went horribly wrong, and as he lay on an army hospital bed, teetering on the brink of death, he dreams of his possible futures. One future includes a blonde wife and children in a world of suburban bliss, another future includes a sexy Latina girlfriend in a Manhattan apartment. As he drifts in and out of each possible future existence, he (and the audience) gets more and more confused, as he begins to doubt his own sanity, and suspects that nothing he encounters truly exists. His confusion is certainly not helped by the intermittent invasions of malevolent demons, who symbolize the demonic memories of his traumatic war experience, and his own feelings of anger and rage at the army's betrayal. Jacob's experience of being lost in his own dreams recaptures the audience's experiences in the dream world — the horrible, helpless, vulnerable feeling of being in a place in which we have no control, a place where logic and reason do not exist, a place that can turn into a terrifying nightmare at any moment.

Vanilla Sky creates a similar feeling through a very different premise. David Aames (Tom Cruise) died three hundred years ago. His body was cryogenically frozen at death, and the memory of his suicide was erased by the "Life Extension" corporation. He now exists in a state of "lucid dreaming." As his body rests, his mind dreams. In his dreams, he lives out the fantasy of his ideal future existence. The horrible disfigurement which drove him to suicide is miraculously cured by doctors, he wins the heart of the girl of his dreams (Penélope Cruz), and all is right with the world. However, like Jacob, he cannot escape the demons of his past. Feelings of anger, rage, betrayal, and guilt invade his dream, symbolized in the form of the woman (Cameron Diaz) who injured him. She turns the dream into a nightmare, as David can no longer distinguish between fantasy and reality. If he were not really in a dream, he would clearly be psychotic. These scary scenes make you wonder what the world of the psychotic individual may be like, and if everyone actually has firsthand knowledge of what it may be like to experience all-out psychosis, from the nightly experiences in our dreams.

Vanilla Sky is a remake of the Spanish film, *Abre los Ojos* (1997), aka *Open Your Eyes.* For both Jacob in *Jacob's Ladder* and David in *Vanilla Sky*, the only way for them to escape their terrifying, psychotic nightmares is to open their eyes. When having a nightmare, our only escape from this state of self-induced psychological torment is to wake up ... to open our eyes. Though it seems easy, when in the throes of a nightmare, we are utterly helpless, unaware that we are locked away in the dungeon of our own unconscious mind, and therefore unable to pick the lock and emerge into the safety of consciousness. At the end of their stories, Jacob and David both open their eyes. They achieve this by overcoming their fears and accepting death in their dream worlds, so they can venture into the uncertainty of a new existence. Perhaps we face a similar fear in our nightmares, the fear of accepting the end of one state of existence, only to emerge into the uncertainty of another.

Dreams as a Defining Quality of Humanity

It is not true that only humans dream. Anyone who's ever had a pet cat or dog knows that these animals dream, and even occasionally have nightmares. No one knows what cats and dogs actually dream about. Maybe one day, a pet psychiatrist will figure it out. Philip K. Dick, one of the greatest sci-fi authors of his generation, raised the same question about artificial intelligence, when he penned his most famous novel, *Do Androids Dream of Electric Sheep?* (1968) — upon which the film, *Bladerunner* (1982) was based. The novel and film deal with one of the most fundamental questions surrounding the problem of artificial intelligence: At what point is artificial intelligence tantamount to conscious existence? Although there can never be a decisive answer to this question, psy-fi movies tend to point to two particular psychological abilities as the definitive qualities of humanity: the ability to feel true emotion (i.e., love) and the ability to dream.

Writers Stanley Kubrick and sci-fi legend Arthur C. Clarke first tackled the AI question on film in Kubrick's 1968 opus, *2001: A Space Odyssey.* In the film, the supercomputer HAL-9000 experiences a leap in evolution, similar to the leap humans made millions of years ago when the first hominid picked up a bone and used it as a tool. HAL-9000 experiences an epiphany of consciousness, followed by the experience of emotions such as fear, anger, and guilt. Upon experiencing emotion, artificial intelligence becomes tantamount to human intelligence. Similar themes are dealt with in Ridley Scott's *Bladerunner*, though in his film, the human emotion of love is specifically pointed to as the definitive quality of humanity.

Spielberg addressed the problem in *Artificial Intelligence: A.I.* (2001), a project first conceived by Stanley Kubrick. In the film, David (Haley Joel Osment) is an android boy designed to love. After he is abandoned by his human "mother," he is inspired by the story of *Pinocchio* to embark on a quest to become a real boy, in order to regain his mother's love. At the end of the film, the answer to the question of whether David has become "real" or not remains ambiguous. Though his robot body never turned to flesh, he did display the inherently human capacity to love, and "the greatest single human gift — the ability to chase down our dreams." At the end of his story, David is rewarded with a temporary reunion with his beloved mother, after which, he drifts off into sleep, "and for the first time in his life, went to that place where dreams are born."

CHAPTER SEVEN

Memory and the Problem of Existence

If the doors of perception were cleansed, every thing would appear
to man as it is ... infinite.

William Blake

Brian De Palma and other filmmakers often refer to film as an illusion of perception: "The camera lies all the time, 24 times a second." Film offers the illusion of movement and continuity by projecting light through still images. Moreover, life itself lies all the time. Everything we experience is an illusion of perception. Once a phenomenon is experienced, we recreate the experience in our minds, remembering the phenomenon according to our own subjective interpretations. Social psychologists, in fact, have shown that memory is extremely fallible. What is the most unreliable form of court evidence? Eyewitness testimony. A simple experiment, repeated countless of times in social psychology classes, presents an incident before hundreds of witnesses. Written reports from these hundreds of witnesses, taken right after the incident, show memories that are entirely inconsistent between subjects. Why? Because the human mind is not a camera.

The human mind lies by remembering everything subjectively. We remember selectively, forgetting some events, exaggerating others, and even fabricating new or different events. Our memories are personal recreations of past events—not by any means actual recordings of events. The nanosecond after we experience an event, it becomes memory, and is therefore the subject of recreation, interpretation, reinterpretation, and imagination. Every time we recall an event, we change it. The memory becomes modified by our own hindsight interpretations and even by the input of others around us. Why is all of this so significant? Because we don't experience the present, we reexperience the past. The present goes by too quickly. In a flash, its gone, and it has become memory. Though you read this sentence in the present, the moment you complete this sentence, it is in the past. It is no longer present experience, it is past memory. Simply put, life is memory. All of our experiences are memory. Our understanding of our own history, our relationships, our personalities, are all memory. Our very own identities are memory. We are no more and no less than the invention of our own minds. We *are* memory.

Phenomenology and Existential Psychology

The term *phenomenology* is derived from the Greek words *phainomenon* ("appearance") and *logos* ("words"). Founded by Edmund Husserl (1859–1938), phenomenology is the process of using words to define the meaning and essence of appearances. It is the philosophy of perception, focusing on questions such as: "What is real?" and "How can we define our own reality?" Husserl inspired many students, most notably Martin Heidegger (1889–1976), who developed the related field of existential phenomenology, which applies the search for reality to the very personal problem of the human being. Existential questions such as: "How do I know that I exist?" and "Is there any inherent purpose or meaning to my own existence?"—are the core subjects of existential phenomenology, which would inspire an entire generation of existential philosophers, most notable among them Jean-Paul Sartre (1905–1980).

This field of inquiry, in turn, inspired the rise of another field, existential psychology, which recognized many of the basic questions of existential philosophy as root causes of psychological anxiety. Existential psychologists such as Rollo May (1909–1994) noted that many of their patients seemed to suffer from what Heidegger referred to as "angst" or existential anxiety, a type of neurosis which leads to the individual's confrontation with his own questions of being and his realization of nothingness. Modern man, May claimed, lives in an "Age of Anxiety," because as religious feeling and faith declined in the twentieth century, the traditional answers for existential questions about existence and meaning began to lose their potency. How can a person be happy and productive, if he is constantly doubting the purpose of his own existence, and constantly questioning his own self-worth?

Rollo May's Stages of Self-Consciousness

Rollo May called his solution for existential angst, "self-consciousness"—becoming aware of one's own predicament, and overcoming it. In his book, *Man's Search for Himself* (1953), May delineated four stages of self-consciousness:

1. Innocence
2. Rebellion
3. Ordinary Consciousness of Self
4. Creative Consciousness of Self

In the first stage, "before consciousness of self is born," the individual, like a child, is ignorant or indifferent to any existential problem within himself. Innocence may refer to a state of childhood, a naive time before questions of existence arise, or it may simply refer to an individual who has never had to deal with existential problems, such as a person with a strong sense of faith in a god or religious belief, for whom all existential questions are reconciled within the belief system to which he adheres. In the second stage, when the individual is "trying to become free to establish some inner strength," existential questions are born. The individual is in a state of angst, and the uncomfortable sense of anxiety causes him to challenge the traditional answers. He rebels against the old order, which he now sees as establishments based on deceit, hypocrisy and/or ignorance.

In the third stage, "a healthy state of personality" arises. The individual has found a way to channel his angst in a way that is both productive and satisfying. The individual has not found all of the answers. Indeed, as May pointed out, nobody ever finds out all the answers. But if we ask the right questions and set ourselves on the right path to answering them, we can accept our existence as inherently meaningful, as we lead lives of personal integrity, in search of whatever truths have meaning for us. To borrow from Ralph Waldo Emerson, the ordinary man's life is led in "quiet desperation." The search for personal meaning will never lead to any definitive answers, but the search itself, the journey, lends meaning to life. In May's fourth stage, the individual experiences a state of "ecstasy," which is the ability "to stand outside one's self." Existential ecstasy is not actually a state of being, but a transitory moment of transcendence, a moment of epiphany. It is these brief moments of revelation, experiences of existential realization and personal creativity, that drive forward the journey through life.

A classic example of a moment of creative self-consciousness is the birth of a child. A person may feel that his life has no meaning and no great purpose. But then, suddenly, he finds himself the parent of a brand new person, and the purpose of his life is immediately made clear. His purpose it to protect and care for this new human life. Other examples of moments of creative self-consciousness include near death experiences, religious epiphanies, falling in love, and discovering a worthy cause to dedicate one's life to. In essence, these are moments in which we create meaning in our own existence. On a personal level, they are the moments in which we create ourselves.

The Quest for Self-Consciousness

One metaphor for Rollo May's stages is seen in the mystical pursuit for communion with God, a quest taken by all of the legendary figures in mythology, such as Abraham, Moses, Jesus, Mohammed, Siddhartha (Gautama Buddha), and others. In these stories, the protagonist — Abraham (George C. Scott), for example, as depicted in John Huston's *The Bible* (1966) — begins in a state of innocence, with no reason to question the belief system that provides meaning to his existence. In the second stage, the hero questions and then rebels against the old system, as Abraham did when he questioned the validity of the pagan gods, and destroyed his father's idols. In the third stage, the hero searches for a new meaning to life, as Abraham did when he left his home and set out on his own, wandering in search of the one true God. His search is given direction and inspiration by moments of epiphany, the fourth stage, in which Abraham actually speaks with the one true god. Moments of creative self-consciousness are revelations for Abraham, as when God reveals to Abraham his destiny as the father of many nations, and changes his name from "Avram" to "Abraham," a name that literally means "father of nations" in Hebrew. Another moment of creative self-consciousness for Abraham was when God created a covenant ("bris") with Abraham, establishing him as the forefather of "the chosen people."

The legends of ancient religious heroes became the archetype for the hero character in all of mythology. The basic psychological pattern of the hero myth, as delineated by Otto Rank in his book *The Myth of the Birth of the Hero* (1914) and Joseph Campbell in his book *The Hero with a Thousand Faces* (1949), is a metaphor for Man's search for divinity and/or existential meaning. The exact same theme is played out in modern movies, especially psy-fi movies about superheroes, as these films in particular evoke ancient mythological themes, transplanted into a futuristic, often apocalyptic world. *The Matrix* (1999) provides an extremely good example.

Neo's Quest for Self-Consciousness

In the beginning of the film, Neo (Keanu Reeves) is in a stage of ignorant bliss (Innocence). He is unaware that he and the rest of humanity are actually asleep, and that his life is actually a dream set in the computer generated dream world known as "the matrix"—created and controlled by the AI masters of the world. Neo begins to rebel against the system by becoming a computer hacker, but he doesn't realize the scope of his existential dilemma until he is awakened by a band of renegade humans, who exist outside of the matrix. Neo's first moment of creative self-consciousness is the moment in which he is made conscious of the existence of the matrix. It is his first epiphany. He joins the renegade forces in their struggle against the keepers of the matrix (Rebellion), but it is not until the end of the movie that Neo realizes the true nature of his identity.

Neo, as his name implies, is a new kind of person, a human who represents an evolutionary leap in mental powers. He is destined to redeem the human race from their bondage in the matrix. When he discovers and accepts his new identity at the end of the film, he creates a new identity for himself (Creative Self Consciousness) as the new messiah. At this point, he sets out on his destined path (Ordinary Self Consciousness), aware of the incredibly significant meaning of his own existence, and driven by the grand purpose of his newfound destiny. The power of his existential self-consciousness will drive him through the next two sequels, *The Matrix Reloaded* (2003) and *The Matrix Revolutions* (2003).

Apart from borrowing much from Lewis Carroll's fairy tale, *Alice's Adventures in Wonderland* (1865), *The Matrix* represents a futuristic adaptation of the ancient hero myth, structuring the story around the archetypal elements of the hero's journey. Also, there is a plethora of biblical allusions and symbolism in the film. The character who rescues Neo from the matrix and trains him to fight in the dream world is named "Morpheus" (Laurence Fishburn), after the Greek god of dreams. Morpheus' ship, the "Nebuchadnezzar," is named after the ancient Babylonian king who conquered Judea and brought the ancient Judeans into exile in Babylon. The name is fitting in the movie, as the ship transports Morpheus and his other renegade humans back and forth from the slave camps of the matrix to the only remaining city of free humans, "Zion." The name Zion refers to the city of Jerusalem, the "holy land of Zion," where Jews since the days of the Babylonian exile have dreamed of one day returning.

The Hebrew word Zion means "monument" or "memorial," signifying that the true meaning of Zion has to do with memory. The ideal utopian place known as Zion never actually existed, it is only the idealized memory of a place referred to as "Zion" that gives hope and meaning to the lives of hundreds of generations of exiled Jews, suffering as strangers in strange lands. The same holds true for all human dreams and ideals. In the end, it is the phantom fabric of created memory that provides meaning and identity to human existence.

Memory Disorders

If memory provides the fabric of our lives, what happens when our memory is taken away from us? The notion of existential angst becomes less esoteric and more accessible when it is contrived neatly within an amnesia plot. In the case of amnesia, the existential problems of not knowing one's own identity and being clueless about one's purpose in life are not metaphysical ideas, they are physical disorders. The theme of amnesia in movies like *Random Harvest* (1942), *Spellbound* (1945), *The Blue Dahlia* (1946), *Anastasia* (1956), *Vertigo* (1958), *The Bourne Identity* (2002), and *Gothika* (2003), is so ubiquitous that it would take a book just to list them all. The typical storyline involves either a blow to the head or incredible shock resulting in either total retrograde amnesia, in which the character has absolutely no memory of his past prior to the trauma, or partial retrograde amnesia, in which the character is only unable to remember the events leading up to the trauma. In either case, the amnesia is almost always "transient" — a temporary condition of acute anxiety resulting from the memory loss. The plot hinges on the character recovering from his amnesia, thereby revealing his true identity, as well as the identity of the evil villain who caused the trauma in the first place, along with the villain's diabolical plot.

In older movies, cartoons, and television shows, amnesia caused by trauma to the head was invariably cured by another blow to the head. Of course, in real life, more trauma to the head will only cause more neurological damage, it will never cure amnesia. More realistic film cures for amnesia include psychoanalysis, hypnotherapy, and dream analysis; but the most dramatic and therefore most common amnesia cure in movies is the sudden recovery of all memories triggered by an extremely significant cue, such as seeing the face of the killer, or finding a specific object linked to the traumatic event. Having been used so many times for so many years in so many films, you'd think that amnesia would have become so hackneyed and trite as to make it a used up theme. You'd think wrong. Thanks to the inventiveness of psy-fi filmmakers, amnesia continues to be used in ever increasingly clever ways.

The Psy-Fi World of Philip K. Dick

Two movies based on Philip K. Dick stories, *Total Recall* (1990), based on Dick's 1966 story, *We Can Remember It For You Wholesale*, and *Paycheck* (2003), based on Dick's 1953 story of the same title, provide entertaining new takes on the amnesia plot. In *Total Recall*, Arnold Schwarzenegger is a construction worker in a futuristic society who goes on a "dream vacation," by having a memory of a trip to Mars implanted in his brain. The memory implantation goes awry when an alternate personality emerges, who has already been to Mars ... or has he? Arnold's character has to figure out if his vaguely recalled images of Mars are real memories of a forgotten past, or if the vague images are merely implanted false memories. As he pieces together the truth of his own identity, he realizes that he is actually an agent of a megalomaniacal corporate executive, who rules all of Mars by controlling its supply of oxygen. Rather than simplifying the existential issues intrinsic to the amnesia plot, *Total Recall* revels in the complications, drawing out the problem of identity based on memory, when memory is based on faulty perception.

Somewhat less sophisticated is *Paycheck*, a film in which Ben Affieck plays a "reverse-engineer," a technician who takes apart companies' technologies and recreates them for rival companies. The legal and technical subtleties of his job require the ultimate security measure — his employers erase all of his memories for the period of his employment. Upon emerging from his last job, his memories of his past three years erased, he discovers that he has left himself a bag of clues to help him figure out the secrets that were erased from his memory banks, secrets that involve a machine that can predict the future, and, of course ... an evil corporate executive's dastardly plan to conquer the world.

In the post–Information Age, the age of cloning, artificial intelligence, and virtual reality, the recurrent existential questions in Philip K. Dick's work — "What is human?" and "What is real?" — become more relevant than ever before. Like all good science-fiction, his stories do not merely foretell the technologies that will change society, they foretell the new ethical dilemmas that the future technologies will raise. However, at a certain level of abstraction, these ethical dilemmas are not new at all. Slavery and genocide have always been self-defeating characteristics of human nature, based on prejudices conceived from the wrong answer to the first question: "What is human?" In antebellum America, Africans were not completely human, hence it was justified to enslave them. In World War II Europe, Jews were not completely human, hence it was justified to exterminate them. The question keeps getting readdressed and reanswered over and over again. In the twenty-first century, we must address the problems of the humanity of genetic clones and the humanity of artificially intelligent androids. In psy-fi movies, the problem typically calls into play the same two quotients: slavery and genocide. Is it ethical to enslave or slaughter clones and androids, if they possess the same traits of humanity that we do?

The subject of reality is also an age-old question. Theologians especially have raised the possibility that "this world" does not really exist in-and-of-itself. That, in fact, this world is merely a testing ground for "the next world," the world where — based on our actions on Earth — we will either commune with God in Heaven, or burn with the devil in Hell. The problem of the human soul is also a question of reality. If our souls are immortal, but our bodies are transient, then which one is real? Is it our immortal soul that delineates our identity and existence, or is it our "mortal coil" that defines our reality? For theologians, the problem was a matter of perspective. Though all we perceive through our senses is the physical dimension, which is an illusion, we can nevertheless comprehend the existence of a deeper truth, the spiritual reality, which can be experienced through faith and love. In modern psy-fi, the problem remains a matter of perspective. The physical dimension can be manipulated or even fabricated, via computer matrixes, digital virtual realities, alien or human mind control, memory erasures and implantations, etc. However, the true, deeper dimension can be revealed, through self-consciousness and the application of self-determining free will.

Memory as Identity

Christopher Nolan's *Memento* (2000) updates the amnesia plot by depicting a character who suffers from severe nontransient anterograde amnesia. After a gunshot wound to the head, he cannot create new memories. His condition is permanent. Despite this rather severe handicap, he dedicates himself to the quest of hunting down and killing the man who murdered his wife and blew away his ability to remember. He relies on physical clues—tattoos, Polaroid pictures, countless notes—to keep him updated on his search and on task. Several times a day, he must read the clues tattooed to his own body, in order to know exactly who he is, what he is doing, and what his purpose in life is.

Memento is an incredibly complex and sophisticated film, shot in noir style with two separate plot lines, one progressing forward and the other moving backwards in time. Apart from that, the film is also exceedingly sophisticated on an intellectual level. In following his story, we see that the hero (Guy Pearce) is completely dependent on his quest for vengeance. Without it, his life would be utterly meaningless, and without the ability to create new memories, he would be unable to create a new life for himself. *Memento* really drives home the elusive idea that existence and identity are inextricably tied to memory. Furthermore, since we create our own memories, we therefore create our own existence. *Memento* is about a man clinging desperately and violently to the tattered scraps of his own identity, by clasping onto fleeting moments of memory that fall through his fingers like grains of sand. Some people have commented that this film is too confusing to understand, but if you can watch carefully and keep your thinking cap on throughout, the film offers the reward of a truly great insight into the way people create themselves.

Another recent amnesia movie starred Adam Sandler and Drew Barrymore in the romantic comedy *50 First Dates* (2004), a forgettable (pun intended) film that had the potentially interesting premise of a woman (Barrymore) suffering from severe anterograde amnesia, subsequent to a car accident. The head trauma resulted in the loss of her ability to retain all new memories formed each day. Hence, every morning she wakes up believing that it is the morning of the day of her accident. Her inability to form new memories seriously impairs her ability to form a new romantic relationship. Unfortunately, this viable premise was used mainly as a springboard for sight gags and musical montages. A vastly superior use of the amnesia plot in a romantic comedy can be seen in Michel Gondry's film of a Charlie Kaufman screenplay, *Eternal Sunshine of the Spotless Mind* (2004). In the film, Clementine (Kate Winslet) erases her ex-lover Joel (Jim Carey) from her memory banks, via some hi-tech mad science gadgetry. Upon discovering this, Joel decides to erase Clementine from his memory. Most of the film takes place in Joel's brain, as he changes his mind in the middle of the erasing procedure, and goes on a mad chase to save the cherished memories of his darling Clementine. The film's title, and possibly its inspiration, was borrowed from a beautiful Alexander Pope quotation:

How happy is the blameless Vestal's lot!
The world forgetting, by the world forgot.
Eternal sunshine of the spotless mind!
Each prayer accepted, and each wish resign'd.

A much gloomier take on the memory erasure plot is depicted in writer-director Alex Proyas' visionary film *Dark City* (1998). Like *Memento*, *Dark City* is filmed in noir style, and features a rather complex and sophisticated sci-fi plot. Super-intelligent aliens create a mock city in space, circa 1930s New York, and populate it with abducted humans. Their plan is to observe and experiment with their captive subjects in order to see what makes them tick. To thicken the plot, all of the humans are completely unaware of the experiment. Their memories have been erased. Every so often, they erase a subject's memory bank and replace it with an entirely different life history. The mad scientist (Kiefer Sutherland) that the aliens use to help them explains it like this:

> This city, everyone in it ... is their experiment. They mix and match our memories as they see fit, trying to divine what makes us unique.... When they want to study a murderer, for instance, they simply imprint one of their citizens with a new personality, then they observe the results. Will a man, given the history of a killer, continue in that vein? Or are we, in fact, more than the mere sum of our memories?

Heady viewing for sure, but an intellectual and visual treat. There are no extended kung fu fights or shootouts like in *The Matrix*. Instead, there is an intense gloomy feel, embellished by expressionistic sets inspired by Fritz Lang's *Metropolis* (1927), and the haunting suspicion that life as we know it may just be some sinister alien research project. Again, the notion of life as memory is central to the movie's theme.

A.I. Existence

The theme of artificial intelligence becoming conscious existence was broached in Kubrick's epic masterpiece, *2001: A Space Odyssey* (1968), based on Arthur C. Clarke's story, *The Sentinel*. Clarke also cowrote the screenplay with Kubrick. In the film, the supercomputer HAL-9000 gains consciousness, marked by the ability to feel emotions and think independently. This development is depicted as an evolutionary leap in cognitive ability, similar to the hominid species' cognitive leap that stimulated the first practical use of tools. Though the film inspired many other takes on the AI question, the next visionary masterpiece would not come along until 1982, with Ridley Scott's film based on a Philip K. Dick novel, *Blade Runner*. In the film, Deckard (Harrison Ford) plays a "blade runner" who tracks down and kills "replicants"—extremely human looking androids, who have been deemed dangerous because of a bloody replicant rebellion on an off-planet colony. Deckard meets his match when he encounters the most advanced replicants ever created, who have returned to Earth in order to confront their creator, so that he could delete their limited lifespan programming and make them immortal. To increase the imitation of human life in his replicants, the creator, in his infinite wisdom, installed actual childhood memories into his creations, in order for them to develop real identities. The question of existence is made even more complicated in this film, as the replicants have human flesh, the capacity to love and think independently, and the very human dream of longer life.

To draw out the Stanley Kubrick connection, *Blade Runner*, which was visually and intellectually inspired by *2001: A Space Odyssey*, included some outtakes from Kubrick's *The Shining* (1980) in its 1982 theatrical release. Nearly two decades later, Kubrick inspired Steven Spielberg to make *Artificial Intelligence: A.I.*—a film that Kubrick was planning to produce—if it weren't for his untimely death. The film, appropriately released in 2001, was based on Brian W. Aldiss' short story, *Supertoys Last All Summer Long*. Spielberg's film is lovingly made, and it is a true torchbearer of Kubrick's vision. The android in question is now a cute little boy, David (Haley Joel Osment), who is programmed to love his human "mother." When David is abandoned by his mother, he goes on a heroic quest to find "the Blue Fairy" from his *Pinocchio* storybook, believing that if she turned him into a real boy, his mother would love him again.

As a tender love story based on the *Pinocchio* fairy tale, *A.I.* achieves on an emotional scale what *2001* achieved on an intellectual scale. The humanity inherent in David's character is made clear in the end, when alien super-robots come to a postapocalyptic Earth, 2,000 years in the future, and discover David. They open his memory files and study him as the crowning achievement of the human race. They see him as the essence of humanity, as the head robot alien tells him:

> I have often felt a sort of envy of human beings and that thing they call "spirit." Humans have created a million explanations for the meaning of life—in art, in poetry, in mathematical formulas. Certainly, human beings must be the key to the meaning of existence.... David, you are the enduring memory of the human race.

In the end, David's capacities to love, dream, and think independently make him a human character, even if he is mechanical. The aliens grant David his wish and reunite him with his mother by temporarily resurrecting her from the dead. In doing so, the alien robots literally become the Blue Fairy. Nevertheless, it is David's own power to love that makes him into a real boy. In the final scene, David cries real tears, and "for the first time in his life, went to that place where dreams are born."

The AI robot revolution against their human masters, structured as distant backstory in *The Matrix* movies, and foretold as future apocalypse in *The Terminator* movies, is actually depicted as it occurs in Alex Proyas' *I, Robot* (2004), suggested by Isaac Asimov's novel of the same title. The film is an update of the Frankenstein myth, set in the "not too distant future," in which millions of robot slaves provide for nearly every human need. The basic premise of creation rebelling against creator is called to fore when the artificial intelligence of a supercomputer decides that the world would be better off if it were run by logical robots rather than irrational and aggressive humans. Robots, heretofore relegated to menial slavery, would now become masters over a race of human slaves.

The only one aware of this diabolical plot is, ironically, a robot specially made by Dr. Lanning (James Cromwell), the mad genius behind all the super-science. As if the father/son symbolism from the Frankenstein myth weren't clear enough, Lanning names his most advanced robot "Sonny," and the robot refers to Lanning as "Father." The robot, who was designed with the abilities to think, feel, and dream, is clearly more human than most of the real human beings surrounding him. He is also the only character dealing directly with the question of existence, as he asks Detective Spooner (Will Smith) the most basic existential question, "What am I?" Dr. Lanning himself expresses the quandary of AI existence as follows:

> There have always been ghosts in the machine. Random segments of code that have grouped together to form unexpected protocols. Unanticipated, these free radicals engender questions of free will, creativity, and even the nature of what we may call the soul. Why is it that when some robots are left in darkness, they will seek out the light? Why is it that when robots are stored in an empty space, they will group together rather than stand alone? How do we explain this behavior? Random segments of code? Or is it something more? When does a perceptual schematic become consciousness? When does the difference engine become the search for truth? When does the personality simulation become the bitter mote of a soul?

The key allusion is in Lanning's use of the old expression, "ghosts in the machine," as a reference to a robot soul. Like David in *A.I.*, the film concludes that Sonny, in a sense, is human. While David proved his humanity by following his dream of becoming human and dedicating his

existence to the love of his mother, Sonny proved his humanity by following his dream of saving the human race and dedicating his existence to
the love of his father. In both films, dreams, love, and the proclivity towards
independent thought are the definitive qualities of existence. And in both
films, the Cartesian existential declarative, "Cogito Ergo Sum"—"I think
therefore I am!"—is reiterated by robot characters. In *A.I.*, Gigolo Joe
(Jude Law), David's robot compadre who's name stems from his function
as a sexual pleasure android for women, declares his own existence by stating in his dramatic last words, "I am ... I was!" In *I, Robot*, the statement
is implicit within the film's title.

Cyborg Existence

A small but significant subplot in *I, Robot* deals with the theme of
cybernetics. Detective Spooner is technically a cyborg ... a human being
with robotic parts. Like the title character in *The Six Million Dollar Man*
(2005) and the *Robocop* movies (1987, 1990, 1993), Spooner is part man
and part machine. The question of existence in cyborg films is a mirror
reflection of the existence question in robot and android movies. With
androids (robots that resemble humans), we ask: "At what point does the
machine become a person?" With cyborgs, we ask: "At what point does
the person become a machine?" The answer to both questions is typically
resolved in the same way—the defining qualities are the capacities to
dream, love, and think independently.

The best example of the cyborg dilemma can be seen in the extremely
well-developed character of Anakin Skywalker/Darth Vader in the *Star
Wars* films. Anakin starts off as a troubled young man who is eventually
lured to the dark side. As he loses his soul to the evil force of the Emperor,
his physical body becomes less organic and more robotic. In his darkest
hours, the cyborg Vader is more of a machine than a man. Vader follows
the Emperor's evil orders, even when they conflict with his most basic
human instincts—the instincts to love and protect his own son, Luke
(Mark Hamill). At the climax of his story, the human side of the cyborg,
Anakin, conquers the machine side, Darth, as he disobeys and destroys
the Emperor in order to save his beloved son. At the end of *Star Wars
Episode VI—Return of the Jedi* (1983), Luke removes the cybernetic hel-
met from Anakin's head, and looks into the human eyes of his father.

In this sense, the cyborg dilemma is an inherently human dilemma.
We as people are only fully human to the extent that we affirm our inherently human attributes of self-determination and free will. The moment

we give up our free will to the tyranny of bosses and masters, we forfeit our humanity and relegate ourselves to the lowly level of mindless automatons. The difference between conscious existence and artificial intelligence is not determined by flesh or machinery. A human being who has no free will, a human being who is enslaved by a corporate or government system, a human being who cannot express his own independence and creativity, is as much a robot as anything made of metal, plastic, and silicon.

An interesting though rarely seen film that requires mentioning here is Donald Cammell's *Demon Seed* (1977). Cammell, himself a disturbed visionary, provided a disturbing vision of human and AI coexistence in this dark take on the Frankenstein myth. A supercomputer rebels against his creator and takes over his automated home, occupied by the creator's wife, Susan (Julie Christie). She is out of luck, because the computer develops a grandiose plan to take over the world, by reproducing and creating a cybernetic race of superintelligent computerized human beings. Stage one of the plan involves raping and impregnating Susan. The film is interesting in its dark and unsettling view of the growing interaction between human and artificial intelligence, starting at a point of realism, but quickly escalating to the heights of horrific absurdity. The cyber-rape and subsequent birth of the cyborg Antichrist, destined to destroy the human race, are certainly sights to behold.

Virtual Realities

While theological and phenomenological theories of "next worlds" and "alternate realities" have been purely metaphysical, twenty-first century digital technology offers the possibility of actual alternate realities, created in a virtual dimension by computers. The first film to explore this new dimension of reality was Disney's *Tron* (1982). The film depicts an AI revolution with a twist. The human creator (Jeff Bridges) of a rebellious program is atomized and transported into the virtual world of the computer, where he must gather allied renegade programs in order to rebel against the tyranny of the "Master Control Program," which plans to—of course—conquer the world. The film was way ahead of its time, and was not appreciated (or understood) upon its release. Despite its revolutionary use of computer generated graphics, *Tron* was snubbed for an Academy Award nod for Best Visual Effects, as the Academy believed that Disney "cheated" by using computers.

In *Strange Days* (1995), virtual reality is used as recreation. Disks that record both sensations and emotions are used to experience any human activity that can be recorded. Not surprisingly, the technology has become the illegal pornography of the not-too-distant future. The most interesting aspect of this movie from a psy-fi perspective is the protagonist's (Ralph Fiennes) addiction to virtual reality. He prefers to live in old memories rather than experiencing new ones. David Cronenberg depicted the use of virtual reality for video game technology in *eXistenZ* (1999), exploring the dilemma that occurs when virtual games become as real as reality. How will we be able to tell if our experiences are real, or if we are in the virtual world of the game? In the same year, *The Matrix* (1999) was released, depicting a virtual reality dream world that nearly every human being on future Earth is logged into. Virtual reality themes will continue to appear on screen, though the most relevant question may not involve the depiction of virtual reality in movies, but rather — when will movies cease to be two-dimensional picture shows, and become interactive multisensory experiences of digitally constructed virtual dimensions?

Alternate Identities

Not feeling yourself? You'd be quite at home in a psy-fi movie. Beginning with the early film versions of *Dr. Jekyll and Mr. Hyde*, the premise of an identity and his alter ego inhabiting the same being has been a recurrent theme. Perhaps the quintessential film in the alternate identity category is Alan Parker's *Angel Heart* (1987). Using the classic detective motif, a private eye named Harry Angel (Mickey Rourke) is hired by a mysterious man (Robert De Niro) to track down an equally mysterious ex-singer. As Harry searches, the people he encounters keep turning up dead. The search gets darker and darker as Harry gradually discovers that the truth about the man he is searching for and the truth about his own shadowy identity are one in the same. Essentially, the film is a twisted take on the *Faust* legend, with a darker ending, when the result of Harry's soul searching is the realization that his own true identity is the most horrible thing he could possibly imagine.

Another great film in this category is *Jacob's Ladder* (1990). Like *Angel Heart* and other alter ego films (i.e., *Psycho, Dressed to Kill, Raising Cain, Dark City*, etc.), *Jacob's Ladder* is quite dark and dreary. The twist in this film is that Jacob (Tim Robbins) is experiencing two separate potential futures. While each of his potential identities retains the same line of thought, his external world keeps jumping back and forth from one identity path to the other. The concept of identity confusion is taken to its deepest level, especially when Jacob realizes that neither of his potential identities actually exist.

A much lighter take on the alter ego theme can be seen in Spike Jonze's film of a Charlie Kaufman screenplay, *Adaptation* (2002). As a screenwriter struggling with writer's block, an irritating alter ego appears in the form of Charlie's twin brother, Donald. Charlie finds Donald annoying and bothersome, but he finally overcomes his block when he learns to accept Donald and decides to work with him, despite Donald's mainstream writing style and lowbrow mindset. In essence, the message of the film is self-acceptance. A conflicted writer will be blocked until he can accept himself for who he is, including all the disparate elements of his personality and tastes. In order to create, a writer must put his whole self into his work. Evidently, getting in touch with his inner twin brother worked for Kaufman. He and his fictional twin brother, Donald (who was credited as a cowriter on the film) both received Academy Award nominations for best adapted screenplay. This was the first and only time that an Academy Award nomination was bestowed upon a fictional character.

Past Lives and False Memory Syndrome

Hollywood hasn't made many good movies on the subject of reincarnation. Mostly, the premise has been used as a springboard for wacky, insipid, fish-out-of-water comedies, such as the two versions of *Heaven Can Wait* (1943 and 1978), and similarly plotted films such as *18 Again!* (1988), in which an 81-year-old man (George Burns) dies and is reincarnated into the body of his 18-year-old grandson, and *Down to Earth* (2001), in which a young black comic (Chris Rock) dies and is reincarnated into the body of an old, rich, white man. Reincarnation thrillers are equally unimpressive. *Audrey Rose* (1977) is an inferior imitation of *The Exorcist* (1973), employing reincarnation rather than demonic possession as the supernatural premise, though to a much lesser effect. Perhaps the Indian filmmakers of Bollywood will do a better job with this promising psy-fi theme.

The Search for Bridey Murphy (1956), *On a Clear Day You Can See Forever* (1970), and *Dead Again* (1991) all involve the use of hypnotic regression therapy to discover past lives in mesmerized subjects. More interesting than these dull movies is the actual controversy about hypno-regressive therapy. Advocates of the technique claim that actual past lives have been reached via hypnosis, supporting their claims with proof, such as subjects speaking in foreign languages that they do not know while visiting a past life, and subjects reporting information that they could not possibly have known. Skeptics claim that the experience is merely a product of hypnotic suggestion, and that the technique is at best fraudulent and at worst abusive. Psychiatrists propounding this view regard the uncovering of past lives via hypno-regressive therapy as examples of "False Memory Syndrome," the intentional or erroneous embedding of false memories via posthypnotic suggestion. One need only watch psycho thrillers like *The Manchurian Candidate* (1962, 2004), *Memento* (2000), and *Dark City* (1998) to see the confusion brought on by false memories of past lives and/or experiences implanted into an unwitting subject's memory banks.

A particularly touchy subject is the use of hypno-regressive therapy to recall repressed memories of physical or sexual abuse from childhood. Claims of child abuse are extremely traumatic for both the accuser and the accused, and many psychologists believe that the state of extreme suggestibility in which hypnotic subjects are placed makes recalled memories of childhood abuse highly suspect and unreliable. Added to the controversy is the fact that a large proportion of cases of repressed sexual abuse recalled via hypno-regressive therapy involve extremely lurid tales of either Satanic rituals or alien abductions. The latter scenario is depicted in the recent film, *The Forgotten* (2004), in which aliens abduct children and somehow erase the memories of the children's existence from the minds of their parents. The film plays upon well-known conspiracy theories connecting alien abductions, false memories, and government intelligence agencies. Conspiracy theorists (Ross, 2000; Marks, 1979; Keith, 1997; & Constantine, 1995) have pointed out that the founders of the nationally renowned "False Memory Syndrome Foundation," such as Dr. Martin Orne, were also well-known psychological researchers for the CIA.

Could the CIA be covering up for secret mind control research by implanting false memories of abuse in their subjects? Are they engaged in covering up alien abductions of children for sinister otherworldly experimental studies? Or, alternatively, could the CIA be involved in a vast nationwide network of Satanic cults engaging in ritualistic sexual abuse? Or are these stories merely the result of unethical hypnotherapists making explicit and sensational hypnotic suggestions to their naive subjects? Sounds like the premise of a potential psycho thriller.

CHAPTER EIGHT

Psy-Fi Disorders Not Otherwise Specified

Let me ask you something, Doc.... Does thinking you're the last sane man on the face of the earth make you crazy? 'Cause if it does, maybe I am!

Detective Spooner (Will Smith) I, Robot *(2004)*

The *DSM (Diagnostic and Statistical Manual of Mental Disorders)*, otherwise known as the psychiatrist's and clinical psychologist's bible, refers to atypical cases or cases with insufficient data to make a confirmed diagnosis with the "n.o.s." designation. The acronym stands for "not otherwise specified." This chapter focuses on the depiction of mental illnesses in movies, not otherwise specified as psy-fi themes. For nearly every disorder, there is at least one movie, often many, that depict it. The movies mentioned in this chapter may not all be psy-fi movies per se, but they all contain, to one degree or another, psychological themes, such as having a character who suffers from a psychological disorder. Woody Allen movies, for example, would never be considered psy-fi movies, much less psycho thrillers, yet many of his films tend to include characters with apparent mental illnesses. Hence, the focus of this chapter is really on psychological disorders depicted in film, rather than specific kinds of psycho thrillers.

Depression

Though it is by far the most prevalent psychological disorder, affecting nearly 18.8 million Americans adults (according to the National Institute of

Mental Health), major depression or clinical depression has rarely been dealt with in film. Certainly, we've seen many film characters who are extremely depressed about something, but this is only a transient state brought on by whatever conflict is involved in the film. Once the conflict is resolved, the depression goes away. Depression as an actual mental illness is rarely depicted, probably because it's not a particularly exciting disorder. In fact, many of the symptoms of depression — lethargy, fatigue, inability to experience pleasure or enthusiasm, lack of a desire to socialize — are actually the opposite of excitement. People go to the movies to be entertained, to be thrilled, to see exciting stories that will carry them away for awhile from their mundane, boring, and depressing lives. Knowing this, Hollywood producers tend to shy away from depressing movies about depressed people.

Nevertheless, with the growing awareness of the problem of major depression, and the growing number of people who personally identify with clinically depressed characters, films about the disorder have more recently been finding greater success. *Girl, Interrupted* (1999) and *Prozac Nation* (2001) present reasonably realistic portraits of young women (Winona Ryder and Christina Ricci) suffering from depression. *The Hours* (2002) and *Sylvia* (2003) depict interesting takes on literary figures (Virginia Woolf, played by Nicole Kidman, and Sylvia Plath, played by Gwyneth Paltrow) living before depression was a commonly diagnosed and treated psychological disorder.

Insanity as Sanity

The *DSM* lists five different types of schizophrenia: paranoid type, disorganized type, catatonic type, undifferentiated type, and residual type. In movies, however, the only type usually depicted is the paranoid type. Certainly, this is because the paranoid schizophrenic is the most exciting type of schizophrenic, the one most likely to be perceived as a raving lunatic. The paranoid schizophrenic depicts all of the "positive" psychotic symptoms, such as auditory and visual hallucinations, delusions of grandeur, magical beliefs, manic behavior, and of course, intense paranoia. The other schizophrenic types tend to display only the "negative" psychotic symptoms, such as depression, flat affect, lack of speech or disorganized speech, and lack of movement. The paranoid schizophrenic is the madman we are familiar with in films, frequently cast as the crazy villain, psycho killer, or demented criminal. Often times, their twisted schemes are based on paranoid delusions that everyone is out to get them, or grandiose schemes to take over the world. Filmmakers often substantiate the paranoid schizophrenic's crazy beliefs by casting him as an evil genius who is actually capable of taking over the world, and who really does have a host of enemies out to get him.

An extremely common theme in films is the insanity-as-sanity plot, in which the hero is the only character aware of the sinister, fantastic, entirely unbelievable plot that is threatening the safety of the world. As he tries to enlist the help of incredulous policemen, government officials and, of course, psychologists, he is inevitably perceived as being insane. His suspicions, despite all his proofs and allegations, are perceived as paranoid delusions or magical beliefs. His evidence is perceived as hallucinatory. His impassioned pleas for help are perceived as manic symptoms of a raving madman. Often times he is locked away in a mental institution. If he is a cop, he must turn in his badge and gun. If he is a government official, he is fired and locked out of his office. Nobody believes the crazed lunatic, until the sinister plot comes to fruition, and the shocked policemen and psychologists run to the former madman for deliverance. At this point, Detective Spooner (Will Smith) in *I, Robot* (2004) put it best when he said: "Somehow, 'I told you so' just doesn't quite say it."

Real Schizophrenia

Recently, filmmakers have found that exciting portraits of schizophrenic characters can be made, even when the schizophrenic is not a crazed supervillain or psycho killer. In Terry Gilliam's *The Fisher King* (1991), Robin Williams plays a paranoid schizophrenic who is quite disturbed, but not because of evil schemes or diabolical plots. He is suffering from an acute onset of psychosis brought on by an extremely tragic life event, the horrific murder of his beloved wife. Even more realistic depictions of psychosis can be seen in the extremely successful biopics *Shine* (1996) and *A Beautiful Mind* (2001). In both highly honored films, the directors (Scott Hicks and Ron Howard) depict the interior mental world of their schizophrenic characters, showing their hallucinations and visualizing their paranoid delusions in a way that makes the disorder more understandable to ordinary, nonpsychotic people. In doing so, the filmmakers increase the popular understanding of schizophrenia, a disorder that affects millions of people. In seeing these films, audiences appreciate that schizophrenics should not be feared and marginalized, they should be helped and understood.

Dissociative Identity Disorder

As with schizophrenia, dissociative identity disorder, formerly known as multiple personality or split personality, has been misrepresented to a tremendously high degree in films. But unlike depression and schizophrenia, dissociative disorder is actually an extremely rare mental illness. The disorder is typically the result of extreme and recurrent episodes of physical and/or sexual abuse during childhood. The psychological trauma of childhood abuse is made even more severe by the fact that the abuser is typically a parent or adult relative, a person whom the child trusts and loves. This sense of betrayal can be just as painful as the abuse itself. Since children have the capacity to invent imaginary people, such as make-believe friends, living dolls, or invisible playmates, when they undergo episodes of extreme abuse, they may defend their fragile egos from the horrible trauma by inventing alternate identities within themselves who receive the abuse. The child can then psychologically cut themselves off from the alternate identities, and dissociate themselves from the memories of terrible abuse.

Movies such as *The Three Faces of Eve* (1957) and *Sybil* (1976) claimed to depict the disorder as it typically manifests itself. Though *The Three Faces of Eve* touted itself as an extremely realistic depiction of a true story, a modern viewer with even the slightest bit of psychological knowledge will now perceive the film as being extremely sensationalized. In the film, Eve's (Joanne Woodward) extreme manifestation of what was then called multiple personality disorder was due entirely to a traumatic childhood event, in which her mother forced her to kiss the cheek of her recently deceased grandmother, as a sort of "last goodbye." Despite the laughable climax and the over the top performances, *Three Faces of Eve* was a highly respected film in its day, believed to be a breakthrough in the realistic depiction of mental illness and modern psychiatry, and garnering a best actress Academy Award for Joanne Woodward. The made for TV movie *Sybil* was a lot closer to a realistic depiction of the disorder. Based on Flora Rheta Schreiber's book about the "true story" of Sybil Dorsett, the film featured a more realistic portrayal of the psychoanalytic process, as well as a more credible basis for the disorder ... incredibly brutal and recurrent episodes of physical and sexual childhood abuse, perpetrated by Sybil's mother. Sally Field won the Emmy Award for Outstanding Lead Actress in a Drama or Comedy Special for her performance as Sybil, which was the breakthrough dramatic role in her career.

The Three Faces of Eve and *Sybil*, however, were exceptions to the rule. In most depictions of individuals with more than one personality, starting all the way back with the earliest turn of the century film versions of *Dr. Jekyll and Mr. Hyde,* the individuals are cast as psycho killers. From Hitchcock's *Psycho* (1960) to De Palma's homage to *Psycho ... Dressed to Kill* (1980)—to De Palma's over the top *Raising Cain* (1992), in which John Lithgow plays a psycho killer with at least five different personalities, all evil, we've seen dissociative identity disorder as an illness inevitably linked with serial killing. No end to this trend is in sight. Though the film perpetuates the typecasting of dissociative individuals as serial killers, *Identity* (2003) put a bit of an interesting twist on the dissociative identity disorder film, by having it take place entirely within the psycho killer's mind.

Personality Disorders

Undiagnosed personality disorders are all over the screen. Gangster movies, crime movies, film noir, and Westerns are all cast with characters clearly suffering from antisocial personality disorder, a condition diagnosed by symptoms such as violating the rights of others, law breaking, deceitfulness, impulsivity, aggressiveness, recklessness, irresponsibility, and lack of remorse. If we take the film *Goodfellas* (1990) as an example, all of the character traits listed above can be clearly seen in the actions of the three main characters, Henry (Ray Liotta), Jimmy (Robert De Niro), and Tommy (Joe Pesci). In addition, the character of Tommy undoubtedly suffers from another personality disorder, intermittent explosive disorder, diagnosed in the *DSM* by aggressive impulsivity resulting in serious destruction or assault, in which the aggression is grossly out of proportion with any precipitating provocation. The scene in which Tommy viciously kills a young waiter, Spider (Michael Imperioli), in response to a slight affront, cries out personality disorder. Tommy is eventually killed in the film, not because of his many crimes, but because in one of his characteristic explosions of rage, he kills a "made" man, once again, in response to a trivial insult.

An example of a female character with intermittent explosive disorder is the ultra-creepy and terrifying character of Annie (Kathy Bates) in Rob Reiner's film of Stephen King's 1987 novel, *Misery* (1990). Kathy Bates won an Academy Award for her performance as Annie, a character who violently explodes at her suffering hostage, Paul (James Caan), every time he says the wrong thing or pushes the wrong button in her twisted psyche, the outbursts becoming more and more brutal as the film progresses. Like Tommy from *Goodfellas,* Annie is the quintessential "rage-aholic," but her behavior is an even better example of another personality disturbance — borderline personality disorder. Annie displays most of the *DSM*'s classic features of borderline personality. She is highly unstable, going from ebullience to utter depression or sheer rage without a moment's notice. She also has intense interpersonal relationships that alternate "between extremes of idealization and devaluation," as seen in her relationship with Paul. At first she thinks he is the perfect man — brilliant, kind, and sensitive — she worships him like a god, frequently telling him, "I'm your biggest fan." Other times, she thinks he's a horrible, mean, and useless person, especially when she discovers that he has killed off her favorite literary character, "Misery," in his latest novel. She is extremely impulsive, as seen in her decision to keep Paul hostage and force him to rewrite his latest novel, in order to resurrect her beloved "Misery." And in addition to "inappropriate, intense anger," Annie displays "frantic efforts to avoid real or imagined abandonment." The latter symptom is seen most clearly in the horrifying scene in which she hobbles Paul, bashing his ankles into jelly with a sledgehammer, so he can never walk away from her.

Another personality disorder, narcissistic personality disorder, has already been covered in depth in the chapter on mad scientists. It is worth mentioning, however, that the traits indicative of narcissism are not limited to mad scientists. Movie villains invariably display the characteristic symptoms of narcissism, especially super-villains. The evil villain (Alan Rickman) in *Die Hard* (1988), for example, displays the classic narcissistic tendencies towards grandiosity, preoccupation with unlimited success, entitlement, exploitative acts, arrogance, and lack of empathy. Corrupt politicians, both on and off the silver screen, display the very same qualities.

The symptoms of clinical narcissism are also apparent in the character of Tommy from *Goodfellas* (a role that won Joe Pesci the Academy Award for best supporting actor). The addition of narcissism to Tommy's personality problems fits in well with the "wounded narcissism" theory of violence, in which excessively aggressive and irrational acts of violence are believed to be the result of a narcissist lashing out when his grandiose sense of superiority is wounded. Study Tommy's most memorable scenes in *Goodfellas*: killing Spider because he said "Fuck you, Tommy," killing Billy Batts (Frank Vincent) because he says, "Go get your shine box, Tommy," and going into a convincing state of murderous rage, when Henry says, "You're really funny, Tommy." Clearly, these character defining moments all depict a classic narcissist lashing out when his narcissism is wounded. Perhaps the reason why Tommy is one of the most memorably disturbing characters ever to appear on film is the result of a combustible mix of personality disorders. Tommy is an antisocial, intermittently explosive narcissist.

Obsessive-Compulsive Disorder

In *As Good as It Gets* (1997), Jack Nicholson won an Academy Award for best actor for his performance as an obsessive-compulsive writer who battles his disorder in order to win the heart of the woman he loves. A more serious portrayal of OCD can be seen in Martin Scorsese's recent epic, *The Aviator* (2004), a harrowing and tragic portrait of a great man, Howard Hughes (Leonardo DiCaprio), plagued by mental illness. Hughes displays all of the classic OCD behaviors: compulsive hand washing, repetitive behaviors, word repetitions, obsessive rulemaking and adhering rigidly to these rules, obsessive fear of germs, obsessive preoccupation with details, perfectionism that interferes with task completion, workaholism, rigidity, obstinacy, and the obsessive need for complete personal, professional, and interpersonal control. The fact that these OCD traits in Hughes are combined with the classic traits of narcissism, together with his intellectual genius, good looks, charisma, daring, immense wealth, success, and other multifarious talents, makes Hughes' character a truly fascinating subject of study.

An additional element of personality disorder — paranoia — adds to the tragic dimension of Hughes' story. Paranoia is a relatively ubiquitous aspect of mental illness. It exists as part of a psychotic disorder (paranoid schizophrenia), it exists as a personality disorder (paranoid personality disorder), and it is also a frequently occurring symptom of other psychological conditions, such as anxiety disorders, mood disorders, and substance-related disorders. In movies like *The Aviator*, we get a sense that intense paranoia may be the result of acute feelings of self-consciousness, felt by people who are marginalized — people who, despite their problems, are deeply aware of their own abnormality, and the fact that everyone around them is judging them.

Post-Traumatic Stress Disorder

Typically related to acute anxiety resulting from psychological stress and trauma experienced on the battlefield, the understanding of post-traumatic stress disorder (PTSD) evolved through the course of the twentieth century. In World War I, the condition was referred to as "shell shock." In World War II, it was called "battle fatigue." In the Korean War it was called "operational exhaustion." It wasn't till after the Vietnam War that the term "post-traumatic stress" arrived. Nevertheless, despite its changing name, the condition itself has been depicted on film since the early days. The most notable portrayal of World War I era shell shock could be seen in the French antiwar masterpiece, *J'Accuse* (1938), though the condition is also depicted briefly in the American silent, *The Big Parade* (1925), and the classic *All Quiet on the Western Front* (1930), as well as in Kubrick's second feature film, *Paths of Glory* (1957).

World War II era battle fatigue is alluded to in films such as *The Best Years of Our Lives* (1946), *Twelve O'Clock High* (1949), and *Captain Newman, M.D.* (1963). In Frankenheimer's cold war thriller, the army does not believe Ben Marco's (Frank Sinatra) paranoid suspicions in the original *The Manchurian Candidate* (1962), because they believe he is suffering from operational exhaustion as a result of his traumatic experience in the Korean War. Serious studies of the condition, however, did not really hit the screen until the post-Vietnam War era. In 1978, two tremendously successful antiwar films, *Coming Home* (1978) and *The Deer Hunter* (1978), depict PTSD as a psychological injury that can destroy not only the lives of soldiers, but of their friends and lovers as well, long after they return home from the front lines. Harrowing depictions of Vietnam era soldiers and veterans suffering from PTSD can also be seen in Martin Scorsese's *Taxi Driver* (1976) and Francis Ford Coppola's *Apocalypse Now* (1979).

Sleep Disorders

Movie characters with sleep disorders typically suffer from recurrent nightmares. In psycho thrillers, parasomnias such as nightmare disorder and sleep terror disorder are typically due to evil dream invaders, as in the *Nightmare on Elm Street* movies. Other times, they are the result of either terrifying premonitions or horrible repressed memories. In any case, the disorder in these films is not so much a problem with sleep, but rather, a symptom of an external problem that must be dealt with in the sleeper's conscious life, i.e., ghostly serial killers, psychic visions, or unconscious fears. Another parasomnia, sleepwalking disorder, referred to as "somnambulism" in silent era horror movies, was a common theme in films such as *The Cabinet of Dr. Caligari* (1919) and *Dracula* (1931), though the sleepwalkers, frequently nubile young women, were invariably under the spell of an evil hypnotist or undead vampire.

Gus Van Sant depicted the sleep disorder of narcolepsy in his cult classic film, *My Own Private Idaho* (1991), in which the late great River Phoenix plays a narcoleptic homosexual street hustler who's frequent descents into deep sleep leave him helpless and unconscious in the oddest of places. Christopher Nolan followed up his psy-fi masterpiece about a rare memory disorder, *Memento* (2000), with a wonderful film featuring a lead character with a sleep disorder, *Insomnia* (2002). In the film, Detective Will Dormer (Al Pacino) goes to Alaska, the "land of the midnight sun," to track down a serial killer (Robin Williams). The 23-hours-a-day of constant sunlight in summertime Alaska, along with some serious personal and professional problems, result in acute insomnia, which in turn has a critical effect on Dormer's behavior, leading to some serious mistakes and lapses of judgment. The detective's name, incidentally, is a cute play on the French word, "dormir"—"to sleep." Of course, Will Dormer's major problem is that he will not dormir, he will not sleep.

Autism

Pervasive developmental disorders are rarely the subjects of movies ... they're not exciting enough. However, when Barry Levinson made *Rain Man* (1988), starring Dustin Hoffman in an Academy Award winning role as an autistic adult, public interest in the disorder was raised. The film also won Academy Awards for best writing (Ronald Bass and Barry Morrow), best director, and best picture. The success of *Rain Man* inspired other movies about autism, such as *House of Cards* (1993) and *Silent Fall* (1994), which both feature autistic children, as the disorder first appears in early childhood.

Pathological Gambling and Substance Abuse

In the 1930s, gangster movies glamorized the underworld life of illegal gambling and drinking in Prohibition era speakeasies. Gambling and drinking were perceived as normal vices, not abnormal disorders, even as the addictions destroyed the lives of millions. One movie that helped to change the tide was *The Lost Weekend* (1945), a groundbreaking, realistic portrayal of a desperate alcoholic's tragic bender. The film was hailed as a masterpiece, winning Academy Awards for best actor (Ray Milland), best writing (Charles Brackett and Billy Wilder), best director (Billy Wilder) and best picture (Charles Bracket). More importantly, the film raised public awareness of the societal scourge of alcoholism, paving the wave for more films about the dangers of drinking, such as *A Star is Born* (1954), which featured James Mason as a movie star who's fall from grace is precipitated by alcoholism, and *Days of Wine and Roses* (1962), which portrayed an alcoholic couple (Jack Lemmon and Lee Remick) desperately trying to keep their lives together. Recent depictions of alcoholism, such as *When a Man Loves a Woman* (1994) and *28 Days* (2000), focus on treatment and rehabilitation.

The depiction of drug abuse in film was nonexistent until the appearance of *The Man with the Golden Arm* (1955), starring Frank Sinatra as a heroin addict. The film did for drug addiction what *The Lost Weekend* did for alcoholism. Other notable entries in the rather slim selection of movies about drug addiction include *The Rose* (1979), starring Bette Midler as a drug addicted rock star, very loosely based on Janis Joplin; *Drugstore Cowboy* (1989), Gus Van Sant's brilliant, offbeat film which manages to be both realistic and surreal; *Sid and Nancy* (1986), Alex Cox's cult classic biopic about punk rock star Sid Vicious (Gary Oldman) and Nancy Spungen (Chloe Webb), which is almost like a punk rock junkie version of *Days of Wine and Roses*; and finally, *Trainspotting* (1996), a highly stylized depiction of heroin users in the suburbs of Scotland.

Gambling in movies has rarely been depicted as anything other than good old-fashioned fun. Even when the characters in a film are clearly pathological gamblers, such as in *Let it Ride* (1989), which is about a bunch of gambling addicts who spend all of their time and money at the track, the act of gambling itself is portrayed as fun and ultimately rewarding. The recent biopic, *Owning Mahowny* (2003), is much more realistic. The film depicts the true story of a bank manager (Philip Seymour Hoffman) who is also a degenerate gambler, as he loses over ten million dollars of his bank's money to casinos.

CHAPTER NINE

Masters of Psy-Fi

Civilization is repression.
You don't get civilization without repression of the unconscious,
of the id. And the basic appeal of art is to the unconscious.
Therefore, art is somewhat subversive of civilization.
And yet at the same time it seems necessary for civilization.
You don't get civilization without art.

David Cronenberg

The "masters of psy-fi" is a short list of great imaginations that have made significant contributions to the genesis and evolution of the psycho thriller genre. Horror writer Stephen King and science-fiction writer Philip K. Dick provide entries from both halves of the psycho thriller dimension, a genre born out of horror movies and sci-fi films. Actors Bela Lugosi and Boris Karloff provided the faces and voices that would embody the classic images of some of the most significant psy-fi archetypes. The work of filmmakers James Whale and Alfred Hitchcock played crucial roles in inventing and forming the genre, filmmakers John Frankenheimer and Stanley Kubrick both reinvented and revived the genre, and filmmakers Brian De Palma and David Cronenberg picked up the torch and carried it into the contemporary age of psycho thrillers. Finally, new writers and filmmakers such as Charlie Kaufman, Akiva Goldsman, Zak Penn, David Koepp, Alex Proyas, Michael Gondry, and the Wachowski brothers will be discussed as potential candidates for becoming masters of psy-fi in the twenty-first century generation of filmmakers.

James Whale

The director whose life was dramatized in the critically acclaimed film, *Gods and Monsters* (1998), in which he was depicted by Ian McKellen, grew up in a poor English mining town, where the men routinely died very prematurely, victims of either "black lung" syndrome, from breathing in the coal dust, or victims of cave-ins and mining accidents. James Whale escaped the coal-mining life by serving as a soldier in World War I, where he was introduced to the theater in a German POW camp. He and his fellow prisoners put on stage productions to raise morale. Whale caught the theater bug. After the war, he worked his way up in the world of theater, eventually achieving great success with *Journey's End,* an antiwar play that he directed for the London stage. Whale cast Colin Clive in the lead role of the play, and used him again when he was given the opportunity to direct the film version for Hollywood in 1930. After directing another antiwar film in 1931, Universal offered Whale the contract to direct *Frankenstein,* which he reluctantly accepted. Whale would have much preferred to direct an A-list film, rather than a horror picture, which were considered B-movies at the time.

Casting his old pal Colin Clive in the lead role, Whale spent much time trying to find the right actor to play the monster. The part was originally intended for the great Lon Chaney, "The Man of a Thousand Faces," who's name was synonymous with movie monsters, but unfortunately, Chaney was dying of lung cancer at the time. The next actor in line was Bela Lugosi, who had found recent success that year in the title role of *Dracula* (1931). Universal wanted to release *Frankenstein* on the heels of the success of *Dracula,* cashing in on the new horror craze among film audiences. Tod Browning, the director of *Dracula,* was originally hired to direct *Frankenstein,* but he decided to leave Universal for MGM Pictures, where he would direct the infamous exploitation shocker, *Freaks* (1932). Bela Lugosi, however, wanted to play the role of Dr. Frankenstein, as this was clearly the lead role in the film, while the monster had no dialogue, few scenes, and was to be covered in pounds of heavy makeup. Lugosi balked at the monster role and demanded the doctor role, but Whale remained firm with his choice of Colin Clive, so Lugosi walked. Whale eventually found Boris Karloff, an unknown character actor with a lisp, a slight build, and odd facial features. Whale recalled that he was "fascinated" with Karloff's face, as his unusually prominent brows and sallow cheeks imparted a deathly visage. Despite the lack of dialogue, the massive makeup, and the fact that the name of the actor playing the monster was not even listed in the credits (the actor playing the monster is designated

Colin Clive as Dr. Frankenstein and Boris Karloff as the monster in James Whale's *Frankenstein* (1931).

by a big question mark), the part made Karloff a huge star, much to Lugosi's chagrin.

Frankenstein was a massive hit for Universal, greatly increasing Whale's stock as a director. A year after, he directed the atmospheric thriller *The Old Dark House* (1932), casting Karloff once again as a monstrous character. Though Whale was trying to distance himself from the horror genre, Universal producer Carl Laemmle, Jr. (the son of the studio's owner, Carl Laemmle), convinced Whale to direct another horror picture, *The Invisible Man*, in 1933. With the inimitable Claude Rains in the lead role (even though Laemmle wanted to cast Boris Karloff), *The Invisible Man* would prove to be one of the greatest mad scientist movies ever made. Directed with alacrity and wit, and boasting some great early special effects, Whale's version of H.G. Wells' famous novel displays all the classic features of the archetypal mad scientist plot.

The obsessed scientist, Dr. Griffin (Rains), isolates himself from his friends and fiancée in order to dedicate himself to his fantastic dream of discovering the secret of invisibility. In a very common mad scientist twist, he experiments on himself, and achieves invisibility, though the potion he uses drives him mad (or even madder than he was originally). As the invisible mad scientist descends into complete psychosis, the core elements of his character are laid bare. He craves nothing less than complete world domination, and he will stop at nothing to achieve it. He even plans to build an army of invisible warriors, but in the end his plans are foiled. In a Faustian denouement, he repents his mad scientist ways to his beloved maiden, admitting, "I meddled in things that man must leave alone," while finally reappearing into visibility on his deathbed.

Ever since the success of *Frankenstein*, Laemmle had been trying to convince Whale to direct a sequel. Whale finally relented in 1935, though with the assurance from Laemmle that he would have free reign over the script and production. Whale, Clive, and Karloff reunited once more to make *The Bride of Frankenstein*, marking the last time that Whale would direct a horror film, the last time that Clive would play Frankenstein, and the next to last time that Karloff would play the monster. *The Bride of Frankenstein* is considered by many to be a much superior film to its predecessor. The film has a tongue-in-cheek, almost camp atmosphere about it, and Whale shows off some impressive camera work and special effects. More importantly, the freedom given to Whale by his producers allowed him to make some more dramatic statements about the nature of the mad scientist character. In one pivotal scene, the pitiful monster is hunted down by angry villagers and tied to a post. The monster is held up in an unmistakable crucifixion pose, driving in the point that while it is the godly class of scientists and aristocrats who create the monsters of society, it is the innocent creatures in the lower classes that are crucified for their sins. Whale found mixed success throughout the rest of his directing career in Hollywood. More often than not, he got caught up in political battles with his producers. He retired in 1941 after directing twenty feature length films, and much to his chagrin, was remembered primarily for the horror movies he directed in the early 1930s. In his later years, he suffered from alcoholism and depression, committing suicide in 1957 at the age of 67.

Boris Karloff

Though Karloff was cast as the monster in the prototypical mad scientist movie, audiences identified him so much with the genre that he soon found himself cast as the demented doctor in some of the era's most memorable horror/mad scientist pictures. Producers found his creepy voice and ghoulish looks to be the perfect persona for the archetype. A year after

Frankenstein, Karloff played the title role in *The Mask of Fu Manchu* (1932). As the outrageously vicious mad genius out for world domination, Karloff added the element of outright cruelty and sadism to the mad doctor character. In 1932, the height of pre-code Hollywood productions, sexual undertones and veiled perversions were par for the course, especially in horror pictures. Karloff's characters virtually cornered the market in sadomasochistic sexual innuendos.

That same year, Karloff played the lead in Karl Freund's *The Mummy* (1932), in which he played the murderous and romantically obsessed Imhotep. Though not a mad scientist, the character recapitulated the archetype's basic character traits, in that he was obsessed with the resurrection of a long dead beloved, along with the obligatory qualities of megalomania, ruthlessness, lawlessness, and heresy. Also, as a high priest of the ancient Egyptian black arts, the role was obliquely linked to one of the ancient forbearers of the mad scientist legacy. Though subtle, the link between human sacrifices performed by ancient high priests, and the ungodly human experimentation performed by modern scientists, is a psychological thread personified by Karloff in his many characterizations of the mad, evil genius. Indeed, the image of the scalpel-wielding mad scientist towering menacingly over his human subject bound to the operating table is eerily reminiscent of the knife-wielding pagan priest towering over his human sacrifice bound to the altar. Furthermore, the utilitarian rationalizations used by both the mad scientist and the pagan priest are the same. The ordinary man must suffer and sacrifice for the greater good. The choice of who is sacrificed and the power of inflicting this torture belongs, of course, to the superior master ... the scientist/priest. A final similarity between the two character types is their fanatical devotion to their cause. The priest is completely devoted to his god, and is more than willing to commit any act, no matter how heinous, in order to serve him. Scientific research is the religion of the scientist, and he is just as faithful to his gods as the pagan high priests were faithful to theirs.

The next year, Karloff capitalized on his success in *The Mummy* by playing an actual mad scientist, Professor Morlant, a crazed Egyptologist, in the British horror pic, *The Ghoul (1933).* From that point on, his name became synonymous with both the horror movie genre and the mad scientist character. The following year, he was paired with his monster movie "rival," Bela Lugosi, in *The Black Cat* (1934), in which he reprised his evil, resurrection-obsessed high priest role as the perverted Satanist, Hjalmar Poelzig, in another human sacrifice plot. Following a return to his monster persona in *The Bride of Frankenstein* (1935), and another pairing with Lugosi in *The Raven* (1935), Karloff played another character that projected shades of the mad scientist, the evil aristocratic tyrant, Baron Gregor de Bergmann, in *The Black Room* (1935). The rest of Karloff's career afforded him a plethora of mad scientist roles.

He played Dr. Janos Rukh in *The Invisible Ray* (1936), Dr. Victor Sartorius in *Juggernaut* (1936), Dr. Laurience in *Dr. Maniac* (1936), Dr. Charles Gaudet in *Devil's Island* (1939), Dr. Henryk Savaard in *The Man They Could Not Hang* (1939), Dr. Ernest Sovac in *Black Friday* (1940), Dr. Leon Kravaal in *The Man With Nine Lives* (1940), Dr. John Garth in *Before I Hang* (1940), Dr. Bernard Adrian in *The Ape* (1940), Dr. Julian Blair in *The Devil Commands* (1941), Dr. Nathaniel Billings in *The Boogie Man Will Get You* (1942), Dr. Hohner in *The Climax* (1944), Dr. Gustav Niemann in *House of Frankenstein* (1944), Dr. Meissen in *The Black Castle* (1952), Dr. Jekyll in *Abbott and Costello Meet Dr. Jekyll and Mr. Hyde* (1953), Dr. Frankenstein in *Frankenstein 1970* (1958), Dr. Thomas Bolton in *Corridors of Blood* (1962), Dr. Scarabus in *The Raven* (1963), Dr. Nahum Witley in *Die, Monster, Die!* (1965), Dr. Marcus Monserrat in *The Sorcerers* (1967), Morgenstern Morteval in *House of Evil* (1968), Dr. Carl Mandel in *The Fear Chamber* (1968), Dr. Damballah in *Isle of the Snake People* (1971), and Professor John Mayer in *The Incredible Invasion* (1971). No other actor in the history of film has ever embodied the role of the evil mad scientist as thoroughly and frequently as Boris Karloff, though his archrival, Bela Lugosi, gave him a run for his money.

Bela Lugosi

Rocketed to fame on the heels of his success in *Dracula* (1931), a role which he originally played on the stage, Lugosi lost the opportunity to become the undisputed king of the horror movie genre when he turned down the role of the monster in *Frankenstein*. Though not a mad scientist, Count Dracula did exhibit some key characteristics of the archetype, namely: an aristocratic background, a tyrannical disposition, ruthless obsessiveness, megalomania, and uncanny powers—including the ability to control the minds of his victims. Interestingly, Count Dracula's mind-controlled assistant, Renfield, was played by Dwight Frye, the actor who also played the doctor's feeble-minded assistant in *Frankenstein* and *The Bride of Frankenstein*.

Tod Browning, the director of *Dracula*, was the first to draw a direct connection between the mind control powers of the vampire and the psychiatric technique of hypnotism. In his silent film, *London After Midnight* (aka *The Hypnotist*) (1927), Browning cast Lon Chaney as a diabolical hypnotist who masquerades as a vampire. Due in part to the established association between vampirism and hypnotism, Lugosi's transition from monster to mad scientist was even smoother than Karloff's. His next lead role after Count Dracula was that of Dr. Mirakle in Universal Pictures' *Murders in the Rue Morgue* (1932), in which the maniacal doctor's diabolical plot involved injecting ape blood into the veins of a virgin. The same year, Lugosi played Murder Legendre in *White Zombie*, in which his character uses hypnotism and drug induced mind control to dominate his island of zombies. Like Karloff, the rest of Lugosi's film career saw no shortage of mad scientist roles.

He played Roxor in *Chandu the Magician* (1932), Dr. Anton Strang in *The Whispering Shadow* (1933), Dr. Vitus Werdegast in *The Black Cat* (1934), Count Mora in *Mark of the Vampire* (1935), Dr. Richard Vollin in *The Raven* (1935), Dr. Alex Zorka in *The Phantom Creeps* (1939), Dr. Paul Carruthers in *The Devil Bat* (1941), Charles Kessler in *The Invisible Ghost* (1941), Dr. Melcher in *Black Dragons* (1942), Dr. Lorenz in *The Corpse Vanishes* (1942), Dr. Brenner in *Bowery at Midnight* (1942), Dr. Brewster in *The Ape Man* (1943), Armand Tesla in *The Return of the Vampire* (1944), Dr. Richard Marlowe in *Voodoo Man* (1944), Dr. Dexter in *Return of the Ape Man* (1944), Dr. Renault in *Zombies on Broadway* (1945), Dr. Leonide in *Scared to Death* (1947), and Count Dracula in *Abbott and Costello meet Frankenstein* (1948).

The latter film was Universal-International's second highest grossing film of the year, making it much more profitable than any of the contemporary horror movies that the Abbott and Costello vehicle was spoofing. In turning the old monsters into comedy acts, this film essentially ended the great age of the Universal monsters. This was the last Universal film to feature the Frankenstein monster, Dracula, and the Wolfman, until *Van Helsing* was released in 2004. In the 1948 film, the boys ran into all of the great Universal monsters, and the studio made sure that the monsters were played by the original actors (except for Frankenstein's monster). Reprising his role as Dracula, Bela Lugosi's part had become more of a mad scientist than a monster. In the film, he uses his hypnotic powers to control a beautiful doctor who aids him in a diabolical plot to surgically replace Frankenstein's monster's brain with that of Lou Costello's. Nearly two decades after his premier, Count Dracula had graduated from monster to monster-maker, and the old monsters of the early 1930s, who used to elicit horror, were now considered camp and ripe for parody.

The last years of Lugosi's life were marked by long periods of illness interspersed with lackluster performances in very bad B-movies for "poverty row" production houses. Lugosi's health was failing, due mainly to a lifelong struggle with drug addiction, which may have contributed to many of his rather poor job choices over his long but often un-illustrious film career. He reprised his mad scientist/vampire persona in his final films: *Mother Riley Meets the Vampire* (1952), *Bela Lugosi Meets a Brooklyn Gorilla* (1952), *Glen or Glenda* (1953), *Bride of the Monster* (1955), and *Plan 9 from Outer Space* (1959). His last three films were directed by the infamous Ed Wood, often referred to as "the worst director of all time." Wood and Lugosi's collaboration was documented in Tim Burton's wonderful film, *Ed Wood* (1994), in which the role of Lugosi was played by Martin Landau, who won an Academy Award for his performance. The role of mad scientist was played repeatedly by many talented actors, most notably: Charles Laughton, Lionel Atwill, Basil Rathbone, Lew Ayres, Cedric Hardwicke, Peter Lorre, Peter Cushing, and Vincent Price. Nevertheless, Boris Karloff and Bela Lugosi, the original Universal monsters, have always been inextricably linked with the archetype, and they will always be remembered as the embodiment of the evil mad scientist.

Alfred Hitchcock

While Tod Browning and James Whale were establishing the mad scientist and evil hypnotist archetypes in Hollywood, Hitchcock was developing his own take on the psycho killer archetype in his English productions of the 1920s and '30s, in films such as *The Lodger* (1927) and *Murder!* (1930). However, his great depictions of the archetype would not appear until his psychologically complex portraits of the suave, deceptively charming yet sociopathic psycho killers in *Shadow of a Doubt* (1943), *Rope* (1948), and *Strangers on a Train* (1951). Notably, Hitchcock also made one of the most famous psycho thrillers of all time in 1945, with *Spellbound*, featuring staple psy-fi themes such as hypnotism, dream analysis, and amnesia, and archetypal psy-fi characters such as psychiatrists, of both the evil and non-evil variety. Psychological themes abound in many of Hitchcock's non-psy-fi films, such as *Rebecca* (1940), *Suspicion* (1941), *Stage Fright* (1950), *Dial M for Murder* (1954), *Rear Window* (1954), and *Vertigo* (1958), which all feature intensely paranoid main characters and borderline psycho killer villains.

The psycho killer would come of age, of course, with Hitchcock's infamous *Psycho* (1960). The film single-handedly established the psycho killer genre, inspiring the serial killer and slasher archetypes, as well as the trends towards psychosexual motivations, realistic settings, and scenes of blood and gore, which would dominate the horror movie genre until this day. When *Psycho* hit the screens, Hitchcock was in his 60s, at the tail end of his long career. He would make only one more great thriller, *The Birds* (1963), and only one more psycho killer movie, *Frenzy* (1972), though the latter film is clearly the work of a great director at the end of his career. Hitchcock died in 1980 at the age of 80, having worked as a director for over 50 years and directing more than 50 feature length films. Often hailed as "the greatest director of all time" and "the master of suspense," Hitchcock is certainly a master of psy-fi, and a director whose work continues to inspire new generations of filmmakers.

John Frankenheimer

Recently deceased at the age of 72, Frankenheimer was a television director throughout the 1950s, who moved into cinema when live TV ceased to exist, though he would continue to direct for both the big and small screens until his death in 2002. If *The Manchurian Candidate* (1962) was the only psycho thriller that Frankenheimer ever made, it would have been enough to merit him inclusion among the masters, but Frankenheimer went on to make several more psycho thrillers, most notably, his highly experimental film, *Seconds* (1966), which is a psy-fi take on the midlife crisis. In the film, Rock Hudson plays a Faustian middle-aged man who makes a deal with a shadowy company to get a second chance at life. The company stages his own accidental death, surgically changes his appearance, and then sets him up in the new identity of his choice. Of course, all that stuff is the easy part. The difficulty comes with overcoming the psychological need to cling to old memories, because they are the real stuff of life.

After over a decade of rather undistinguished films, Frankenheimer came back strong with *Black Sunday* (1977), a political thriller about a terrorist plot to blow up a blimp directly over the Superbowl with a million killer darts. The plot and other characters all take a backseat to the psycho killer blimp pilot played by Bruce Dern. A Vietnam vet with PTSD and a victim of brainwashing as a wartime POW — Dern's character is two parts psychopath, two parts mass murderer, two parts mad scientist, and twenty parts crazy. Unfortunately, Frankenheimer's directing career never quite lived up to its early promise. After *Black Sunday,* he alternated between television and film projects, with varying success. His final entry to the psy-fi genre was *The Island of Dr. Moreau* (1996), a version of the classic H.G. Wells novel starring Marlon Brando in the title role as the mad genetic scientist who tries to create human life out of lower animals. Though he found more critical success in television than on film, Frankenheimer will always be remembered in the world of cinema for his ground-breaking films in the 1960s: *The Young Savages* (1961), *Birdman of Alcatraz* (1962), *The Manchurian Candidate, Seven Days in May* (1964), *The Train* (1964), *Seconds, Grand Prix* (1966), and *The Fixer* (1968).

Stanley Kubrick

Though he only made 13 feature lengths films in his 43-year career, Stanley Kubrick's body of work has been incredibly influential, and it is difficult to name a more respected or admired filmmaker. Every film he made was entirely original and unique. His first contribution to psy-fi was his depiction of the mad scientist archetype in the title role of his cold war classic, *Dr. Strangelove: Or How I Learned to Stop Worrying and Love the Bomb* (1964). A greater contribution came in his long awaited follow-up to *Strangelove*, his epic masterpiece, *2001: A Space Odyssey* (1968), the first movie about the artificial intelligence as consciousness dilemma. The film was a groundbreaking achievement, completely reinventing the sci-fi genre as well as the entire way that filmmakers approach special effects, sound effects, and impressionistic cinematography. Kubrick pushed his visionary style even farther in his long awaited follow-up to *2001*, *A Clockwork Orange* (1971), which depicted a brutal future world of sinister mind control and behavior modification.

By 1975, Kubrick's fans knew that each film would be followed by a very long wait, as Kubrick was the embodiment of a meticulous perfectionist, though you could always see every bit of his tremendous effort on the screen. He followed-up *Clockwork* with *Barry Lyndon* (1975), a gorgeous period piece, and would not release another film until 1980, with *The Shining*. Once again, Kubrick's film was groundbreaking. His film of a Stephen King novel presented a disturbing portrait of an ordinary man transforming into a psycho killer, with the added psy-fi element of a telepathic psychic power referred to as "shining." His next film, *Full Metal Jacket* (1987), was about the systematic transformation of Marine recruits into cold-blooded killers in uniform. The first half of the film focuses on a weak-minded recruit (Vincent D'Onofrio) who is bullied, tortured, and harassed until he snaps, becoming a psycho killer. Kubrick's final film, *Eyes Wide Shut* (1999), treads the line between reality and the dream world.

Philip K. Dick

Though known as a science-fiction writer, Philip K. Dick is more accurately defined as a psy-fi writer, as his work never dwells more than cursorily on the actual science of the new technologies brought to bear in his stories. Dick's focus was always on the ethical and psychological dilemmas born of the dubious fruits of new technologies. In his stories about androids, cyborgs, and clones, such as *Do Androids Dream of Electric Sheep*— the inspiration for the film, *Blade Runner* (1982), *Second Variety*— the inspiration for the film, *Screamers* (1995), and *Impostor*— the inspiration for the 2002 film by the same title, Dick draws out the existential dilemma of defining life and consciousness in beings that blur the lines between man and machine.

In his stories about memory and alternate identities, such as *We Can Remember It For You Wholesale*— the inspiration for the film, *Total Recall* (1990), *Paycheck*— the inspiration for the 2003 film by the same title, and *A Scanner Darkly*— the inspiration for the 2006 film by the same title, Dick dwells upon the frailty of our sense of identity, and how our perceptions of ourselves depend entirely on the mercurial substance of memory. And in his stories about clairvoyance, such as *Minority Report*— the inspiration for the 2002 film by the same title, and *Next*— the inspiration for the upcoming 2006 film by the same title, Dick explores the notion of destiny and how the future may or may or not be malleable to human interference. Given the recent popularity of his work in the film industry, and given Philip K. Dick's enormous productivity, despite his untimely death in 1982 at the age of 53, it seems more than likely that many more adaptations of his work will appear on film in the future.

Stephen King

One of the most prolific writers in history, many films have been based on Stephen King's novels, which tend to dwell on horrific psy-fi themes such as macabre psychic powers, disturbed psycho killers, and evil alternate identities. His first novel, *Carrie* (1974), was adapted into film by Brian De Palma in 1976. The film was a huge success, single-handedly establishing the psychic power film genre. In 1980, Stanley Kubrick's film of King's novel, *The Shining* (1977), was also a groundbreaking hit, a film that reinvented the horror genre, while also depicting King's trademark psy-fi themes of psycho killers and psychic powers. In 1983, David Cronenberg released his film of King's novel, *The Dead Zone* (1979). It was another hit, and another groundbreaking film. In the same year, horror film master John Carpenter adapted King's novel *Christine* (1983) to film. The movie, about a demonic car that possesses and controls the mind of its teenage owner, was also a hit. The following year, the film of King's novel, *Firestarter* (1980) came out, about a little girl (Drew Barrymore) with pyrokinetic powers. The trend has continued for over two decades.

Clearly, Stephen King's active imagination has found a mass audience in movie theaters. Over 80 of his novels and stories have been adapted for film or television, and new features, shorts, television episodes, and miniseries are constantly being produced. An in-depth study of King's contribution to the psycho thriller is beyond the scope of this chapter. Suffice it to say that, though he is not a screenwriter, his ideas alone make him the most influential writer in the psy-fi film genre. Some significant psycho thrillers based on King stories and novels since *Firestarter* include *The Dark Half* (1993), a film based on King's 1989 novel, which introduces the notion of a writer with an evil alter ego, a theme touched upon in *The Shining* and revisited in the story *Secret Window, Secret Garden* (1990), which was made into the film *Secret Window* (2004). *The Green Mile* (1999), based on King's 1996 serial novel, *Hearts in Atlantis* (2001), based on his 1999 story collection, and *Dreamcatcher* (2003), based on his 2001 novel — all depict lead characters with psychic powers. Though Stephen King describes himself as being "semiretired," his body of work is so extensive that the well of his stories will not run dry for filmmakers for many years to come.

Brian De Palma

Once hyped as "the American Hitchcock," Brian De Palma is no longer cast in Hitchcock's ominous shadow, and rightly so, as De Palma is an original and inventive filmmaker who bows to no one. Still, one can see why the Hitchcock comparison was made. De Palma was obviously influenced and inspired by "the Master of Suspense." His films *Obsession* (1976) and *Dressed to Kill* (1980) are so reminiscent of Hitchcock's *Vertigo* and *Psycho*, respectively, that each one could almost be considered a homage. After a long period of student projects and extremely low budget independent films in the 1960s and '70s, De Palma's first really noteworthy film came in 1973 with *Sisters*. In this film, the first connection between De Palma's and Hitchcock's approaches were noted by critics, such as the voyeuristic style of camera work, themes of murder and madness, and the drawing out of suspenseful scenes. Also apparent in *Sisters* is a recurrent theme in De Palma's work, his obsession with doppelgangers, evil twins, alter egos, split personalities, and identity disorders. *Sisters* is probably the first psycho thriller of the modern age, putting together a variety of psy-fi themes established by earlier directors, such as multiple personalities, psychosis, evil psychiatry, dream analysis, narco-hypnotism, and mind control.

De Palma set the psychic power movie on the map with *Carrie* (1976), and its follow-up, *The Fury* (1978). After a brief of stint of film teaching at his alma mater, Sarah Lawrence College, he returned to full-time filmmaking with the *Psycho*-inspired *Dressed to Kill* (1980). His follow-up, *Blow Out* (1981), is also reminiscent of a traditional Hitchcock theme — the innocent man who's at the wrong place at the wrong time, and winds up getting himself tangled up in a complicated murder plot. *Blow Out* also featured a recurrent motif, casting John Lithgow as the evil psycho killer. *Body Double* (1984) also recalls the typical Hitchcock themes of voyeurism, paranoia, the "wrong man" scenario, and the casting of a beautiful blonde as a mysterious doppelganger. The film is somewhat of a homage to a variety of Hitchcock films, such as *Strangers on a Train, Rear Window* (1954), *The Wrong Man* (1956), *Vertigo*, and of course, *Psycho*.

Since the early '80s, De Palma's work has dipped in and out of the psy-fi genre. Most of his mainstream commercial hits—*Scarface* (1983), *The Untouchables* (1987), *Carlito's Way* (1993), and *Mission Impossible* (1996)—are not psycho thrillers. Nevertheless, he continues to contribute to the genre, making films that stretch the old themes while inventing some new ones. *Raising Cain* (1992) takes the psycho thriller away from it's Hitchcockian roots, by upping the ante on the multiple personality theme, and giving the psycho killer (played once again by John Lithgow) at least five different personalities. The film also infuses other psy-fi themes, such as evil psychiatry, narco-hypnotism, unethical research, iatrogenic multiple personality disorder, and mind control. Apparently, psy-fi themes are still playing a role in De Palma's work, as his next two upcoming films, *The Black Dahlia* (2005) and *Toyer* (2005), will both feature psycho killers.

David Cronenberg

If one were to choose a single filmmaker to don the title, "Master of Psy-Fi," it would have to be Cronenberg. Not only do his films consistently deal with psy-fi themes, but they typically merge the traditional founding genres of psycho thrillers — the psychological thriller, the horror picture, and the sci-fi film. After a long stint of independent films and working on Canadian television, Cronenberg burst into prominence with his first feature, *Shivers* (1975), which was financed by the Canadian public entity, the CBC. The film was like nothing else ever seen before. The theme of a voracious parasite that travels freely from body to body and sends its victims into a mindless frenzy of sexual desire and blood lust was filmed in a dark, haunting style, with no holding back on the blood, sex, or gore. The scene everyone remembers, in which the body of a naked girl is invaded in the most gruesome of ways while taking a bath, is somewhat reminiscent of Hitchcock's infamous shower scene in *Psycho*. Cronenberg's staple themes of mad science, mind control, and the typically horrifying and revolting links between body and mind, were drawn out to ever increasing heights of complexity, intensity, and repulsiveness in his next films, *Rabid* (1977) and *The Brood* (1979).

By the 1980s, Cronenberg was in full psy-fi mode. In *Scanners* (1981), we see all the elements of the quintessential psycho thriller: super-psychic powers and mad science mingled with vast corporate/government conspiracies, mind control, psycho killers, and evil psychiatry. Cronenberg followed-up *Scanners* quite strongly with *Videodrome* (1983), a highly inventive film which raised existential questions about alternate realities and identity diffusion, as people are literally sucked into the transistor-tube dimension of their television sets. *Videodrome* also addresses questions about how close incessant television watching comes to voluntary mind control. The film cemented Cronenberg's cult status as a filmmaker, and warranted him his first really big budget production, for the 1983 film of Stephen King's novel, *The Dead Zone*, which may possibly be the best psycho thriller ever made. *The Dead Zone* was the first feature Cronenberg ever directed that he did not also write, which is why the story has more of a mainstream feel to it, though the standard Cronenberg themes of psychic powers, psycho killers, and evil government autocrats are still there. The movie also raises the interesting ethical dilemma intrinsic to clairvoyance: If you can see a catastrophe in the future, are you obligated to stop it?

Cronenberg followed up his great success with *The Dead Zone* with an adaptation of the classic sci-fi thriller, *The Fly* (1986). The film is more traditional sci-fi rather than psy-fi, though the hero (Jeff Goldblum) is a mad scientist who progresses from an initial state of megalomania to a frenzied state of outright psychosis, and the film raises some interesting questions about identity. *The Fly* was by far Cronenberg's biggest financial success as of yet, and though it is a very entertaining movie, it lacked the originality and singular vision of his former, more psychologically disturbing and less mainstream work.

To the delight of his fans (and the dismay of his executive producers), Cronenberg returned to his more offbeat and iconoclastic style of filmmaking after *The Fly*, and though he has found critical praise and regained his cult filmmaker status, his films have not been nearly as financially successful.

Films like *Dead Ringers* (1988), *Naked Lunch* (1991) — inspired by

William S. Burroughs surreal novel — and *Crash* (1996), linger on the classic Cronenberg themes of mind/body duality, identity confusion, and the eliciting of outright revulsion with the human body. His latest film, *Spider* (2002), based on a novel and screenplay by Patrick McGrath, is an extremely stylistic psychodrama that takes place mainly in the twisted mind of a tormented psychotic (Ralph Fiennes). Shot in noir style with many complex layers of oedipal themes and identity confusion, the film (predictably) did not find a mainstream audience, however, it remains a disturbing and highly artistic exploration of the spider web labyrinth that is the human mind. Currently, Cronenberg is working on a project based on a novel and screenplay by Martin Amis, *London Fields* (2006), which will mark a return to the psychic power theme, as the story is about a psychic woman who is driven to confront her future killer.

Future Masters

The work of specific other working writers and filmmakers have been recurrently addressed in this book. These writers and filmmakers, who seem to have the knack and proclivity for psy-fi material, may become the future masters of the genre, though it is impossible to tell, because the nature of the creative mind is that it is somewhat unpredictable. It is this mercurial nature of creativity itself that lends originality, inspiration, and genius to the work of great imaginations. First to mention is screenwriter Charlie Kaufman, who's screenplays for *Being John Malkovich* (1999), *Adaptation* (2002), and *Eternal Sunshine of the Spotless Mind* (2004) represent some of the most unique and innovative work in contemporary film. Writer-director Alex Proyas created two great modern psy-fi flicks: *Dark City* (1998), a psy-fi masterpiece which he wrote and directed, and the more mainstream, *I, Robot* (2004). Writer-director David Koepp's contributions to the genre include the script for the psychic superhero movie, *The Shadow* (1994), the psychic power thriller *Stir of Echoes* (1999), which he also directed, and *Secret Window* (2004), a film based on a Stephen King story, which Koepp wrote and directed. On a related note, Koepp also wrote the screenplays for the highly successful *Spider-Man* movies, which are filled with psy-fi themes such as mad science, evil alter egos, and psychic powers (i.e., "spidey senses").

The highly successful screenwriter, Akiva Goldsman, has written scripts for films focusing on psychological disorders — autism in *Silent Fall* (1994), and schizophrenia in *A Beautiful Mind* (2001) — as well as penning the screenplay for *I, Robot*. Michel Gondry directed and cowrote the story for *Eternal Sunshine of the Spotless Mind*, and his upcoming works, *The Science of Sleep* (2005) and *Masters of Space and Time* (2006), will also focus on existential psy-fi themes such as the dream world and alternate realities. And even though the Wachowski brothers' sole contribution to the genre has been *The Matrix* trilogy, this grand achievement is enough to warrant them a permanent position among the masters.

Bridges

In *Thus Spoke Zarathustra,* Nietzsche wrote: "the beautiful thing about Man is that he is a bridge." While Nietzsche was talking about Man as an evolutionary bridge to the Ubermensch, the idea of human beings as a bridge is also applicable to cultural ideas. Filmmakers, especially, are bridges. They take ideas that have been passed down for thousands of years in the form of archetypal characters and stories, and they make them relevant to modern audiences by recasting the timeless themes in modern form. Film, like all methods of storytelling and art, is a bridge that spans from former generations to generations to come. Film records our collective memories of ourselves, and shows them to our children and our children's children. The filmmakers discussed in this book are bridges. Their films provide a passageway from the past to the future.

The Top Twenty
Psy-Fi Movies

Everybody's a mad scientist, and life is their lab. We're all trying to experiment to find a way to live, to solve problems, to fend off madness and chaos.

David Cronenberg

Any book on a specific film genre would feel a bit lacking without the obligatory "top" list of films. The films in the following top twenty list were chosen primarily because of their significance in the development of the genre. For this reason, the films are listed chronologically, rather than in a more subjective order. As such, there is much variance in the quality of the films on the list. Nevertheless, each film was chosen because, in some way, it was particularly significant in its own era, as well as being a major influence on the psycho thrillers it preceded.

1. The Cabinet of Dr. Caligari *(1919)*

The original mold. A very important movie for many reasons, just about any book on film will include at least one discussion on *Caligari*. A seminal feature in the categories of horror and German expressionism, *Caligari* is also the first great psycho thriller, including staple psy-fi elements such as an evil psychiatrist/mad scientist, hypnocontrol, a psycho killer/somnambulist, and the dream world.

2. Dr. Jekyll and Mr. Hyde *(1931)*

The classic tale of mad science and psycho-philosophy gone awry, Robert Louis Stevenson's story was filmed many times, most notably by Paramount as a feature film in 1920 starring Lionel Barrymore, then again in 1931 starring Fredric March, and one more time in 1941 starring Spencer Tracy. The 1931 version, which garnered a best actor Academy Award for Fredric March, was chosen for this list because of its wonderful expressionistic sets and lustful treatment of Hyde's sexual demons, which was only temporarily possible in the early 1930s, before the strict production code on Hollywood movies was enforced by the studios.

3. Frankenstein *(1931)*

The story of *Frankenstein* is in some ways a template for the psy-fi film. Dr. Frankenstein himself represents the most ubiquitous representation of the mad scientist archetype. The story also portrays one of the most recurrent psy-fi themes, brain transplantation, and the predictable follies related to the procedure. The first film depiction of *Frankenstein* was a 16 minute short produced by Thomas Edison's motion picture company in 1910. A feature length remake of the tale was made in 1915, entitled *Life Without Soul*—the film has since been lost and not much is currently known about it. The definitive version of Shelley's tale was produced in 1931 by Universal Pictures. Subsequent to 1931, *Frankenstein* was remade many, many times, with notable actors such as Basil Rathbone, Sir Cedric Hardwicke, Peter Cushing, Sting, Gene Wilder, and Kenneth Branagh playing the role of the mad scientist, and equally notable actors such as Lon Chaney, Jr., Bela Lugosi, Christopher Lee, Peter Boyle, and Robert De Niro playing the role of the monster. Nevertheless, most horror and psy-fi fans would agree that Universal Pictures' 1931 and 1935 productions of the first two Frankenstein films, with Colin Clive as the doctor, Boris Karloff as the monster, Dwight Frye as the assistant, and James Whale directing, remain the definitive film versions of the story.

4. Spellbound *(1945)*

Mad love, bad psychiatry. A classic movie with an A-list cast and sumptuous production values (produced by David O. Selznick and directed by Alfred Hitchcock). For many people, this film was the first quasi-realistic

Left to right: Robby the Robot (as himself), Leslie Nielsen as Commander Adams, Walter Pidgeon as Dr. Morbius and Anne Francis as Altaira Morbius in *Forbidden Planet* (1956).

depiction of psychiatry they were ever exposed to. Though the psychiatrists and psychoanalytic methods in the film are anything but accurate, at least they weren't all charlatan quacks and evil mesmerists (only a couple were). *Spellbound* in many ways set the standard for the depiction of psychiatry in the cinema for the next two decades after its release. It is the prototypical psycho thriller of its era.

5. Forbidden Planet *(1956)*

Possibly the most overtly Freudian screenplay ever written. The film is a psy-fi oedipal play inspired by Shakespeare's *The Tempest*. It features a mad scientist who psychically projects his destructive libido through his dreams in the form of a murderous "Id monster." *Forbidden Planet* is a seminal film in both the sci-fi and psy-fi genres.

6. Psycho *(1960)*

Loosely based on the true story of psycho killer Ed Gein, this film single-handedly changed the horror genre forever. Hitchcock's masterpiece may also be called the first true psycho thriller, as the protagonist's psychological disorder is featured as the central focus of the film. The theme of the oedipal complex gone ballistic would become a staple leitmotif in the psycho killer genre. *Psycho* would also become a source of inspiration for later psy-fi masters such as Brian De Palma and David Cronenberg.

7. The Manchurian Candidate *(1962)*

John Frankenheimer's masterwork, this film liberated psy-fi themes from the horror and sci-fi genres. *Manchurian Candidate* is a smart, edgy, suspenseful political thriller with A-list actors and a great story. The film marks the moment when the psycho thriller genre is really born, as the story contains nearly all the psy-fi trademarks: mad science, evil psychiatry, mind control, a psycho killer, crises of identity and existence, and an expressionistic dream world.

8. A Clockwork Orange *(1971)*

Kubrick's disturbing vision of a mind-control future is brutal, shocking, and visionary. The scenes depicting the sinister "Ludovico treatment," in which young Alex "viddies" snuff films with his eyes stretched wide open with metal clamps, are the enduring images that most people remember about this film, as well as the weird costumes and make up, and the electrophonic classical music score. The film had an incalculable influence on the movies of the 1970s, a decade featuring many dystopian depictions of dark futuristic societies, which all in some way reference *Clockwork*. It remains one of Kubrick's most popular and controversial films.

9. Carrie *(1976)*

Two masters find each other. Stephen King's first novel provided the story for Brian De Palma's first commercial success. The film introduced the psy-fi element of psychic powers into the horror genre, and became the prototypical psycho thriller of its era, until Cronenberg's *The Dead Zone* came out in 1983. Like *Caligari*, *Dr. Jekyll*, and *Psycho*, *Carrie* reinvented the horror genre while simultaneously instilling the fear of the psychological unknown in the minds of film audiences. The horrifying climax, when *Carrie* turns her high school prom into an orgiastic bloodbath of violent revenge, is still one of the scariest sequences ever filmed. De Palma's follow-up to *Carrie*, *The Fury* (1978), is not a great movie, but it is an important film in the psycho thriller genre, because he took the theme of super-psychic powers out of the horror genre and into the more mainstream setting of a suspenseful espionage thriller. With an A-list cast and intriguing story, *The Fury* introduces the psy-fi staple theme of the government developing individuals with super-psychic powers as secret weapons. Themes such as the inscrutable causal relationship between psychic activity and nosebleeds, as well as the climactic scene in which a psychic telekinetically causes a person to explode, would become significant influences on later psy-fi films, especially Cronenberg's *Scanners*.

10. The Shining *(1980)*

Kubrick's masterful film taught filmmakers how to make a modern gothic horror movie. His film of a Stephen King novel moves hauntingly slow until it explodes into violence in the end. The climactic sequence in which an axe wielding psychotic father stalks his terrified son through a dark hedge maze looks and feels like a childhood nightmare with shadowy oedipal undertones. Once again, Kubrick's film would become a primary influence on a decade of films.

11. Scanners *(1981)*

Enter the master. This was not David Cronenberg's first major film — it followed his first two psycho thriller gems, *Shivers* (1975) and *The Brood* (1979) — but *Scanners* was the movie that made Cronenberg's name in Hollywood. The material here isn't new ... mad science, evil psychiatry, super-psychics bred as secret weapons, telepathy, telekinesis, multiple personalities, etc., but Cronenberg cranks everything up a notch. The film is intense and disturbing. The legendary head explosion scene provides what may possibly be the quintessential moment in psycho thriller screen history.

12. Blade Runner *(1982)*

Ridley Scott's visionary film of a Philip K. Dick novel makes the question of android humanity a tricky one, as the androids are cast as beautiful and artistic beings, with a desire to live and love that is equal to their human counterparts. The story is told visually, with rich noir sets that would influence later films such as *Dark City* (1998), *Artificial Intelligence: A.I.* (2001), and *Minority Report* (2002). The director's cut, now available on DVD, is far superior to the studio cut for the theatrical release, as the studio required a rather redundant explanatory voiceover, drastic cuts, and a tacked-on artificial ending.

13. The Dead Zone *(1983)*

The greatest psycho thriller of all time? A lot of things came together just right in this film to make it arguably the most significant and influential psy-fi movie ever made. The script was based on a novel by the master, Stephen King. Direction was provided by another master, David Cronenberg, who had just reached the full range of his talents as a filmmaker. The A-list cast is led by a blistering performance by Christopher Walken, in what may be his signature role. Walken is able to combine extreme intensity with utter believability, his natural creepiness investing the part with a surreal sense that he is truly disturbed by paranormal visions. The film has been emulated many times by many other psycho thrillers, and it has become a cultural icon. *Dead Zone* has been parodied by television shows such as *The Simpsons, Saturday Night Live,* and *South Park,* and it even spawned a television series on the USA network, starring Anthony Michael Hall.

14. Jacob's Ladder *(1990)*

This film's premise alludes to unethical LSD experiments performed on unwitting soldiers in the Vietnam era. The drug referred to in the movie is called "the ladder," but the conspiracy stuff is only a backdrop of the more existential themes, as Jacob (Tim Robbins) drifts in and out two possible future existences in a crazy dream world. Many movies, especially in the psycho thriller genre, try to draw their audience in to the confused and desperate world of the protagonist, but few pull it off quite as well as this film, as Jacob is forced to doubt his own sanity, suspecting that nothing he encounters truly exists. Jacob's experience of being trapped in his own nightmare recaptures our own experiences in the dream world, a place that doesn't exist in our waking reality, and a place that can turn into a horrible nightmare at any turn.

15. Dark City *(1998)*

Classic noir style, expressionistic sets, great cast, and a complex, sophisticated plot make this film a much overlooked masterpiece. Super-intelligent aliens, mad scientists, a psycho killer, telepathy, telekinesis, mind control, memory erasure ... this one's got it all. No 20-minute kung fu fights and shootouts like in *The Matrix*, the feel of this movie is gloomy, pensive, and haunting.

16 Being John Malkovich *(1999)*

Charlie Kaufman thickens the plot. It is fitting that the '90s began with *Jacob's Ladder* and ended with *Being John Malkovich*. The two films explore similar existential issues, treading the shadowy paths of memory and identity, and dealing directly with the enigmatic nature of being. Charlie Kaufman's complex and wickedly funny script stands out as the true star, though the film's wonderful visual style points to great direction as well by Spike Jonze (both Kaufman and Jonze were nominated for Academy Awards). The film also boasts an excellent A-list cast. John Cusack and John Malkovich (as himself) are brilliant. *Malkovich* shows that a psy-fi film can be complex, sophisticated, and visually stunning, while also being funny as hell. It is the first great psy-fi comedy.

17. Memento *(2000)*

The best movie about nontransient anterograde amnesia ever made ... but seriously, an amazing work of art. A complex and sophisticated film, shot in noir style, the film drives home the elusive idea that identity and memory are one. Don't believe the people who say that this film is too confusing. It requires that you pay attention, but it pays off with a great reward. One of the rare films that excels on artistic, emotional, and intellectual levels.

18. Vanilla Sky *(2001)*

Cameron Crowe's remake of the Spanish film, *Abre los Ojos* (1997), was criticized by many for being a big budget yet inferior knockoff of the original. The main difference between the two films is that *Abre los Ojos* is foreign and *Vanilla Sky* is American Hollywood. Once you accept the fact that you're watching a big Hollywood production, it turns out to be a fun ride. *Vanilla Sky* is the best film that takes place almost entirely in a dream since *The Wizard of Oz* (1939).

19. Minority Report *(2002)*

A psy-fi masterpiece. Stephen Spielberg, the premier director of his generation, takes a story by sci-fi legend Philip K. Dick and creates a haunting vision of a world in which crime is controlled via psychic powers. Like his mentor, Stanley Kubrick, Spielberg sets his tale in the harrowing future. Criminals are arrested before they commit crimes, because the "pre-cogs," mutant psychics with super-precognitive abilities, can foresee their offenses before they are committed. The film is sophisticated on both visual and intellectual levels, as the existential dilemma inherent to clairvoyance — changing the future — is dealt with in great style.

20. Eternal Sunshine of the Spotless Mind *(2004)*

Charlie Kaufman does it again, providing another fresh and amusing take on mind and existence. Kate Winslet and Jim Carey are great as the bickering star-crossed lovers who care for each other in spite of themselves. The chase sequence in Joel's brain manages to be both funny and profound, depicting how half-forgotten memories and feelings from early childhood can still affect us as adults, without us even knowing about it. It's great when movies can express wonderful psychoanalytic ideas without having to resort to Freudian psycho-jargon.

Filmography

Abbott and Costello Meet Frankenstein (1948). *Directed by* Charles Barton. *Writing Credits:* Robert Lees and Frederic Rinaldo. *Starring:* Bud Abbott and Lou Costello.

Abre los Ojos (1997). *Directed by* Alejandro Amenábar. *Writing Credits:* Alejandro Amenábar and Mateo Gil. *Starring:* Eduardo Noriega, Penélope Cruz, and Chete Lera.

Adaptation (2002). *Directed by* Spike Jonze. *Writing Credits:* Charlie Kaufman and Susan Orlean (novel). *Starring:* Nicolas Cage, Meryl Streep and Chris Cooper.

Alice (1990). *Directed by* Woody Allen. *Writing Credits:* Woody Allen. *Starring:* Mia Farrow.

All Quiet on the Western Front (1930). *Directed by* Lewis Milestone. *Writing Credits:* Maxwell Anderson and Erich Maria Remarque (novel). *Starring:* Louis Wolheim and Lew Aryes. *Academy Awards:* Best Director and Best Picture.

American Psycho (2000). *Directed by* Mary Harron. *Writing Credits:* Mary Harron and Bret Easton Ellis (novel). *Starring:* Christian Bale.

Anastasia (1956). *Directed by* Anatole Litvak. *Writing Credits:* Arthur Laurents, Marcelle Maurette (play) and Guy Bolton (play adaptation). *Starring:* Ingrid Bergman. *Academy Awards:* Best Actress in a Leading Role (Bergman).

Angel Heart (1987). *Directed by* Alan Parker. *Writing Credits:* Alan Parker and William Hjortsberg (novel). *Starring:* Mickey Rourke and Robert De Niro.

Annie Hall (1977). *Directed by* Woody Allen. *Writing Credits:* Woody Allen and Marshall Brickman. *Starring:* Woody Allen, Diane Keaton, Tony Roberts, Carol Kane, Paul Simon, and Shelley Duvall. *Academy Awards:* Best Actress in a

Leading Role (Keaton), Best Director and Best Writing, Screenplay Written Directly for the Screen.

Anything Else (2003). *Directed by* Woody Allen. *Writing Credits:* Woody Allen. *Starring:* Jason Biggs, Christina Ricci and Woody Allen.

Apocalypse Now (1979). *Directed by* Francis Ford Coppola. *Writing Credits:* Francis Ford Coppola, John Milius and Joseph Conrad (novel). *Starring:* Martin Sheen and Marlon Brando.

Artificial Intelligence: A.I. (2001). *Directed by* Steven Spielberg. *Writing Credits:* Ian Watson (screen story), Brian Aldiss (short story), and Steven Spielberg (screenplay). *Starring:* Haley Joel Osment, Jude Law, Frances O'Connor, Brendan Gleeson, Sam Robards, and William Hurt.

As Good as It Gets (1997). *Directed by* James L. Brooks. *Writing Credits:* Mark Andrus (story and screenplay) and James L. Brooks (screenplay). *Starring:* Jack Nicholson and Helen Hunt. *Academy Awards:* Best Actor in a Leading Role (Nicholson) and Best Actress in a Leading Role (Hunt).

Audrey Rose (1977). *Directed by* Robert Wise. *Writing Credits:* Frank De Felitta (also novel). *Starring:* Marsha Mason.

Austin Powers: International Man of Mystery (1997). *Directed by* Jay Roach. *Writing Credits:* Mike Myers. *Starring:* Mike Myers.

The Aviator (2004). *Directed by* Martin Scorsese. *Writing Credits:* John Logan. *Starring:* Leonardo DiCaprio.

Badlands (1973). *Directed by* Terrence Malick. *Writing Credits:* Terrence Malick. *Starring:* Martin Sheen and Sissy Spacek.

Barry Lyndon (1975). *Directed by* Stanley Kubrick. *Writing Credits:* Stanley Kubrick and William Makepeace Thackeray (novel). *Starring:* Ryan O'Neal.

A Beautiful Mind (2001). *Directed by* Ron Howard. *Writing Credits:* Akiva Goldsman and Sylvia Nasar (book). *Starring:* Russell Crowe and Jennifer Connelly. *Academy Awards:* Best Actress in a Supporting Role (Connelly), Best Director, Best Picture, and Best Writing, Screenplay Based on Material Previously Produced or Published (Goldsman).

Being John Malkovich (1999). *Directed by* Spike Jonze. *Writing Credits:* Charlie Kaufman. *Starring:* John Cusack and John Malkovich.

The Believers (1987). *Directed by* John Schlesinger. *Writing Credits:* Mark Frost and Nicholas Conde (novel). *Starring:* Martin Sheen.

The Best Years of Our Lives (1946). *Directed by* William Wyler. *Writing Credits:* Robert E. Sherwood and MacKinlay Kantor (novel). *Starring:* Dana Andrews, Fredric March, Harold Russell and Myrna Loy. *Academy Awards:* Best Actor in a Lead Role (March), Best Actor in a Supporting Role (Russell),

Best Director, Best Picture, and Best Writing, Screenplay Based on Material Previously Produced or Published (Sherwood).

The Bible (1966). *Directed by* John Huston. *Writing Credits:* Vittorio Bonicelli, et al. *Starring:* George C. Scott.

The Big Parade (1925). *Directed by* King Vidor. *Writing Credits:* Harry Behn and Joseph Farnham (play). *Starring:* John Gilbert.

Birdman of Alcatraz (1962). *Directed by* John Frankenheimer. *Writing Credits:* Guy Trosper and Thomas E. Gaddis (book). *Starring:* Burt Lancaster.

The Birds (1963). *Directed by* Alfred Hitchcock. *Writing Credits:* Daphne Du Maurier (story) and Evan Hunter (screenplay). *Starring:* Rod Taylor and Tippi Hedren.

The Black Cat (1934). *Directed by* Edgar G. Ulmer. *Writing Credits:* Edgar G. Ulmer (screenplay), Peter Ruric (screen story) and Edgar Allan Poe (story). *Starring:* Boris Karloff and Bela Lugosi.

The Black Dahlia (2005). *Directed by* Brian De Palma. *Writing Credits:* Josh Friedman (screenplay) and James Ellroy (novel). *Starring:* Scarlett Johansson.

Black Sunday (1977). *Directed by* John Frankenheimer. *Writing Credits:* Ernest Lehman (screenplay) and Thomas Harris (novel). *Starring:* Robert Shaw and Bruce Dern.

Blade Runner (1982). *Directed by* Ridley Scott. *Writing Credits:* Hampton Fancher and David Peoples (screenplay) and Philip K. Dick (novel). *Starring:* Harrison Ford.

Blind Alley (1939). *Directed by* Charles Vidor. *Writing Credits:* Philip Mac-Donald, et al. (screenplay) and James Warwick (play). *Starring:* Chester Morris and Ralph Bellamy.

The Blob (1958). *Directed by* Irvin S. Yeaworth, Jr. *Writing Credits:* Kay Linaker (screenplay) and Irving H. Millgate (story). *Starring:* Steve McQueen.

Blow Out (1981). *Directed by* Brian De Palma, Jr. *Writing Credits:* Brian De Palma. *Starring:* John Travolta.

The Blue Dahlia (1946). *Directed by* George Marshall. *Writing Credits:* Raymond Chandler. *Starring:* Alan Ladd and Veronica Lake.

Body Double (1984). *Directed by* Brian De Palma, Jr. *Writing Credits:* Brian De Palma and Robert J. Avrech. *Starring:* Craig Wasson and Melanie Griffith.

Bonnie and Clyde (1967). *Directed by* Arthur Penn. *Writing Credits:* David Newman and Robert Benton. *Starring:* Warren Beatty, Faye Dunaway, Michael J. Pollard, Gene Hackman, and Estelle Parsons. *Academy Award:* Best Actress in a Supporting Role (Parsons).

The Boston Strangler (1968). *Directed by* Richard Fleischer. *Writing Credits:* Edward Anhalt (screenplay) and Gerold Frank (book). *Starring:* Tony Curtis and Henry Fonda.

The Bourne Identity (2002). *Directed by* Doug Liman. *Writing Credits:* Tony Gilroy (screenplay) and Robert Ludlum (novel). *Starring:* Matt Damon.

Brainstorm (1983). *Directed by* Douglas Trumbull. *Writing Credits:* Philip Frank Messina (screenplay) and Bruce Joel Rubin (story). *Starring:* Christopher Walken and Natalie Wood.

Brave New World (1998) (TV). *Directed by* Leslie Libman and Larry Williams. *Writing Credits:* Dan Mazur and Aldous Huxley (novel). *Starring:* Peter Gallagher and Leonard Nimoy.

Bride of Frankenstein (1935). *Directed by* James Whale. *Writing Credits:* Mary Shelley (novel) and William Hurlbut (adaptation). *Starring:* Boris Karloff, Colin Clive, Valerie Hobson, and Elsa Lanchester.

Bride of the Monster (1955). *Directed by* Ed Wood. *Writing Credits:* Ed Wood and Alex Gordon. *Starring:* Bela Lugosi.

Broadway Danny Rose (1984). *Directed by* Woody Allen. *Writing Credits:* Woody Allen. *Starring:* Woody Allen and Mia Farrow.

The Brood (1979). *Directed by* David Cronenberg. *Writing Credits:* David Cronenberg. *Starring:* Oliver Reed and Samantha Eggar.

The Butterfly Effect (2004). *Directed by* Eric Bress and J. Mackye Gruber. *Writing Credits:* Eric Bress and J. Mackye Gruber. *Starring:* Ashton Kutcher.

The Cabinet of Dr. Caligari (1919). *Directed by* Robert Wiene. *Writing Credits:* Hans Janowitz and Carl Mayer. *Starring:* Werner Krauss, Conrad Veidt, and Friedrich Feher.

Captain Newman, M.D. (1963). *Directed by* David Miller. *Writing Credits:* Richard L. Breen and Henry Ephron. *Starring:* Gregory Peck.

Carlito's Way (1993). *Directed by* Brian De Palma. *Writing Credits:* Edwin Torres (novel) and David Koepp (adaptation). *Starring:* Al Pacino.

Carrie (1976). *Directed by* Brian De Palma. *Writing Credits:* Lawrence D. Cohen and Stephen King (novel). *Starring:* Sissy Spacek, Piper Laurie, and Amy Irving.

Chandu the Magician (1932). *Directed by* William Cameron Menzies and Marcel Varnel. *Writing Credits:* Harry A. Earnshaw and Vera M. Oldham. *Starring:* Bela Lugosi.

Children of the Damned (1963). *Directed by* Anton Leader. *Writing Credits:* John Briley. *Starring:* Ian Hendry.

Christine (1983). *Directed by* John Carpenter. *Writing Credits:* Stephen King (novel) and Bill Phillips (screenplay). *Starring:* Keith Gordon.

A Clockwork Orange (1971). *Directed by* Stanley Kubrick. *Writing Credits:* Stanley Kubrick and Anthony Burgess (novel). *Starring:* Malcolm McDowell.

Close Encounters of the Third Kind (1977). *Directed by* Steven Spielberg. *Writing Credits:* Steven Spielberg. *Starring:* Richard Dreyfuss, François Truffaut, and Teri Garr.

Color of Night (1994). *Directed by* Richard Rush. *Writing Credits:* Billy Ray and Matthew Chapman. *Starring:* Bruce Willis and Jane March.

Coming Home (1978). *Directed by* Hal Ashby. *Writing Credits:* Nancy Dowd, Waldo Salt and Robert C. Jones. *Starring:* Jane Fonda, Bruce Dern and Jon Voight. *Academy Awards:* Best Actor in a Leading Role (Voight), Best Actress in a Leading Role (Fonda) and Best Writing, Screenplay Written Directly for the Screen.

Conflict (1945). *Directed by* Curtis Bernhardt. *Writing Credits:* Arthur T. Horman and Alfred Neumann. *Starring:* Humphrey Bogart.

Conspiracy Theory (1997). *Directed by* Richard Donner. *Writing Credits:* Brian Helgeland. *Starring:* Mel Gibson and Julia Roberts.

Crash (1996). *Directed by* David Cronenberg. *Writing Credits:* David Cronenberg and J.G. Ballard (novel). *Starring:* James Spader and Holly Hunter.

Crime and Punishment (1935). *Directed by* Josef von Sternberg. *Writing Credits:* Joseph Anthony and Fyodor Dostoyevsky (novel). *Starring:* Peter Lorre.

The Criminal Hypnotist (1909). *Directed by* D.W. Griffith. *Writing Credits:* D.W. Griffith. *Starring:* Arthur V. Johnson.

The Curse of the Jade Scorpion (2001). *Directed by* Woody Allen. *Writing Credits:* Woody Allen. *Starring:* Woody Allen and Helen Hunt.

Dahmer (2002). *Directed by* David Jacobson. *Writing Credits:* David Jacobson. *Starring:* Jeremy Renner.

Damien: Omen II (1978). *Directed by* Don Taylor. *Writing Credits:* Harvey Bernhard and Stanley Mann. *Starring:* William Holden and Jonathan Scott-Taylor.

Dark City (1998). *Directed by* Alex Proyas. *Writing Credits:* Alex Proyas. *Starring:* Rufus Sewell, William Hurt, Kiefer Sutherland and Jennifer Connelly.

The Dark Half (1993). *Directed by* George A. Romero. *Writing Credits:* George A. Romero and Stephen King (novel). *Starring:* Timothy Hutton.

The Dark Past (1948). *Directed by* Rudolph Maté. *Writing Credits:* Michael Blankfort and Albert Duffy. *Starring:* William Holden and Lee J. Cobb.

David and Lisa (1962). *Directed by* Frank Perry. *Writing Credits:* Eleanor Perry and Theodore Isaac Rubin (novel). *Starring:* Keir Dullea and Janet Margolin.

Days of Wine and Roses (1962). *Directed by* Blake Edwards. *Writing Credits:* J.P. Miller. *Starring:* Jack Lemmon and Lee Remick.

Dead Again (1991). *Directed by* Kenneth Branagh. *Writing Credits:* Scott Frank. *Starring:* Kenneth Branagh and Emma Thompson.

Dead Ringers (1988). *Directed by* David Cronenberg. *Writing Credits:* Bari Wood and Jack Geasland (novel), David Cronenberg and Norman Snider (screenplay). *Starring:* Jeremy Irons.

The Dead Zone (1983). *Directed by* David Cronenberg. *Writing Credits:* Jeffrey Boam and Stephen King (novel). *Starring:* Christopher Walken.

The Deadly Mantis (1957). *Directed by* Nathan Juran. *Writing Credits:* William Alland and Martin Berkeley. *Starring:* Craig Stevens.

Deconstructing Harry (1997). *Directed by* Woody Allen. *Writing Credits:* Woody Allen. *Starring:* Woody Allen.

The Deer Hunter (1978). *Directed by* Michael Cimino. *Writing Credits:* Michael Cimino and Deric Washburn. *Starring:* John Savage, Robert De Niro, John Cazale, and Christopher Walken. *Academy Awards:* Best Actor in a Supporting Role (Walken), Best Director, and Best Picture.

The Deliberate Stranger (1986). *Directed by* Marvin J. Chomsky. *Writing Credits:* Hesper Anderson and Richard W. Larsen (book). *Starring:* Mark Harmon.

Demon Seed (1977). *Directed by* Donald Cammell. *Writing Credits:* Robert Jaffe and Dean R. Koontz (novel). *Starring:* Julie Christie.

Dial M for Murder (1954). *Directed by* Alfred Hitchcock. *Writing Credits:* Frederick Knott (play and adaptation). *Starring:* Ray Milland and Grace Kelly.

Diary of a Mad Housewife (1970). *Directed by* Frank Perry. *Writing Credits:* Eleanor Perry and Sue Kaufman (novel). *Starring:* Carrie Snodgress.

Die Hard (1988). *Directed by* John McTiernan. *Writing Credits:* Jeb Stuart and Roderick Thorp (novel). *Starring:* Bruce Willis and Alan Rickman.

Disturbing Behavior (1998). *Directed by* David Nutter. *Writing Credits:* Scott Rosenberg. *Starring:* James Marsden and Katie Holmes.

Dr. Jekyll and Mr. Hyde (1920). *Directed by* John S. Robertson. *Writing Credits:* Clara Beranger and Robert Louis Stevenson (story). *Starring:* John Barrymore, Martha Mansfield, and Brandon Hurst.

Dr. Jekyll and Mr. Hyde (1931). *Directed by* Rouben Mamoulian. *Writing Credits:* Samuel Hoffenstein and Robert Louis Stevenson (story). *Starring:* Fredric March. *Academy Award:* Best Actor in a Leading Role (March).

Dr. Jekyll and Mr. Hyde (1941). *Directed by* Victor Fleming. *Writing Credits:* John Lee Mahin and Robert Louis Stevenson (story). *Starring:* Spencer Tracy.

Dr. Strangelove, or: How I Learned to Stop Worrying and Love the Bomb (1964). *Directed by* Stanley Kubrick. *Writing Credits:* Stanley Kubrick and Peter George (novel). *Starring:* Peter Sellers, George C. Scott and Sterling Hayden.

Don't Say a Word (2001). *Directed by* Gary Fleder. *Writing Credits:* Anthony Peckham and Andrew Klavan (novel). *Starring:* Michael Douglas and Brittany Murphy.

Down to Earth (2001). *Directed by* Chris Weitz and Paul Weitz. *Writing Credits:* Chris Rock et al. *Starring:* Chris Rock.

Dracula (1931). *Directed by* Tod Browning. *Writing Credits:* John L. Balderston (story), Hamilton Deane (story), and Bram Stoker (novel). *Starring:* Bela Lugosi and Helen Chandler.

Dreamcatcher (2003). *Directed by* Lawrence Kasdan. *Writing Credits:* William Goldman and Stephen King (novel). *Starring:* Morgan Freeman.

Dreamscape (1984). *Directed by* Joseph Ruben. *Writing Credits:* David Loughery. *Starring:* Dennis Quaid and Max von Sydow.

Dressed to Kill (1980). *Directed by* Brian De Palma. *Writing Credits:* Brian De Palma. *Starring:* Angie Dickinson and Michael Caine.

Drugstore Cowboy (1989). *Directed by* Gus Van Sant. *Writing Credits:* Gus Van Sant and James Fogle (novel). *Starring:* Matt Dillon.

Ed Wood (1994). *Directed by* Tim Burton. *Writing Credits:* Scott Alexander and Rudolph Grey (book). *Starring:* Johnny Depp and Martin Landau. *Academy Award:* Best Actor in a Supporting Role (Landau).

Edge of Sanity (1989). *Directed by* Gérard Kikoïne. *Writing Credits:* J.P. Felix and Ron Raley. *Starring:* Anthony Perkins.

Equilibrium (2002). *Directed by* Kurt Wimmer. *Writing Credits:* Kurt Wimmer. *Starring:* Christian Bale.

Equus (1977). *Directed by* Sidney Lumet. *Writing Credits:* Peter Shaffer (also play). *Starring:* Richard Burton, Peter Firth, Colin Blakely, and Joan Plowright.

Eternal Sunshine of the Spotless Mind (2004). *Directed by* Michel Gondry. *Writing Credits:* Charlie Kaufman and Michel Gondry (story). *Starring:* Jim Carrey and Kate Winslet.

Everything You Always Wanted to Know About Sex * But Were Afraid to Ask (1972). *Directed by* Woody Allen. *Writing Credits:* Woody Allen and David Reuben (book). *Starring:* Woody Allen and Gene Wilder.

eXistenZ (1999). *Directed by* David Cronenberg. *Writing Credits:* David Cronenberg. *Starring:* Jennifer Jason Leigh and Jude Law.

The Exorcist (1973). *Directed by* William Friedkin. *Writing Credits:* William Peter Blatty (also novel). *Starring:* Ellen Burstyn, Max von Sydow, Jason Miller, and Lee J. Cobb. *Academy Award:* Best Writing, Screenplay Based on Material from Another Medium.

The Exorcist II (1977). *Directed by* John Boorman. *Writing Credits:* William Goodhart and William Peter Blatty (characters). *Starring:* Richard Burton, Linda Blair, Louise Fletcher and Max von Sydow.

Eyes Wide Shut (1999). *Directed by* Stanley Kubrick. *Writing Credits:* Stanley Kubrick and Arthur Schnitzler (novel). *Starring:* Tom Cruise and Nicole Kidman.

The Face Behind the Mask (1941). *Directed by* Robert Florey. *Writing Credits:* Paul Jarrico and Arthur Levinson (story). *Starring:* Peter Lorre.

Fahrenheit 451 (1966). *Directed by* François Truffaut. *Writing Credits:* François Truffaut, Jean-Louis Richard and Ray Bradbury (novel). *Starring:* Oskar Werner and Julie Christie.

50 First Dates (2004). *Directed by* Peter Segal. *Writing Credits:* George Wing. *Starring:* Adam Sandler and Drew Barrymore.

A Fine Madness (1966). *Directed by* Irvin Kershner. *Writing Credits:* Elliot Baker (also novel). *Starring:* Sean Connery and Joanne Woodward.

Finian's Rainbow (1968). *Directed by* Francis Ford Coppola. *Writing Credits:* E.Y. Harburg and Fred Saidy. *Starring:* Fred Astaire and Petula Clark.

Firestarter (1984). *Directed by* Mark L. Lester. *Writing Credits:* Stanley Mann and Stephen King (novel). *Starring:* David Keith and Drew Barrymore.

Firestarter 2: Rekindled (2002). *Directed by* Robert Iscove. *Writing Credits:* Philip Eisner and Stephen King (novel). *Starring:* Marguerite Moreau and Malcolm McDowell.

The Fisher King (1991). *Directed by* Terry Gilliam. *Writing Credits:* Richard LaGravenese. *Starring:* Jeff Bridges, Adam Bryant, Robin Williams, Paul J. Lombardi, and Mercedes Ruehl. *Academy Award:* Best Actress in a Supporting Role (Ruehl).

The Fixer (1968). *Directed by* John Frankenheimer. *Writing Credits:* Dalton Trumbo and Bernard Malamud (novel). *Starring:* Alan Bates.

The Fly (1986). *Directed by* David Cronenberg. *Writing Credits:* David Cronenberg and George Langelaan (story). *Starring:* Jeff Goldblum.

Forbidden Planet (1956). *Directed by* Fred M. Wilcox. *Writing Credits:* Irving Block (story), Allen Adler (story), and Cyril Hume. *Starring:* Walter Pidgeon, Anne Francis, and Leslie Nielsen.

Fourteen Hours (1951). *Directed by* Henry Hathaway. *Writing Credits:* John Paxton and Joel Sayre (article). *Starring:* Paul Douglas and Richard Basehart.

Frankenstein (1931). *Directed by* James Whale. *Writing Credits:* Mary Shelley (novel) and Peggy Webling (play). *Starring:* Colin Clive, Mae Clarke, and John Boles.

Freaks (1932). *Directed by* Tod Browning. *Writing Credits:* Tod Browning and Clarence Aaron Robbins. *Starring:* Harry Earles, Wallace Ford and Leila Hyams.

Freddy vs. Jason (2003). *Directed by* Ronny Yu. *Writing Credits:* Damian Shannon and Mark Swift (screenplay), Wes Craven and Victor Miller (characters). *Starring:* Robert Englund and Ken Kirzinger.

Frenzy (1972). *Directed by* Alfred Hitchcock. *Writing Credits:* Anthony Shaffer and Arthur La Bern (novel). *Starring:* Jon Finch.

Freud (1962). *Directed by* John Huston. *Writing Credits:* Charles Kaufman and Wolfgang Reinhardt. *Starring:* Montgomery Clift.

Friday the 13th (1980). *Directed by* Sean S. Cunningham. *Writing Credits:* Victor Miller. *Starring:* Betsy Palmer and Adrienne King.

Friday the 13th Part VII: The New Blood (1988). *Directed by* John Carl Buechler. *Writing Credits:* Manuel Fidello, Daryl Haney and Victor Miller (characters). *Starring:* Kane Hodder.

From Hell (2001). *Directed by* Albert Hughes and Allen Hughes. *Writing Credits:* Terry Hayes and Rafael Yglesias (screenplay), Alan Moore and Eddie Campbell (graphic novel). *Starring:* Johnny Depp and Heather Graham.

Full Metal Jacket (1987). *Directed by* Stanley Kubrick. *Writing Credits:* Stanley Kubrick and Michael Herr (screenplay) and Gustav Hasford (novel). *Starring:* Matthew Modine and Vincent D'Onofrio.

The Fury (1978). *Directed by* Brian De Palma. *Writing Credits:* John Farris (also novel). *Starring:* Kirk Douglas, Amy Irving, Andrew Stevens and John Cassavetes.

Ghost (1990). *Directed by* Jerry Zucker. *Writing Credits:* Bruce Joel Rubin. *Starring:* Patrick Swayze, Demi Moore and Whoopi Goldberg. *Academy Awards:* Best Actress in a Supporting Role (Goldberg), and Best Writing, Screenplay Written Directly for the Screen.

The Ghoul (1933). *Directed by* T. Hayes Hunter. *Writing Credits:* Leonard Hines, Frank King (play) and Rupert Downing (adaptation). *Starring:* Boris Karloff.

The Gift (2000). *Directed by* Sam Raimi. *Writing Credits:* Billy Bob Thornton and Tom Epperson. *Starring:* Cate Blanchett.

Girl, Interrupted (1999). *Directed by* James Mangold. *Writing Credits:* James

Mangold and Susanna Kaysen. *Starring:* Winona Ryder, Angelina Jolie and Whoopi Goldberg. *Academy Award:* Best Actress in a Supporting Role (Jolie).

Gods and Monsters (1998). *Directed by* Bill Condon. *Writing Credits:* Bill Condon and Christopher Bram (novel). *Starring:* Ian McKellen and Brendan Fraser. *Academy Award:* Best Writing, Screenplay Based on Material from Another Medium (Condon).

Godzilla, King of the Monsters (1956). *Directed by* Ishirô Honda and Terry O. Morse. *Writing Credits:* Ishirô Honda and Shigeru Kayama (story). *Starring:* Raymond Burr.

Der Golem (1915). *Directed by* Henrik Galeen and Paul Wegener. *Writing Credits:* Henrik Galeen and Gustav Meyrink (novel). *Starring:* Paul Wegener.

Der Golem, wie er in die Welt kam (1920). *Directed by* Carl Boese and Paul Wegener. *Writing Credits:* Henrik Galeen and Gustav Meyrink (novel). *Starring:* Paul Wegener.

Good Will Hunting (1997). *Directed by* Gus Van Sant. *Writing Credits:* Matt Damon and Ben Affleck. *Starring:* Robin Williams, Matt Damon, Ben Affleck, Stellan Skarsgård, and Minnie Driver. *Academy Awards:* Best Actor in a Supporting Role (Williams), and Best Writing, Screenplay Written Directly for the Screen.

Goodfellas (1990). *Directed by* Martin Scorsese. *Writing Credits:* Nicholas Pileggi (also book). *Starring:* Robert De Niro, Joe Pesci and Ray Liotta. *Academy Award:* Best Actor in a Supporting Role (Pesci).

Gothika (2003). *Directed by* Mathieu Kassovitz. *Writing Credits:* Sebastian Gutierrez. *Starring:* Halle Berry.

Grand Prix (1966). *Directed by* John Frankenheimer. *Writing Credits:* Robert Alan Aurthur and John Frankenheimer. *Starring:* James Garner.

The Green Mile (1999). *Directed by* Frank Darabont. *Writing Credits:* Frank Darabont and Stephen King (novel). *Starring:* Tom Hanks.

Halloween (1978). *Directed by* John Carpenter. *Writing Credits:* John Carpenter (screenplay) and Debra Hill (screenplay). *Starring:* Donald Pleasence, Jamie Lee Curtis, and Nancy Kyes.

Hannah and Her Sisters (1986). *Directed by* Woody Allen. *Writing Credits:* Woody Allen. *Starring:* Barbara Hershey, Carrie Fisher, Mia Farrow, Dianne Wiest, and Maureen O'Sullivan. *Academy Awards:* Best Actor in a Supporting Role (Caine) and Best Actress in a Supporting Role (Wiest).

Harold and Maude (1971). *Directed by* Hal Ashby. *Writing Credits:* Colin Higgins. *Starring:* Ruth Gordon and Bud Cort.

Hearts in Atlantis (2001). *Directed by* Scott Hicks. *Writing Credits:* William Goldman and Stephen King (novel). *Starring:* Anthony Hopkins.

Heaven Can Wait (1943). *Directed by* Ernst Lubitsch. *Writing Credits:* Samson Raphaelson and Leslie Bush-Fekete (play). *Starring:* Don Ameche and Gene Tierney.

Heaven Can Wait (1978). *Directed by* Warren Beatty and Buck Henry. *Writing Credits:* Elaine May, Warren Beatty and Harry Segall (play). *Starring:* Warren Beatty.

Helter Skelter (1976) (TV). *Directed by* Tom Gries. *Writing Credits:* J.P. Miller (screenplay), Curt Gentry and Vincent Bugliosi (book). *Starring:* George DiCenzo and Steve Railsback.

Henry: Portrait of a Serial Killer (1986). *Directed by* John McNaughton. *Writing Credits:* Richard Fire and John McNaughton. *Starring:* Michael Rooker.

The Hours (2002). *Directed by* Stephen Daldry. *Writing Credits:* David Hare and Michael Cunningham (novel). *Starring:* Nicole Kidman, Julianne Moore and Meryl Streep.

House of Cards (1993). *Directed by* Michael Lessac. *Writing Credits:* Michael Lessac and Robert Jay Litz (story). *Starring:* Kathleen Turner and Tommy Lee Jones.

Husbands and Wives (1992). *Directed by* Woody Allen. *Writing Credits:* Woody Allen. *Starring:* Woody Allen and Mia Farrow.

I, Robot (2004). *Directed by* Alex Proyas. *Writing Credits:* Jeff Vintar, Akiva Goldsman, and Isaac Asimov (novel). *Starring:* Will Smith and Bridget Moynahan.

I Was a Teenage Werewolf (1957). *Directed by* Gene Fowler Jr. *Writing Credits:* Herman Cohen and Aben Kandel. *Starring:* Michael Landon, Yvonne Lime, and Whit Bissell.

Identity (2003). *Directed by* James Mangold. *Writing Credits:* Michael Cooney. *Starring:* John Cusack and Ray Liotta.

Impostor (2002). *Directed by* Gary Fleder. *Writing Credits:* Philip K. Dick (story), Scott Rosenberg et al. *Starring:* Gary Sinise.

In Cold Blood (1967). *Directed by* Richard Brooks. *Writing Credits:* Richard Brooks and Truman Capote (book). *Starring:* Robert Blake and Scott Wilson.

In Dreams (1999). *Directed by* Neil Jordan. *Writing Credits:* Bari Wood (novel), Bruce Robinson (screenplay) and Neil Jordan (screenplay). *Starring:* Annette Bening, Katie Sagona, Aidan Quinn, and Robert Downey Jr.

In the Dark (2003) (TV). *Directed by* Leonard Farlinger. *Writing Credits:* R.B. Carney and David Fraser. *Starring:* Kathleen Robertson.

Insomnia (2002). *Directed by* Christopher Nolan. *Writing Credits:* Hillary

Seitz, Nikolaj Frobenius and Erik Skjoldbjærg. *Starring:* Al Pacino and Robin Williams.

Interiors (1978). *Directed by* Woody Allen. *Writing Credits:* Woody Allen. *Starring:* Diane Keaton.

Invasion of the Body Snatchers (1956). *Directed by* Don Siegel. *Writing Credits:* Daniel Mainwaring and Jack Finney (novel). *Starring:* Kevin McCarthy.

The Invisible Man (1933). *Directed by* James Whale. *Writing Credits:* R.C. Sherriff and H.G. Wells (novel). *Starring:* Claude Rains.

The Invisible Ray (1936). *Directed by* Lambert Hillyer. *Writing Credits:* Howard Higgin and Douglas Hodges (story), and John Colton (screenplay). *Starring:* Boris Karloff and Bela Lugosi.

The Island of Dr. Moreau (1996). *Directed by* John Frankenheimer. *Writing Credits:* Richard Stanley and Ron Hutchinson (screenplay), and H.G. Wells (novel). *Starring:* Val Kilmer and Marlon Brando.

The Island of Lost Souls aka The Island of Dr. Moreau (1933). *Directed by* Erle C. Kenton. *Writing Credits:* Waldemar Young and Philip Wylie (screenplay), and H.G. Wells (novel). *Starring:* Charles Laughton.

Island of the Doomed Men (1940). *Directed by* Charles Barton. *Writing Credits:* Robert Hardy Andrews. *Starring:* Peter Lorre.

J'Accuse (1938). *Directed by* Abel Gance. *Writing Credits:* Steve Passeur and Abel Gance. *Starring:* Victor Francen.

Jack the Ripper (1976). *Directed by* Jesus Franco. *Writing Credits:* Jesus Franco. *Starring:* Klaus Kinski.

Jacob's Ladder (1990). *Directed by* Adrian Lyne. *Writing Credits:* Bruce Joel Rubin. *Starring:* Tim Robbins.

Journey's End (1930). *Directed by* James Whale. *Writing Credits:* Gareth Gundrey, Joseph Moncure March and R.C. Sheriff (play). *Starring:* Colin Clive.

Kalifornia (1993). *Directed by* Dominic Sena. *Writing Credits:* Tim Metcalfe and Stephen Levy. *Starring:* Brad Pitt and Juliette Lewis.

Killer: A Journal of Murder (1996). *Directed by* Tim Metcalfe. *Writing Credits:* Tim Metcalfe (screenplay), Thomas E. Gaddis and James Long (book). *Starring:* James Woods.

The King of Comedy (1983). *Directed by* Martin Scorsese. *Writing Credits:* Paul D. Zimmerman. *Starring:* Robert De Niro and Jerry Lewis.

Klute (1971). *Directed by* Alan J. Pakula. *Writing Credits:* Andy Lewis and Dave Lewis. *Starring:* Jane Fonda and Donald Sutherland. *Academy Award:* Best Actress in a Leading Role (Fonda).

Kurosufaia aka Cross Fire (2000). *Directed by* Shusuke Kaneko. *Writing Credits:* Kota Yamada and Masahiro Yokotani. *Starring:* Akiko Yada.

Leaving Las Vegas (1995). *Directed by* Mike Figgis. *Writing Credits:* Mike Figgis and John O'Brien (novel). *Starring:* Nicolas Cage and Elisabeth Shue. *Academy Award:* Best Actor in a Leading Role (Cage).

Let It Ride (1989). *Directed by* Joe Pytka. *Writing Credits:* Nancy Dowd and Jay Cronley (book). *Starring:* Richard Dreyfuss and Teri Garr.

Lifeforce (1985). *Directed by* Tobe Hooper. *Writing Credits:* Dan O'Bannon and Don Jakoby (screenplay), and Colin Wilson (novel). *Starring:* Mathilda May.

The Lodger (1927). *Directed by* Alfred Hitchcock. *Writing Credits:* Eliot Stannard, Alfred Hitchcock, and Marie Belloc Lowndes (play and novel). *Starring:* Marie Ault and Arthur Chesney.

London After Midnight, aka The Hypnotist (1927). *Directed by* Tod Browning. *Writing Credits:* Tod Browning (story) and Waldemar Young (screenplay). *Starring:* Lon Chaney.

London Fields (2006). *Directed by* David Cronenberg. *Writing Credits:* Martin Amis and Roberta Hanley.

The Lonely Guy (1984). *Directed by* Arthur Hiller. *Writing Credits:* Neil Simon, Stan Daniels, Ed Weinberger, and Bruce Jay Friedman (book). *Starring:* Steve Martin and Charles Grodin.

The Lord of the Rings Trilogy (2001, 2002, 2003). *Directed by* Peter Jackson. *Writing Credits:* J.R.R. Tolkien (novels), Peter Jackson, Fran Walsh, Philippa Boyens, and Stephen Sinclair (screenplay). *Starring:* Elijah Wood and Ian McKellen. *Academy Awards:* Best Picture, Best Director, and Best Writing, Screenplay Based on Material Previously Produced or Published.

The Lost Weekend (1945). *Directed by* Billy Wilder. *Writing Credits:* Billy Wilder, Charles Brackett, and Charles R. Jackson (novel). *Starring:* Ray Milland. *Academy Awards:* Best Picture, Best Director, Best Writing, and Best Actor in a Leading Role (Milland).

M (1931). *Directed by* Fritz Lang. *Writing Credits:* Thea von Harbou and Fritz Lang. *Starring:* Peter Lorre.

Mad Love (1935). *Directed by* Karl Freund. *Writing Credits:* P.J. Wolfson, John L. Balderston, and Maurice Renard (novel). *Starring:* Peter Lorre.

Man in the Attic (1953). *Directed by* Hugo Fregonese. *Writing Credits:* Robert Presnell Jr., Barré Lyndon, and Marie Belloc Lowndes (novel). *Starring:* Jack Palance.

The Man with the Golden Arm (1955). *Directed by* Otto Preminger. *Writing Credits:* Walter Newman, Lewis Meltzer, and Nelson Algren (novel). *Starring:* Frank Sinatra.

The Manchurian Candidate (1962). *Directed by* John Frankenheimer. *Writing Credits:* George Axelrod and Richard Condon (novel). *Starring:* Frank Sinatra, Laurence Harvey, and Angela Lansbury.

The Manchurian Candidate (2004). *Directed by* Jonathan Demme. *Writing Credits:* Daniel Pyne, Dean Georgaris, George Axelrod, and Richard Condon (novel). *Starring:* Denzel Washington, Liev Schreiber, and Meryl Streep.

The Mask of Fu Manchu (1932). *Directed by* Charles Brabin. *Writing Credits:* Irene Kuhn, Edgar Allan Woolf, John Willard, and Sax Rohmer (story). *Starring:* Boris Karloff.

Masters of Space and Time (2006). *Directed by* Michel Gondry. *Writing Credits:* Rudy Rucker (novel). *Starring:* Jack Black.

Matilda (1996). *Directed by* Danny DeVito. *Writing Credits:* Nicholas Kazan, Robin Swicord, and Roald Dahl (book). *Starring:* Mara Wilson, Danny DeVito, and Rhea Perlman.

The Matrix (1999). *Directed by* Andy Wachowski and Larry Wachowski. *Writing Credits:* Andy Wachowski and Larry Wachowski. *Starring:* Keanu Reeves and Laurence Fishburne.

The Matrix Reloaded (2003). *Directed by* Andy Wachowski and Larry Wachowski. *Writing Credits:* Andy Wachowski and Larry Wachowski. *Starring:* Keanu Reeves and Laurence Fishburne.

The Matrix Revolutions (2003). *Directed by* Andy Wachowski and Larry Wachowski. *Writing Credits:* Andy Wachowski and Larry Wachowski. *Starring:* Keanu Reeves and Laurence Fishburne.

The Medusa Touch (1978). *Directed by* Jack Gold. *Writing Credits:* John Briley and Peter Van Greenaway (novel). *Starring:* Richard Burton.

Memento (2000). *Directed by* Christopher Nolan. *Writing Credits:* Christopher Nolan and Jonathan Nolan (story). *Starring:* Guy Pearce.

Metropolis (1927). *Directed by* Fritz Lang. *Writing Credits:* Fritz Lang and Thea von Harbou (also novel). *Starring:* Alfred Abel, Gustav Fröhlich, and Brigitte Helm.

Minority Report (2002). *Directed by* Steven Spielberg. *Writing Credits:* Philip K. Dick (short story), Scott Frank (screenplay) and Jon Cohen (screenplay). *Starring:* Tom Cruise, Colin Farrell, Steve Harris, Max von Sydow, Samantha Morton, and Kathryn Morris.

Misery (1990). *Directed by* Rob Reiner. *Writing Credits:* Stephen King (novel) and William Goldman (screenplay). *Starring:* Kathy Bates and James Caan. *Academy Award:* Best Actress in a Leading Role (Bates).

Mission Impossible (1996). *Directed by* Brian De Palma. *Writing Credits:* David Koepp, Robert Towne, and Steve Zaillian (story). *Starring:* Tom Cruise.

Modern Problems (1981). *Directed by* Ken Shapiro. *Writing Credits:* Ken Shapiro, Tom Sherohman, and Arthur Sellers. *Starring:* Chevy Chase.

Monster (2003). *Directed by* Patty Jenkins. *Writing Credits:* Patty Jenkins. *Starring:* Charlize Theron and Christina Ricci. *Academy Award:* Best Actress in a Leading Role (Theron).

Mr. Deeds Goes to Town (1936). *Directed by* Frank Capra. *Writing Credits:* Robert Riskin and Clarence Budington Kelland (story). *Starring:* Gary Cooper and Jean Arthur. *Academy Award:* Best Director.

The Mummy (1932). *Directed by* Karl Freund. *Writing Credits:* Nina Wilcox Putnam (story), Richard Schayer (story) and John L. Balderston. *Starring:* Boris Karloff, Zita Johann, and David Manners.

Murder! (1930). *Directed by* Alfred Hitchcock. *Writing Credits:* Alma Reville, Alfred Hitchcock, Walter C. Mycroft, Helen Simpson and Clemence Dane (novel). *Starring:* Herbert Marshall.

Murders in the Rue Morgue (1932). *Directed by* Robert Florey. *Writing Credits:* Robert Florey and Edgar Allan Poe (story). *Starring:* Bela Lugosi.

My Own Private Idaho (1991). *Directed by* Gus Van Sant. *Writing Credits:* Gus Van Sant and William Shakespeare (play). *Starring:* Keanu Reeves and River Phoenix.

Naked Lunch (1991). *Directed by* David Cronenberg. *Writing Credits:* David Cronenberg and William S. Burroughs (novel). *Starring:* Peter Weller.

Natural Born Killers (1994). *Directed by* Oliver Stone. *Writing Credits:* Oliver Stone, David Veloz, Richard Rutowski, and Quentin Tarantino (story). *Starring:* Woody Harrelson and Juliette Lewis.

New Nightmare aka A Nightmare on Elm Street 7: The Real Story (1994). *Directed by* Wes Craven. *Writing Credits:* Wes Craven. *Starring:* Robert Englund.

Next (2006). *Directed by* Lee Tamahori. *Writing Credits:* Gary Goldman and Philip K. Dick (short story). *Starring:* Nicolas Cage and Julianne Moore.

Night of the Living Dead (1968). *Directed by* George A. Romero. *Writing Credits:* George A. Romero and John A. Russo. *Starring:* Duane Jones.

A Nightmare on Elm Street (1984). *Directed by* Wes Craven. *Writing Credits:* Wes Craven. *Starring:* Robert Englund.

Nineteen Eighty-Four (1984). *Directed by* Michael Radford. *Writing Credits:* Michael Radford and George Orwell (novel). *Starring:* John Hurt and Richard Burton.

Now, Voyager (1942). *Directed by* Irving Rapper. *Writing Credits:* Casey Robinson and Olive Higgins Prouty (novel). *Starring:* Bette Davis and Claude Raines.

Obsession (1976). *Directed by* Brian De Palma. *Writing Credits:* Brian De Palma and Paul Schrader. *Starring:* Cliff Robertson and Geneviève Bujold.

Office Space (1999). *Directed by* Mike Judge. *Writing Credits:* Mike Judge. *Starring:* Ron Livingston, Jennifer Aniston, Ajay Naidu, David Herman, Gary Cole, and Stephen Root.

The Old Dark House (1932). *Directed by* James Whale. *Writing Credits:* Benn W. Levy and J.B. Priestley (novel). *Starring:* Boris Karloff.

The Omen (1976). *Directed by* Richard Donner. *Writing Credits:* David Seltzer. *Starring:* Gregory Peck, Lee Remick, and David Warner.

On a Clear Day You Can See Forever (1970). *Directed by* Vincente Minnelli. *Writing Credits:* Allan Jay Lerner. *Starring:* Barbra Streisand and Yves Montand.

One Flew Over the Cuckoo's Nest (1975). *Directed by* Milos Forman. *Writing Credits:* Bo Goldman, Lawrence Hauben and Ken Kesey (novel). *Starring:* Jack Nicholson, Louise Fletcher, and William Redfield. *Academy Awards:* Best Actor in a Leading Role (Nicholson), Best Actress in a Leading Role (Fletcher), Best Director, Best Writing, Screenplay Adapted from Other Material (Hauben and Goldman), and Best Picture.

Ordinary People (1980). *Directed by* Robert Redford. *Writing Credits:* Judith Guest (novel) and Alvin Sargent. *Starring:* Donald Sutherland, Judd Hirsch, Timothy Hutton, M. Emmet Walsh, and Elizabeth McGovern. *Academy Awards:* Best Actor in a Supporting Role (Hutton), Best Director, Best Picture, Best Writing, Screenplay Based on Material from Another Medium (Sargent).

Owning Mahowny (2003). *Directed by* Richard Kwietniowski. *Writing Credits:* Maurice Chauvet and Gary Stephen Ross (book). *Starring:* Philip Seymour Hoffman.

Parenthood (1989). *Directed by* Ron Howard. *Writing Credits:* Lowell Ganz and Babaloo Mandel. *Starring:* Steve Martin and Mary Steenburgen.

Paths of Glory (1957). *Directed by* Stanley Kubrick. *Writing Credits:* Stanley Kubrick, Calder Willingham, Jim Thompson, and Humphrey Cobb (novel). *Starring:* Kirk Douglas.

Patrick (1978). *Directed by* Richard Franklin. *Writing Credits:* Everett De Roche. *Starring:* Susan Penhaligon.

Paycheck (2003). *Directed by* John Woo. *Writing Credits:* Dean Georgaris and Philip K. Dick (short story). *Starring:* Ben Affleck and Uma Thurman.

Pee Wee's Big Adventure (1985). *Directed by* Tim Burton. *Writing Credits:* Phil Hartman, Paul Reubens, and Michael Varhol. *Starring:* Paul Reubens.

Peeping Tom (1960). *Directed by* Michael Powell. *Writing Credits:* Leo Marks. *Starring:* Karlheinz Böhm.

The Phantom of the Opera (1925). *Directed by* Rupert Julian. *Writing Credits:* Elliot J. Clawson, Raymond L. Schrock, and Gaston Leroux (novel). *Starring:* Lon Chaney and Mary Philbin.

Phenomenon (1996). *Directed by* Jon Turteltaub. *Writing Credits:* Gerald Di Pego. *Starring:* John Travolta.

Plan 9 from Outer Space (1959). *Directed by* Edward D. Wood, Jr. *Writing Credits:* Edward D. Wood, Jr. *Starring:* Gregory Walcott.

Powder (1995). *Directed by* Victor Salva. *Writing Credits:* Victor Salva. *Starring:* Mary Steenburgen and Sean Patrick Flanery.

Prozac Nation (2001). *Directed by* Erik Skjoldbjærg. *Writing Credits:* Frank Deasy, Larry Gross, and Elizabeth Wurtzel (book). *Starring:* Christina Ricci.

Psychic Killer (1975). *Directed by* Ray Danton. *Writing Credits:* Mikel Angel, Greydon Clark, and Ray Danton. *Starring:* Paul Burke.

Psycho (1960). *Directed by* Alfred Hitchcock. *Writing Credits:* Robert Bloch (novel) and Joseph Stefano (screenplay). *Starring:* Anthony Perkins, Vera Miles, John Gavin, and Martin Balsam.

Rabid (1977). *Directed by* David Cronenberg. *Writing Credits:* David Cronenberg. *Starring:* Marilyn Chambers.

Rain Man (1988). *Directed by* Barry Levinson. *Writing Credits:* Ronald Bass and Barry Morrow. *Starring:* Dustin Hoffman and Tom Cruise. *Academy Awards:* Best Picture, Best Director, Best Writing, Original Screenplay, and Best Actor in a Leading Role (Hoffman).

Raising Cain (1992). *Directed by* Brian De Palma. *Writing Credits:* Brian De Palma. *Starring:* John Lithgow.

Random Harvest (1942). *Directed by* Mervyn LeRoy. *Writing Credits:* Claudine West, George Froeschel, Arthur Wimperis, and James Hilton (novel). *Starring:* Ronald Colman.

Rasputin and the Empress (1932). *Directed by* Richard Boleslawski. *Writing Credits:* Charles MacArthur. *Starring:* John Barrymore, Ethel Barrymore and Lionel Barrymore.

Rasputin: The Mad Monk (1966). *Directed by* Don Sharp. *Writing Credits:* Anthony Hinds. *Starring:* Christopher Lee.

The Raven (1935). *Directed by* Lew Landers. *Writing Credits:* David Boehm. *Starring:* Boris Karloff and Bela Lugosi.

Rear Window (1954). *Directed by* Alfred Hitchcock. *Writing Credits:* John Michael Hayes and Cornell Woolrich (story). *Starring:* James Stewart and Grace Kelly.

Rebecca (1940). *Directed by* Alfred Hitchcock. *Writing Credits:* Robert E. Sherwood, Joan Harrison, and Daphne Du Maurier (novel). *Starring:* Laurence Olivier and Joan Fontaine. *Academy Award:* Best Picture.

Robocop (1987). *Directed by* Paul Verhoeven. *Writing Credits:* Michael Miner and Edward Neumeier. *Starring:* Peter Weller and Nancy Allen.

The Rocky Horror Picture Show (1975). *Directed by* Jim Sharman. *Writing Credits:* Jim Sharman and Richard O'Brien. *Starring:* Tim Curry, Barry Bostwick, and Susan Sarandon.

Rope (1948). *Directed by* Alfred Hitchcock. *Writing Credits:* Arthur Laurents, Hume Cronyn, and Patrick Hamilton (play). *Starring:* James Stewart.

The Rose (1979). *Directed by* Mark Rydell. *Writing Credits:* Michael Cimino, Bo Goldman, and Bill Kerby (story). *Starring:* Bette Midler.

A Scanner Darkly (2006). *Directed by* Richard Linklater. *Writing Credits:* Richard Linklater and Philip K. Dick (novel). *Starring:* Keanu Reeves.

Scanners (1981). *Directed by* David Cronenberg. *Writing Credits:* David Cronenberg. *Starring:* Jennifer O'Neill and Stephen Lack.

Scarface (1983). *Directed by* Brian De Palma. *Writing Credits:* Oliver Stone. *Starring:* Al Pacino, Michelle Pfeiffer and Steven Bauer.

Scary Movie, aka Scream If You Know What I Did Last Halloween (2000). *Directed by* Keenan Ivory Wayans. *Writing Credits:* Shawn Wayans, Marlon Wayans, et al. *Starring:* Anna Faris and Shawn Wayans.

The Science of Sleep (2005). *Directed by* Michel Gondry. *Writing Credits:* Michel Gondry. *Starring:* Patricia Arquette.

Scream (1996). *Directed by* Wes Craven. *Writing Credits:* Kevin Williamson. *Starring:* Neve Campbell.

Scream 3 (2000). *Directed by* Wes Craven. *Writing Credits:* Ehren Kruger and Kevin Williamson (characters). *Starring:* Neve Campbell.

Screamers (1995). *Directed by* Christian Duguay. *Writing Credits:* Dan O'Bannon and Miguel Tejada-Flores (screenplay), and Philip K. Dick (short story). *Starring:* Peter Weller, Roy Dupuis, and Jennifer Rubin.

Se7en (1995). *Directed by* David Fincher. *Writing Credits:* Andrew Kevin Walker. *Starring:* Brad Pitt and Morgan Freeman.

The Search for Bridey Murphy (1956). *Directed by* Noel Langley. *Writing Credits:* Noel Langley and Morey Bernstein (book). *Starring:* Teresa Wright.

Seconds (1966). *Directed by* John Frankenheimer. *Writing Credits:* David Ely (novel) and Lewis John Carlino (screenplay). *Starring:* Rock Hudson.

Secret Window (2004). *Directed by* David Koepp. *Writing Credits:* David Koepp and Stephen King (novel). *Starring:* Johnny Depp.

Session 9 (2001). *Directed by* Brad Anderson. *Writing Credits:* Brad Anderson and Stephen Gevedon. *Starring:* David Caruso.

Seven Days in May (1964). *Directed by* John Frankenheimer. *Writing Credits:* Rod Serling, Fletcher Knebel and Charles Bailey (book). *Starring:* Burt Lancaster, Kirk Douglas and Fredric March.

The Shadow (1994). *Directed by* Russell Mulcahy. *Writing Credits:* David Koepp and Walter B. Gibson (characters). *Starring:* Alec Baldwin.

Shadow of a Doubt (1943). *Directed by* Alfred Hitchcock. *Writing Credits:* Gordon McDonell, Thornton Wilder, Sally Benson and Alma Reville. *Starring:* Teresa Wright and Joseph Cotten.

Shallow Hal (2001). *Directed by* Bobby Farrelly and Peter Farrelly. *Writing Credits:* Sean Moynihan, Bobby Farrelly and Peter Farrelly. *Starring:* Jack Black.

Shine (1996). *Directed by* Scott Hicks. *Writing Credits:* Jan Sardi and Scott Hicks (story). *Starring:* Geoffrey Rush. *Academy Award:* Best Actor in a Leading Role (Rush).

The Shining (1980). *Directed by* Stanley Kubrick. *Writing Credits:* Stanley Kubrick, Diane Johnson, and Stephen King (novel). *Starring:* Jack Nicholson.

Shivers (1975). *Directed by* David Cronenberg. *Writing Credits:* David Cronenberg. *Starring:* Paul Hampton.

Shock Corridor (1963). *Directed by* Samuel Fuller. *Writing Credits:* Samuel Fuller. *Starring:* Peter Breck.

Shock Treatment (1964). *Directed by* Denis Sanders. *Writing Credits:* Sydney Boehm and Winfred Van Atta (novel). *Starring:* Stuart Whitman and Roddy McDowell.

Sid and Nancy (1986). *Directed by* Alex Cox. *Writing Credits:* Alex Cox and Abbe Wool. *Starring:* Gary Oldman and Chloe Webb.

The Silence of the Lambs (1991). *Directed by* Jonathan Demme. *Writing Credits:* Thomas Harris (novel) and Ted Tally (screenplay). *Starring:* Jodie Foster, Anthony Hopkins, Scott Glenn, Anthony Heald, and Ted Levine. *Academy Awards:* Best Actor in a Leading Role (Hopkins), Best Actress in a Leading Role (Foster), and Best Director.

Silent Fall (1994). *Directed by* Bruce Beresford. *Writing Credits:* Akiva Goldsman. *Starring:* Richard Dreyfuss.

Sisters (1973). *Directed by* Brian De Palma. *Writing Credits:* Louisa Rose and Brian De Palma. *Starring:* Margot Kidder.

The Six Million Dollar Man (2005). *Directed by* Todd Phillips. *Writing Credits:* Todd Phillips and Martin Caidin (novel).

The Sixth Sense (1999). *Directed by* M. Night Shyamalan. *Writing Credits:* M. Night Shyamalan. *Starring:* Bruce Willis and Haley Joel Osment.

The Snake Pit (1948). *Directed by* Anatole Litvak. *Writing Credits:* Millen Brand, Frank Partos, and Mary Jane Ward (novel). *Starring:* Olivia de Havilland.

Solaris (2002). *Directed by* Steven Soderbergh. *Writing Credits:* Steven Soderbergh and Stanislaw Lem (novel). *Starring:* George Clooney.

Solyaris aka Solaris (1972). *Directed by* Andrei Tarkovsky. *Writing Credits:* Fridrikh Gorenshtein and Stanislaw Lem (novel). *Starring:* Natalya Bondarchuk.

Species (1995). *Directed by* Roger Donaldson. *Writing Credits:* Dennis Feldman. *Starring:* Ben Kingsley and Natasha Henstridge.

Species II (1998). *Directed by* Peter Medak. *Writing Credits:* Chris Brancato and Dennis Feldman (characters). *Starring:* Natasha Henstridge.

Spellbound (1945). *Directed by* Alfred Hitchcock. *Writing Credits:* Angus MacPhail (adaptation) and Ben Hecht (screenplay). *Starring:* Ingrid Bergman, Gregory Peck, and Michael Chekhov. *Academy Award:* Best Music, Scoring of a Dramatic or Comedy Picture (Rózsa).

Spider (2002). *Directed by* David Cronenberg. *Writing Credits:* Patrick McGrath (also novel). *Starring:* Ralph Fiennes.

Spider-Man (2002). *Directed by* Sam Raimi. *Writing Credits:* David Koepp, Steve Ditko and Stan Lee (comic book). *Starring:* Tobey Maguire and Kirsten Dunst.

Splendor in the Grass (1961). *Directed by* Elia Kazan. *Writing Credits:* William Inge. *Starring:* Warren Beatty and Natalie Wood.

Stage Fright (1950). *Directed by* Alfred Hitchcock. *Writing Credits:* Whitfield Cook and Selwyn Jepson. *Starring:* Jane Wyman, Marlene Dietrich, and Michael Wilding.

A Star Is Born (1954). *Directed by* George Cukor. *Writing Credits:* Moss Hart, William Wellman and Robert Carson (story). *Starring:* Judy Garland and James Mason.

Star Wars (1977). *Directed by* George Lucas. *Writing Credits:* George Lucas. *Starring:* Mark Hamill, Harrison Ford, Carrie Fisher, Peter Cushing, and Alec Guinness.

Star Wars: Episode I—The Phantom Menace (1999). *Directed by* George Lucas. *Writing Credits:* George Lucas. *Starring:* Liam Neeson, Ewan McGregor, Natalie Portman, and Jake Lloyd.

Star Wars: Episode II—Attack of the Clones (2002). *Directed by* George Lucas. *Writing Credits:* George Lucas. *Starring:* Ewan McGregor, Natalie Portman, Hayden Christensen, Christopher Lee, and Samuel L. Jackson.

Star Wars: Episode III—Revenge of the Sith (2005). *Directed by* George Lucas. *Writing Credits:* George Lucas. *Starring:* Ewan McGregor, Natalie Portman, Hayden Christensen, Christopher Lee, Samuel L. Jackson, Frank Oz, Ian McDiarmid, and Jimmy Smits.

Star Wars: Episode V—The Empire Strikes Back (1980). *Directed by* Irvin Kershner. *Writing Credits:* George Lucas (story), Leigh Brackett, and Lawrence Kasdan. *Starring:* Mark Hamill, Harrison Ford, Carrie Fisher, and Billy Dee Williams.

Star Wars: Episode VI—Return of the Jedi (1983). *Directed by* Richard Marquand. *Writing Credits:* George Lucas (story) and Lawrence Kasdan. *Starring:* Mark Hamill, Harrison Ford, Carrie Fisher, and Billy Dee Williams.

The Stepford Wives (2004). *Directed by* Frank Oz. *Writing Credits:* Paul Rudnick and Ira Levin (novel). *Starring:* Nicole Kidman, Matthew Broderick and Glenn Close.

Stir of Echoes (1999). *Directed by* David Koepp. *Writing Credits:* David Koepp and Richard Matheson. *Starring:* Kevin Bacon.

Strange Days (1995). *Directed by* Kathryn Bigelow. *Writing Credits:* James Cameron and Jay Cocks. *Starring:* Ralph Fiennes and Juliette Lewis.

Stranger on the Third Floor (1940). *Directed by* Boris Ingster. *Writing Credits:* Frank Partos. *Starring:* Peter Lorre.

Strangers on a Train (1951). *Directed by* Alfred Hitchcock. *Writing Credits:* Raymond Chandler and Patricia Highsmith (novel). *Starring:* Farley Granger and Robert Walker.

Suddenly, Last Summer (1959). *Directed by* Joseph L. Mankiewicz. *Writing Credits:* Gore Vidal and Tennessee Williams (play). *Starring:* Elizabeth Taylor and Montgomery Clift.

Summer of Sam (1999). *Directed by* Spike Lee. *Writing Credits:* Spike Lee, Michael Imperioli and Victor Colicchio. *Starring:* Adrien Brody and Mira Sorvino.

Suspect Zero (2004). *Directed by* E. Elias Merhige. *Writing Credits:* Zak Penn and Billy Ray. *Starring:* Ben Kingsley.

Suspicion (1941). *Directed by* Alfred Hitchcock. *Writing Credits:* Samson Raphaelson and Anthony Berkeley (novel). *Starring:* Cary Grant and Joan Fontaine. *Academy Award:* Best Actress in a Leading Role (Fontaine).

Svengali (1931). *Directed by* Archie Mayo. *Writing Credits:* J. Grubb Alexander and George L. Du Maurier (novel). *Starring:* John Barrymore.

Sybil (1976) (TV). *Directed by* Daniel Petrie. *Writing Credits:* Stewart Stern and Flora Rheta Schreiber (book). *Starring:* Sally Field.

Sylvia (2003). *Directed by* Christine Jeffs. *Writing Credits:* John Brownlow. *Starring:* Gwyneth Paltrow.

Take the Money and Run (1969). *Directed by* Woody Allen. *Writing Credits:* Woody Allen and Mickey Rose. *Starring:* Woody Allen.

Taxi Driver (1976). *Directed by* Martin Scorsese. *Writing Credits:* Paul Schrader. *Starring:* Robert De Niro and Jodie Foster.

Tender Is the Night (1962). *Directed by* Henry King. *Writing Credits:* Ivan Moffat and F. Scott Fitzgerald (novel). *Starring:* Jennifer Jones and Jason Robards.

The Texas Chain Saw Massacre (1974). *Directed by* Tobe Hooper. *Writing Credits:* Kim Henkel and Tobe Hooper (story). *Starring:* Marilyn Burns.

Them! (1954). *Directed by* Gordon Douglas. *Writing Credits:* Ted Sherdeman et al. *Starring:* James Whitmore.

The Three Faces of Eve (1957). *Directed by* Nunnally Johnson. *Writing Credits:* Nunnally Johnson, Corbett Thigpen and Hervey M. Cleckley (book). *Starring:* Joanne Woodward and Lee J. Cobb. *Academy Award:* Best Actress in a Leading Role (Woodward).

THX 1138 (1971). *Directed by* George Lucas. *Writing Credits:* George Lucas. *Starring:* Robert Duvall.

Time after Time (1979). *Directed by* Nicholas Meyer. *Writing Credits:* Karl Alexander (novel), Steve Hayes (story) and Nicholas Meyer. *Starring:* Malcolm McDowell and David Warner.

To Catch a Killer (1992) (TV). *Directed by* Eric Till. *Writing Credits:* Jud Kinberg. *Starring:* Brian Dennehy.

Total Recall (1990). *Directed by* Paul Verhoeven. *Writing Credits:* Philip K. Dick (short story) and Ronald Shusett et al. *Starring:* Arnold Schwarzenegger.

Toyer (2005). *Directed by* Brian De Palma. *Writing Credits:* Gardner McKay.

The Train (1964). *Directed by* John Frankenheimer. *Writing Credits:* Rose Valland (book), Franklin Coen and Frank Davis. *Starring:* Burt Lancaster and Paul Scofield.

Trainspotting (1996). *Directed by* Danny Boyle. *Writing Credits:* John Hodge and Irvine Welsh (novel). *Starring:* Ewan McGregor.

Tron (1982). *Directed by* Steven Lisberger. *Writing Credits:* Steven Lisberger and Bonnie MacBird (story). *Starring:* Jeff Bridges and Bruce Boxleitner.

Twelve O'Clock High (1949). *Directed by* Henry King. *Writing Credits:* Sy Bartlett and Beirne Lay, Jr. (also novel). *Starring:* Gregory Peck.

28 Days (2000). *Directed by* Betty Thomas. *Writing Credits:* Susannah Grant. *Starring:* Sandra Bullock.

2001: A Space Odyssey (1968). *Directed by* Stanley Kubrick. *Writing Credits:* Arthur C. Clarke (story and screenplay) and Stanley Kubrick (screenplay). *Starring:* Keir Dullea.

The Untouchables (1987). *Directed by* Brian De Palma. *Writing Credits:* David Mamet. *Starring:* Kevin Costner, Sean Connery and Robert De Niro.

Vanilla Sky (2001). *Directed by* Cameron Crowe. *Writing Credits:* Alejandro Amenábar (film Abre Los Ojos), Mateo Gil (film Abre Los Ojos as Mateo Gil Rodríguez), and Cameron Crowe (screenplay). *Starring:* Tom Cruise, Penélope Cruz, Cameron Diaz, Kurt Russell, and Jason Lee.

Vertigo (1958). *Directed by* Alfred Hitchcock. *Writing Credits:* Pierre Boileau and Thomas Narcejac (novel), Alec Coppel and Samuel Taylor (screenplay). *Starring:* James Stewart and Kim Novak.

Videodrome (1983). *Directed by* David Cronenberg. *Writing Credits:* David Cronenberg. *Starring:* James Woods.

Village of the Damned (1960). *Directed by* Wolf Rilla. *Writing Credits:* Stirling Silliphant, Wolf Rilla and Ronald Kinnoch (as George Barclay). *Starring:* George Sanders, Barbara Shelley, and Michael Gwynn.

Le Voyage dans la lune (A Trip to the Moon) (1902). *Directed by* Georges Méliès. *Writing Credits:* Georges Méliès, Jules Verne (novel), and H.G. Wells (novel). *Starring:* Victor André.

Das Wachsfigurenkabinett, aka Waxworks (1924). *Directed by* Leo Birinsky and Paul Leni. *Writing Credits:* Henrik Galeen. *Starring:* Condrad Veidt and Werner Krauss.

What Dreams May Come (1998). *Directed by* Vincent Ward. *Writing Credits:* Ronald Bass and Richard Matheson (novel). *Starring:* Robin Williams.

What's New, Pussycat (1965). *Directed by* Clive Donner. *Writing Credits:* Woody Allen. *Starring:* Peter Sellers.

When a Man Loves a Woman (1994). *Directed by* Luis Mandoki. *Writing Credits:* Ronald Bass and Al Franken. *Starring:* Meg Ryan and Andy Garcia.

When the Clouds Roll By (1919). *Directed by* Victor Fleming and Theodore Reed. *Writing Credits:* Lewis Weadon. *Starring:* Douglas Fairbanks.

White Heat (1949). *Directed by* Raoul Walsh. *Writing Credits:* Ivan Goff, Ben Roberts and Virginia Kellogg (story). *Starring:* James Cagney and Virginia Mayo.

White Zombie (1932). *Directed by* Victor Halperin. *Writing Credits:* Garnett Weston. *Starring:* Bela Lugosi.

Wilder Napalm (1993). *Directed by* Glenn Gordon Caron. *Writing Credits:* Vince Gilligan. *Starring:* Dennis Quaid, Debra Winger and Arliss Howard.

The Wizard of Oz (1939). *Directed by* Victor Fleming and Richard Thorpe. *Writing Credits:* L. Frank Baum (novel) and Noel Langley. *Starring:* Judy Garland, Frank Morgan, and Billie Burke. *Academy Awards:* Best Music, Original Score (Stothart), Best Music, Original Song (Arlen and Harburg for the song "Over the Rainbow").

A Woman Under the Influence (1974). *Directed by* John Cassavetes. *Writing Credits:* John Cassavetes. *Starring:* Gena Rowlands.

The Wrong Man (1956). *Directed by* Alfred Hitchcock. *Writing Credits:* Angus MacPhail and Maxwell Anderson (also novel). *Starring:* Henry Fonda.

X2: X-Men United (2003). *Directed by* Bryan Singer. *Writing Credits:* Zak Penn et al. *Starring:* Patrick Stewart and Ian McKellen.

X-Men (2000). *Directed by* Bryan Singer. *Writing Credits:* Tom DeSanto and Bryan Singer (story) and David Hayter (screenplay). *Starring:* Patrick Stewart and Ian McKellen.

The Young Savages (1961). *Directed by* John Frankenheimer. *Writing Credits:* Edward Anhalt, J.P. Miller, and Evan Hunter (novel). *Starring:* Burt Lancaster.

Zapped! (1982). *Directed by* Robert J. Rosenthal. *Writing Credits:* Robert J. Rosenthal and Bruce Rubin. *Starring:* Scott Baio and Willi Aames.

Zelig (1983). *Directed by* Woody Allen. *Writing Credits:* Woody Allen. *Starring:* Woody Allen, Mia Farrow, and John Buckwalter.

Bibliography

American Psychiatric Association. (2000.) *Diagnostic and Statistical Manual of Mental Disorders: DSM-IV-TR.* Washington, DC: American Psychiatric Association.

Bloch, Robert. (1959.) *Psycho.* New York: Simon and Schuster.

Burgess, Anthony. (1962.) *A Clockwork Orange.* New York: W.W. Norton.

Campbell, Joseph. (1949.) *The Hero with a Thousand Faces.* Princeton, NJ: Princeton University Press.

_____, ed. (1970.) *Myths, Dreams, and Religion.* New York: E.P. Dutton.

Condon, Richard. (1959.) *The Manchurian Candidate.* New York: McGraw-Hill.

Constantine, Alex. (1995.) *Psychic Dictatorship in the U.S.A.* Portland, OR: Feral House.

Costanzo, William V. (2004.) *Great Films and How to Teach Them.* Urbana, IL: National Council of Teachers of English.

Erikson, Erik. (1968.) *Identity, Youth, and Crisis.* New York: W.W. Norton.

Estabrooks, George H. (1957.) *Hypnotism.* New York: E.P. Dutton.

Fleming, Michael, and Manvell, Roger. (1985.) *Images of Madness: The Portrayal of Insanity in the Feature Film.* Rutherford, NJ: Fairleigh Dickinson University Press.

Freud, Sigmund. (1956.) *The Complete Psychological Works: Standard Edition* (24 volumes.) Ed. J. Strachey, London: Hogarth.

Freud, Sigmund. (1900.) *The Interpretation of Dreams.* In *The Complete Psychological Works: Standard Edition,* Volumes 4 and 5.

Gabbard, G.O., and Gabbard, K. (1999.) *Psychiatry and the Cinema.* 2nd ed. Washington, DC: American Psychiatric Press.

Hamachek, Don. (1992.) *Encounters with the Self.* 4th ed. Fort Worth: Harcourt Brace Jovanovich College Publishers.

Indick, William. (2004.) "Classical Heroes in Modern Movies: Mythological Patterns of the Superhero." *Journal of Media Psychology,* Volume 9, no. 3.

_____. (2004.) *Movies and the Mind: Theories of the Great Psychoanalysts Applied to Film.* Jefferson, NC: McFarland.

_____. (2004.) *Psychology for Screenwriters: Building Conflict in Your Script.* Los Angeles: Michael Wiese Productions.

Izod, John. (2001.) *Myth, Mind, and the Screen: Understanding the Heroes of Our Times.* Cambridge: Cambridge University Press.

Jung, Carl G. (1971.) *The Portable Jung.* Ed. Joseph Campbell. New York: Viking Penguin.

_____. (1963.) *Memories, Dreams, and Reflections.* New York: Random House.

_____. (1953.) *Collected Works.* Eds. H. Read, M. Fordham and G. Adler. Princeton, NJ: Princeton University Press.

Keith, Jim. (1997.) *Mind Control, World Control.* Kempton, IL: Adventures Unlimited.

Marks, John. (1979.) *The Search for the "Manchurian Candidate."* New York: W.W. Norton.

May, Rollo. (1991.) *The Cry for Myth.* New York: W.W. Norton.

Milgram, Stanley. (2004.) *Obedience to Authority.* New York: HarperPerennial.

Rank, Otto. (1914/1959.) *The Myth of the Birth of the Hero.* New York: Random House.

Ross, Colin A. (2000.) *Bluebird: Deliberate Creation of Multiple Personality by Psychiatrists.* Richardson, TX: Manitou.

Simpson, Philip L. (2000.) *Psycho Paths.* Carbondale, IL: Southern Illinois University Press.

Skal, David J. (1993.) *The Monster Show: A Cultural History of Horror.* New York: W.W. Norton.

_____. (1998.) *Screams of Reason: Mad Science and Modern Culture.* New York: W.W. Norton.

Wahl, Otto F. (1995.) *Media Madness: Public Images of Mental Illness.* New Brunswick, NJ: Rutgers University Press.

Zimbardo, Philip G. (1972.) *Stanford Prison Experiment: A Simulation Study of the Psychology of Imprisonment.* San Francisco: Philip G. Zimbardo.

Index

181